REVISER'S TOOLBOX

written and compiled by

Barry Lane

DWP

DISCOVER
WRITING
PRESS

po box 264
Shoreham, VT 05770
www.discoverwriting.com

Discover Writing Press
PO Box 264
Shoreham, VT 05770
1-800-613-8055 www.discoverwriting.com

ISBN# 0-9656574-4-2

99 00 01 02 03 04 05   10 9 8 7 6 5 4 3 2

For information on the seminar which goes along with this book call 1-800-613-8055 or visit our website at www.discoverwriting.com

Credits and Permissions:
Picture: page 62—Library of Congress. page 95 New York Public Library. page 106—Library of Congress. Page 112 excerpt from *Fig Pudding* by Ralph Fletcher, Clarion Books 1995 reprinted with permission, Picture:page 118—Library of Congress. Page 132,*Chipmunk Bites Toddler* from Manchester Union Leader. Reprinted with permission of the author. Picture:page 135 Marlboro Ads, California State Department of Health, reprinted with permission. page 143: *In Real Life Snow White was Murdered*, reprinted with permission from The Weekly World News. Picture:page 146,*Pony Express*—Library of Congress. page 164, excerpted from *Strength to Your Sword Arm: collected writings of Brenda Ueland* 1992, Holy Cow Press, reprinted with permission. page 179 kid friendly rubric, Atkinson Elementary School, Ky. pages 196-214, *The Power of the Printed Word*, 1984, The International Paper Company, reprinted with permission. pages 215-222, *The Writer's Toolbox* by Laura Harper, reprinted from Language Arts magazine with permission, page 227-232: *Quality in Writing*, excerpted from Writing Teacher Magazine, reprinted with permission. page 233-236,*One Two, Buy Velcro Shoes*, excerpted from *OOps: What Happens When Teaching Fails*, Stenhouse, 1996. Reprinted with permission. pages 256—262 *Good Rubric* from a work in progress by Vicki Spandel, The Write Traits Co. reprinted with permission.
Thanks to Mark Perry and Lorie Duval for work on the manuscript.

To all the students and teachers who keep revising
after THE END

It's a Toolbox, Not a Workbook.

Why a Toolbox?

Last fall, a teacher sent me a worksheet from her district designed to beat the state mastery test. She thought I would be interested to see what had happened to the kid-empowering concepts from my first book on revision, *After THE END*, when they fell into the hands of the enemy. "A snapshot should be 3 sentences long," the worksheet read. "The first sentence should be the topic sentence, the second the first supporting detail....". I cringed. I gagged. I convulsed. Then I got angry. Then I got sad.

In *After THE END*, I warned about the dangers of textbook fundamentalism; now the ideas and concepts from that same book had fallen victim. In the name of education, they had turned a collection of kid-friendly ideas into a kid-torturing workbook. I vowed right then to create a practical book to supplement *After THE END* that did not put to death the ideas. You are reading that book.

How To Use It

The first four chapters of the toolbox take basic concepts of craft such as leads, details, snapshots, thoughtshots. exploding and shrinking time, and give very specific ways to teach them using examples from literature, writing exercises and inspirational posters and quotes. There is no strong sequence to the pages in these chapters just as there is no inherent sequence to how your students learn. You can skim through the chapters with an eye for particular pages to help with this week's lesson. Some pages are cross-referenced with the appendices in the back of the book.

Chapters five and six give practical and fun suggestions for revising expository writing for voice and tone. Chapter seven will give you and your students ideas to make peer conferences more effective. Chapters eight and nine provide articles to help you revise your concept of revision, school and assessment. Please take some time to browse through the appendices. You'll find examples and information to help improve your reading/writing classroom.

What About Grade Level?

This book is primarily designed for teachers of writing grades 2 through 12; some specific pages, however, will be more relevant to primary grades than they'll be to others. As a teacher of writing at all grade levels, I am very wary of saying, "This won't work with second graders" or "This will." I have been proven wrong enough times to know that a young writer's ability often rises or sinks to the level of our expectations. Certain pages in this book, however, will work especially well with primary writers. In order to point these pages out, I've marked them with a "P" at the center top of the page. But most importantly, I urge you to let your instincts and your dauntless teacher spirit be your guide when using this book, not the suggestions of an author who's never personally met you or your students.

Any book for teachers on revision is only as good as the teachers and students who use it and revise it in their own unique way. To encourage this individualistic use, I've put your own personal index on the flip side of the back cover. Here you can reference your favorite lessons for easy retrieval.

A Word About Copyright

I have designed this book so that certain pages can be photocopied for your classes without permission. You are also permitted to use up to five pages for teacher workshops, as long as the source is documented at the bottom of the page. To make it easy for you, we've included source lines at the bottom of most pages. For questions about permission or to order more books, call 1-800-613-8055.

Give us Feedback

Because this book is an experiment of sorts and an ongoing project, I encourage you to let us know how you have used it. We are also collecting student work for the next edition. All student work submitted should have a home address on it so we can contact parents for permission. Students receive a small stipend and 2 copies of the finished book.

Send work to: Student Work PO 264 Shoreham, VT 05770
web page: www.discoverwriting.com email: barry@discoverwriting.com

Concepts of Craft To Aid Revision

* Leads (the magic flashlight)

* Detail (the binoculars)

* Snapshot (physical detail)

* Thoughtshot (thoughts)

* Scene(talk+snapshot+thoughtshot)

* Exploding Moments(slow-mo)

* Point of View(what you leave out)

Table of Contents

It's a Toolbox, not a Workbook

Chapter Three: Snapshots and Thoughtshots

Chapter Four: Playing with Time

Chapter Five: Voice Lessons in Expository Writing

Chapter Six: 15 Wacky Research Reports

Chapter 9   Revising Writing and Teaching

Appendices

1

Digging Potatoes:
Crafting Meaning from Start to Finish

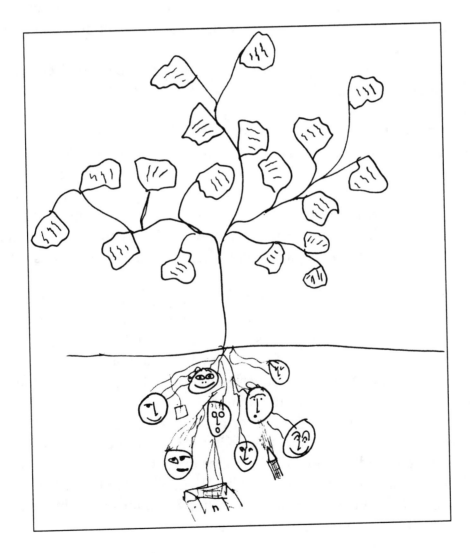

Lead Seed

"DON'T SAY ANYTHING. DON'T EVEN LOOK UP...."
The words were written on a tiny scrap of paper at the edge of route 16 in Newington, New Hampshire. I picked it up and slid it into my pocket. A bored hitchhiker will mindlessly do things like that. It was only later that day when I emptied my pockets on the kitchen counter that one of my roommates found the note and asked, "What was that scrap of paper you left on the counter? It scared me when I read it." When I told her I found it on the side of the road, she suggested I call the police. It was a good suggestion. That night two detectives came to our house and fingerprinted us because we had touched the paper. The day before, the shoe store at the mall had been robbed, and I had found a piece of the hold-up note.

I sometimes think about the writer of that hold-up note when I teach about writing. He knew something about what a strong lead was. I wonder if it was something he learned in school or something that came later in life. I wonder if his first robbery failed because he wrote notes that began. "In this note I will ask you, the teller of this bank, to give me all the money in your drawer..."

You see ,when I was in school we didn't write grabbing leads; we wrote introductions. We said what we were going to say. We said it. And then we said it again. We wrote as if every piece of writing could be planned from start to finish in our brains before we even wrote one word. Writing was dictation from the brain to the hand to the paper, and when it hit the paper it was usually wrong.

Even today when I ask teachers to define leads, they will say, "A lead is a topic sentence." But what if it doesn't state the topic? What if it is leading to the topic? Leads are not topic sentences. Leads are not introductions. Leads are seeds that help a writer begin to figure out where the plant is growing. They are an organizational tool, a motivational tool and a springboard into a piece of writing. They also lead us to endings.

In the next few pages you'll find ideas for making leads a part of your classroom vocabulary. Teach students to value leads and they will know it's worth scribbling ten leads before they begin, or throwing out pages one and two when the real story starts on page three. They'll also be able to see the connection (or lack thereof) between the beginning and the end. Understanding endings has much to do with understanding beginnings.

P

Dig a Potato Today

A potato grows beneath the surface in a   piece of writing. It's the thing that the reader and the writer want to dig up.

Listen to the following leads. What questions arise in your minds as you listen?

I was six years old when my mother taught me the art of invisible strength.
Rules of the Game   Amy Tan

You are not the kind of guy who would be at a place like this at this time of the morning.

Bright Lights Big City   Jay McInerney

"You must not tell anyone," my mother said, "what I am about to tell you."
The Woman Warrior   Maxine Hong Kingston

The name my family calls me is Morning Girl, because I wake up early always with something on my mind."

The Morning Girl   Michael Dorris

1) Tell a story to some friends or read a piece you are working on.

2) Have your friends listen and write curious questions on scraps of paper.

3) Take your favorite question and turn it into a new lead by answering it in a sentence or two.
 For example:
  How big was the dog?
    It was the biggest dog I'd ever seen.
  Is this a true story?
    You may not believe it, but what follows is a true story.

4) Try finding or writing a new lead to a piece from your writing folder.

Great Questions

- Rise from curious minds

- Cluster together like popcorn

- Are preceded by deep silence

- Have no answer

P

Questions to the Future

If you were in Kristina Sullivan's third grade class you might be asked to write a letter to yourself 20 years in the future. Think about it. What would you say to yourself?

Dear Jackie,

How are you? Are you an artist, an animal trainer or a farmer? Do you still love animals? Do you still like to read? What is the world like now? Where are you? What is it like there? Do you sitll like to go on trips? Do you like fruits and vegetables? Do you have a horse? Did you work at Port Defiance Zoo when you were twelve? Do you still have your secret forest? Is Lani still your best friend? Hope you are having fun wherever you are?

Jackie

Dear Clara,

Today we got free popcorn. Right now I'm mad at C.J. because he tripped me and I got a bloody leg. I call him boogerboy because he picks his nose and eats his boogers. I am Clara and in the 3rd grade. I love sweets. I used to think I was this dinky little girl with long legs and glasses, but right now I feel special.   I don't know why. Mrs. Sullivan said life was a gift. That's probably why I feel this way. In fifteen years I hope I can get a good job, my own house and my own dog and cat. A lot of the people think that when you're grown up it's going to be like you are going to use a surfboard and fly to work. They think the world is going to change. Of course, it'll change but not too much. What if it doesn't change at all? But what I don't want to change is animals. I don't want endangered animals to be extinct.

Clara

Leads are magic flashlights that shine down through a story showing the writer what to put in and what to leave out.

John McPhee

The Horserace of Meaning

All writing is a horserace of information, the most important bits taking the lead, the least important falling to the rear and sometimes not even making it to the race. Which horse is in the lead in your story? Which horse needs to fall back?

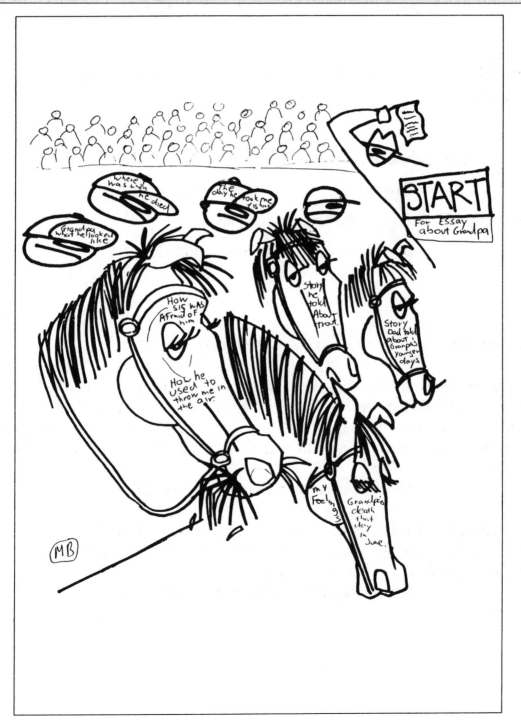

The Lead Board

(define your own species of lead)

Find any great leads lately in your reading or living? Put them up on the lead board. Try coming up with your own classifications or use some I've used below.

Big Potato Leads   *Jump into the middle of your story and leave the reader wanting more.*

And suddenly everything stops.

> ### *Runa*   Alison James

Every so often that dead dog dreams me up again.

> ### *Dog Heaven*   Stephanie Vaughn

Snapshot Leads   *Create a picture in the reader's mind.*

Abraham Lincoln wasn't the sort of man who could lose himself in a crowd. After all, he stood 6 foot 4 inches tall, and to top it off he wore a high silk hat. His height was mostly in his long bony legs, and when he sat in a chair he seemed no taller than anyone else. It was only when he stood up that he towered about other men.

> ### *Lincoln: a photobiography*   Russell Freedman

The doorman of the Kilmarnock was six foot two. He wore a pale blue uniform, and white gloves made his hands look enormous. He opened the door of the yellow taxi as gently as an old maid stroking a cat.

> ### *Smart Alec Kill*   Raymond Chandler

My father came home from work on weeknights long after we had eaten our supper and gotten into our pajamas. The six of us watched from the living room while he sat at the kitchen table to have his supper. My mother sat down his dinner before him, steam rising from the plate she'd kept warm over a pot of boiling water. Loading his fork with his knife, he bent to his dinner, not looking up from his plate until he had pushed it away from him empty.

Daley's Girls   Catherine Brady

Talking Leads   Maybe you want to start with a line or two of dialogue.

"Where is he?"

Barney hopped from one foot to the other as he clambered down from the train, peering through the white-faced crowds flooding eagerly to the St. Austel ticket barrier. "Oh, I can't see him. Is he there?"

Over Sea, Under Stone   Susan Cooper

"Where is Papa going with that ax?" said Fern to her mother as they were setting the table for breakfast.

Charlotte's Web   E.B. White

Thinking Leads   *Start with a thought inside a character or you.*

Mother taught me to be polite to dragons. Particularly polite, I mean; she taught me to be ordinarily polite to everyone. Well, it makes sense. With all the enchanted princess and disguised wizards and transformed kings and so on wandering around, you never know *whom* you might be talking to. But dragons are a special case.

Talking to Dragons   Patricia C. Wrede

As a boy, I never knew where my mother was from--where she was born, who her parents were.

The Color of Water   James McBride

Up until I turned twelve years old the kind of friends I had were what you'd expect. They were my own age more or less. Most of them were born here in Serenity along with me. And all of us went to the same school together.

Onion John   Joseph Krumgold

Misleading Leads[1]   *Set up expectations, then surprise the reader.*

I have a farm. It has lots of animals. (next page) Fooled ya! It's a toy farm."
         Michael, a first grader, from *What a Writer Needs* by Ralph Fletcher

I would like to die peacefully in my sleep like my grandfather, not terrified and screaming like the other people in the car.
                    Prairie Home Companion   Garrison Keillor

Until Columbus reached the New World the people he called "Indians" lived in peace and harmony with one another.
   Not so.   *Not So!*   Paul Boller JR,

Set-up Leads *Set-up the action for the whole story in a few sentences.*

This blind man, an old friend of my wife's, he was on his way to spend the night..... I wasn't enthusiastic about his visit. He was no one I knew. And his being blind bothered me. My idea of blindness came from the movies, the blind moved slowly and never laughed. Sometimes they were led by seeing-eye dogs. A blind man in my house was not something I looked forward to.
                    Cathedral   Raymond Carver

In the early days of America when men wore ruffles on their shirts and buckles on their shoes, when they rode horseback and swore allegiance to the King of England, there lived in Boston a man who cared for none of these things. His name was Samual Adams. His clothes were shabby and plain, he refused to get on a horse, and he hated the King of England.
                    Why Don't You Get a Horse, Sam Adams?   Jean Fritz

This is not a book about my life or yours. It does not hold the secret to success or salvation. It won't strengthen your self-esteem. I don't think it will get me on Oprah.   *I'm Dysfunctional, You're Dysfunctional* Wendy Kaminer

---

[1] *What a Writer Needs* by Ralph Fletcher Portsmouth NH: Heinemann 1993
See appendix A book information.

Macro-Micro Leads

Below are two photos of a streetcar in San Francisco . Notice how the top photo sees the car at a distance and the bottom zooms in closer. The lead in photo 1 might say, "The streetcar pulled up to the curb." In the bottom photo I'm closer to a subject so my lead might describe one of the people on the streetcar, "The man clung to the white rail." or even climb inside a mind, "I'm late again, Harry thought as he clung to the white rail of the streetcar."

Try standing back and using your macro lens about a place you would like to set your story, then zoom in with a lead that zooms right into the life of one person.

P

Write Leads to Photos

Look at the photos beneath and write a lead to one. If you don't want to do it, find or draw some pictures of your own and write leads to them. Create your own book of leads like Chris Van Allsburgs' book, *The Mysteries of Harris Burdick.*

P

Follow My Lead

It's fun to write leads that make the reader want to read and the writer want to write. Read some of these leads and write five or ten of your own. You may want to start by thinking of different genres as the examples below, or just dive right in. After you've written some leads, pick your favorite one and put it at the top of a new piece of paper. Swap it with a partner and see where you lead each other.

Examples from different genres

Science Fiction
The moment the space ship landed I could tell this was not the kind of planet where kids would be appreciated.

Historical Fiction
My name is John Wilkes Boothe and I am a great actor about to give my greatest performance.

Adventure
The more I ran the more I heard the footsteps.

Biography
Why would anyone want to know about my life?

Horror
As I walked up the stairs I could feel my heart pounding with each creak of the steps.

Scientific Research paper
If I were a hummingbird my heart would weigh 80 pounds.

Romance
She said no, but Walker Kirby didn't have the two letter word in his vocabulary.

Dark and Stormy Night

Now it's time to enter the Bulwer-Lytton Fiction contest. You need to write bad beginnings. No, not just bad, awful—so awful they are funny. Here are some examples of past winners.

Loretta had been working as the tattoo artist's assistant for only two weeks and already he had designs on her.

Hugh B. King, Freemont, California

The full moon jutted out like a malevolent speed bump on the blacktop of night.

Donny Philicione, Belleville, New Jersey

There was a considerable consternation among the cats in the coliseum when it was learned that the tigers were taking the lion's share of the prophets.

Gary S. Dunbar, Cooperstown, New York

Paul Revere had just discovered that someone in Boston was a spy for the British, and when he saw the young woman believed to be the spy's girlfriend in an Italian restaurant he said to the waiter, "Hold the spumoni— I'm going to follow the chick an' catch a Tory."

John L. Ashman, 1995 Grand Prize winner

Now get to work. Send your entries to: Bulwer-Lytton Fiction Contest, Department of English, San Jose State University, San Jose, CA 95192-0090 (www.bulwer-lytton.com)

Rules: "Sentences may be of any length (though you venture beyond 50 or 60 words at your peril), and entrants may submit more than one, but all entries must be "original" and previously unpublished.

Mail entries should be submitted on index cards, the sentence on one side and the entrant's name, address, and phone number on the other. (For electronic submissions, see below.)

Entries will be judged by categories, from "general" to detective, western, science fiction, romance, and so on. There will be overall winners as well as category winners.

The official BLFC deadline is April 15 (a date Americans associate with painful submissions and making up bad stories). In truth, though, we will judge anything submitted by the middle of May." (See Appendix B for more information and examples)

Four Beginnings to a Life

Below are four beginnings to the life of Harriet Tubman, the famous leader of the Underground Railroad, from four different biographies. Notice how each biographer finds a different place to start a life. Try writing your own lead to Harriet's life. Where would you begin? Remember you don't have to start at the beginning. You can begin anywhere you find interesting. Try writing several leads to the biography of a friend or a person whose life you have researched.

Harriet Tubman was a runaway slave who worked most of her life to eliminate slavery in the United States. She grew up in the 19th century, born into one of the cruelest systems of slavery ever created by human beings.

Harriet Tubman and the Fight Against Slavery Bree Burns

Two small black children drew with sticks in the dirt in front of a ramshackle cabin. Their older sister, Minty, whose real name was Harriet Ross, watched them. She wished that she could play, too. But she had work to do. It was a warm fall day. The field hands who picked crops for Edward Borodas would be thirsty. She must carry water to them. Minty picked up the heavy buckets. She had no time for play.

The Story of Harriet Tubman, Conductor of the Underground Railroad   Kate McMullan

Chesapeake Bay forms the western boundary of the section of Maryland which is sometimes called Tidewater Maryland, sometimes called the Eastern Shore. Here there are so many coves and creeks, rivers and small streams, that the land areas are little more than heads or necks of land, almost surrounded by water.

Harriet Tubman: Conductor of the Underground Railroad
Ann Petry

Harriet was running.

Freedom Train: The Story of Harriet Tubman   Dorothy Sterling

My Favorite Leads

> Collect some of your favorite leads in your journal or keep them by your writing desk as inspiration. Here are a few of mine. Remember a lead can be more than a sentence. It can be a paragraph or two or even a few pages.
> Try writing a line or two about why you like it.

Hundreds of thousands of years ago, America was very different. There was no civilization: no roads, no cities, no shopping malls, no Honda dealerships. There were, of course, obnoxious shouting radio *commercials* for car dealerships; these have been broadcast toward Earth for billions of years by the evil Planet of Men Wearing Polyester Sport Coats, and there is nothing anybody can do to stop them.
> **Dave Barry Slept Here: A Sort of History of the United States**

(I love the way the way this misleading lead starts serious and keeps getting funnier.)

Many years later, as he faced the firing squad, Colonel Aureliano Buendia was to remember that distant afternoon when his father took him to discover ice.
> **One Hundred Years of Solitude**   Gabriel Garcia Marquez

(I love the way this lead encompasses a whole life in one sentence.)

Every so often that dead dog dreams me up again.
> **Dog Heaven**   Stephanie Vaughn

(I didn't know dead dogs dreamed.)

If you really want to hear about it, the first thing you'll probably want to know is where I was born, and what my lousy childhood was like, and how my parents were occupied and all before they had me, and all that David Copperfield kind of crap, but I don't like going into it, if you want to know the truth.
> **Catcher in the Rye**   J.D. Salinger

(From the start Holden Caulfield tells you more about himself by refusing to tell anything.)

During these last two decades the interest in professional fasting has been markedly diminished.
>   **The Hunger Artist**   Franz Kafka

(I love the way Kafka states something so odd in such a matter- of- fact way. The nonchalance drives the irony of the story.)

Four score and seven years ago our fathers brought forth on this continent, a new nation, conceived in Liberty and dedicated to the proposition that all men are created equal.
>   **The Gettysburg Address**   Abraham Lincoln

(Lincoln knows that his critics call his views on slavery unconstitutional so he leads this famous speech by alluding to the Declaration of Independence. I love the way Lincoln reminds us that America is not all about a book of laws, it's about a central idea.)

Five score years ago, a great American, in whose symbolic shadow we stand, signed the Emancipation Proclamation.
>   **I Have a Dream (speech)**   Martin Luther King

(Martin Luther King, who gave this famous speech standing on the steps of the Lincoln Memorial, knew he didn't have to look far to find his lead. Notice how the lead recalls Lincoln's Gettysburg address in its syntax and the Emancipation Proclamation by name.)

It's a funny thing about mothers and fathers. Even when their own child is the most disgusting little blister that you could ever imagine, they still think he or she is wonderful.
>   **Matilda**   Roald Dahl

(From the start you know this book is not a sweet little story.)

Leads in Expository Writing

What's the most boring way you could begin a research report about the human brain? A rattlesnake? The United States Constitution? We all know.

"In this report I will tell you about...."

Now that we know that, let's experiment with different places to start.

♦ **Start with a Snapshot.** (When you paint a picture, you draw the reader in. Notice the difference between these two leads to a report about ice-skating.)

Boring

Ice-skating is my favorite sport.

Better

It's ten degrees below zero and the river is frozen a foot thick. It makes snapping sounds like the limbs of trees cracking. A lone figure glides along the black ice, moving towards the city. The only sound is the scraping of each blade as it bites into the river. That's me doing my favorite sport, ice-skating.

♦ **Start with one important observation.** (Don't start in the general. Put your most surprising or important observation into your opening.)

General

The human brain is a complex and amazing organ.

Better

Seeing stars, it dreams of eternity. Hearing birds, it makes music. Smelling flowers, it is enraptured. Touching tools, it transforms the earth. But deprived of these sensory experiences, the human brain withers and dies.

Inside the Brain   Ronald Kotulak

+ **Start with a strongly stated question your readers might have.** (In some ways all writing is about trying to answer our best questions. A strong question is the one we all want to know the answer to.)

Weakly-stated
In this paper I will attempt to answer the question why history is important.

Better
What's the point of studying history? Who cares what happened long ago? After all, aren't the people in history books dead?

The History of US   Joy Hakim

+ **Put your connection with the subject in the lead.** (Why are you attracted to the subject? Do you have a personal reason for writing about this subject? What specific memories of the subject come to mind?)

General
The problem of longitude was one of the greatest scientific challenges of its day.

Better
Once on a Wednesday excursion when I was a little girl, my father bought me a beaded wire ball that I loved. At a touch, I could collapse the toy into a flat coil between my palms, or pop it open to make a hollow sphere. Rounded out it resembled a tiny Earth, because its hinged wires traced the same pattern of intersecting circles that I had seen on the globe in my school room—the thin black lines of latitude and longitude

Longitude   Dava Sobel

+ **Flaunt your favorite bit of research in the lead.** (Start with the facts that made you smile, laugh, go "ahaaa!" or just plain grossed you out.)

General
Did you ever wonder why God created flies?

Better
Though we've been killing them for years now, I have never tested the folklore that with a little cream and sugar, flies taste very much like black raspberries.

Where to Look for Titles

Titles are the first impression of any piece of writing. Some extend their hand in a warm embrace; others pull back and demand that you draw them into conversation. Some titles are cute; some are mysterious. Others tell you exactly what to expect. Playing with titles can be a great way to grasp their unique power and how it relates to a particular piece of writing. Below you'll find some ideas about where titles come from. Let your list of titles grow long and pick the one that fits best.

Look for a specific quote within the text
Go Ask Alice   Anonymous
To Kill a Mockingbird Harper Lee
Catcher in the Rye J.D. Salinger
For Whom the Bell Tolls Ernest Hemingway

Title your book after a central character
Hamlet William Shakespeare
Runa   Alison James
Wilfred Gordon McDonald Partridge   Mem Fox

Describe the central idea of your story
Love in the Time of Cholera Gabriel Garcia Marquez
Anatomy of an Illness   Norman Cousins
On Death and Dying   Elizabeth Kubler Ross

Pick one word which sums up the central theme of your story

Affliction Russell Banks
Hunger   Knut Hamson
Patrimony Phillip Roth
Rimwalkers Vicki Grove
Metamorphosis Franz Kafka

The title is the doorway into the story.

Name your piece about a place
Whipple's Castle Thomas Williams
Chesapeake James Michener
Ellis Island Mark Helprin

Funny Headlines

In newspapers titles come as headlines. The great thing about headlines is they try to say a lot in a short amount of space. Sometimes this leads to problems, funny problems. After you read the funny headlines below try writing some of your own.

Include Your Children When Baking Cookies

Police Begin Campaign to Run Down Jaywalkers

Safety Experts Say School Bus Passengers Should Be Belted

Iraqi Head Seeks Arms

British Left Waffles on Falkland Islands

Teachers Strike Idle Kids

Enraged Cow Injures Farmer with Ax

Miners Refuse To Work After Death

Stolen Painting Found by Tree

War Dims Hope for Peace

Deer Kill 17,000

Red Tape Holds Up New Bridge

Hospital Sued by 7 Foot Doctors

Re-Titling is Revising

When we re-title a piece of writing we change its whole shape. To prove this we are going have some fun. Below are some different genres of writing. Try re-naming a story to fit another genre. For example, what would *Hamlet* be called if it was a Broadway musical? Answer: *Decisions. Decisions!* What would Hamlet cereal be called?

Original Title:

Genre

Genre	
Mystery	
Insurance Policy	
Broadway Musical	
Fairy Tale	
Cereal	
Adventure Story	
Pop Song	
Self-help Book	
How-to Book	

Beginnings and Endings

Night creeps around the edges of the gauzy curtains at the Belknap Nursing Home. The TV stares like an empty block of slate. The Puerto Ricans are passed out on the floor by the vase of geraniums. Beside the tray of uneaten food, at the end of her bed, sits the hunchback. He huddles over a tattered prayer book and mutters the Kaddish prayer. Her arms reach in his direction. They caress the rough burlap. They pull him towards her. His hair is a nest of dead trees, his shoulders are mounds of earth falling softly, without weight, over her, like the eyelids of an infant sinking into sleep.

And so the Prince married Jessie and they lived at the farmer's house where she worked in the garden and learned to read and write and do all the things she loved best. And they lived happily ever after, but they had to work at it.

Then one by one, starting at the bottom and rippling to the top, all seven puppets turn their heads and look up at me. What do they want? How can I move them when my hands are stone?

Long ago, in a kingdom far away there lived a very poor farmer and his young daughter Jessie.

My interest in puppetry began when as a five year old I stood beside my grandfather in Berlin's Schauspielhaus and watched the great Gerhard Schweitzer. I found it hard to believe that something made of wood and metal, something hanging from wires could appear so lifelike –yet so much more beautiful than life.

Mrs. Zysblatt sits in the Belknap nursing home and two Puerto Rican men sit across from her, their legs crossed like the guests on the Merv Griffin show. Through the gauzy curtains leaf shadows dance in the whirring breeze and a toothless hunchback man in a potato sack shirt speckled with sawdust sits on the bureau. He rocks from side to side and calls to her but she cannot hear him because it is an evening forty years ago and she is waiting for her son Solly to come home from the dance at PS 54.

The 3 Act Story

Many stories and just about all Hollywood movies can be divided into 3 sections: the Set-up where the basic problem or friction is defined; the Mix-up, where things get more complicated and other problems often arise; and the End-up, the resolution where the problems are resolved one way or another. Below you'll find an analysis of the 3 acts of Cinderella. After you see the analysis try defining the 3 acts of one of your stories.

Cinderella

Set-up: She wants to go to the ball and then the Fairy Godmother shows up and makes magic things happen, but she warns what will happen if Cindy doesn't split by 12:00. The conflict is set up.

Mix-up: Though she makes a big hit at the ball she leaves too late and in running away leaves her glass slipper. Her sisters talk about the Princess but don't believe it was their step-sister.

End-up: The Prince decides to hunt for his Princess and eventually finds the right foot. The story begins sadly and ends happily.

Comments: *I think the end-up in Cinderella is too short. If I were to re-write the story I would add more about the search for Cinderella or make the ending longer. Walt Disney's writers actually did this by having some invented mice help Cinderella get out of a locked room.*

3 Acts of my Story

Below are 3 Boxes for you to define the 3 acts of a story you have written or are about to write. After you write or draw about your 3 acts, ask yourself which act is the strongest, and which could be made stronger by a bigger obstacle or problem or a change in plot line.

Title_____

Set-up

Mix-up

End-up

What's the Goal?
What's the Obstacle?

My friend David Evanier is a screenwriter in Hollywood. He told me a question producers always ask about a script is, where's the obstacle? What's the thing that gets in the way of a character and her goal? Strong stories tend to have big goals and big obstacles for the characters to overcome, and weak stories can be made stronger by upping the ante. For example, your character wants to win a race because he wants to use the $500 first prize to go to college. This is a worthy goal, but what if your character has a grandfather who won't get out of bed because he hasn't paid taxes on the farm and knows he will lose it if he can't come up with $500, and your character is an eleven year-old boy who knows he can get the money by winning the race? Then you have a real story. Add to that an obstacle like your character has a sled with one dog and his rival is a stone-faced Indian who has five of the most beautiful sled dogs the world has ever seen, and then you have a rich story like **The Stone Fox** by John Reynolds Gardiner.

Look at some stories you have read or heard or seen, and ask yourself two questions about the main character.

What's the Goal?

What's the Obstacle?

P

Types of Endings

"Don't write endings, find them," novelist Thomas Williams used to say. Endings grow from beginnings and reveal themselves through clues within the story, characters or ideas. One way to learn about endings is to observe the different ways authors end a story. See appendix A for books with each of the following endings.

The Loop Ending

A loop ending ends at the same place it begins. A good children's book to illustrate this is *If You Give a Mouse a Cookie* by Laura Numeroff. Does your story want to end the same place it began?

The Surprise Ending

A surprise ending usually has a twist to it that takes the reader by surprise. In the *Wizard of Oz* movie, we think Dorothy is going home in the balloon with the wizard, then the balloon flies away. How will she get home now? The good witch Glinda comes and shows her the true power of the slippers.

A good mystery story must have a surprise ending. The least likely suspect must be the one who did it. Is your story one that wants to throw the reader a curve ball in the last inning? If so, try writing a surprise ending.

The Summary

And to round off tonight's newscast, here are the highlights once again. A summary ending repeats the main points of a story, trying to tie together any loose ends. This type of ending works well in speeches that are trying to hammer home a point. Is your piece trying to persuade the reader? If so, you may want to end by summing up your best points.

The Happy Ending

Most fairy tales have happy endings (depending on whether you are a wolf-lover, of course). A happy ending such as the one in Cinderella leaves the reader with no feeling of sadness. Like a good warm blanket, it covers us from the cold of life. Is your story a fairy tale? Does it want to end happily, or would it be stronger and more real if it ended sadly?

The Sad but True Ending

When we read that Charlotte dies at the end of *Charlotte's Web,* we are sad. But it has to end that way. Try saving Charlotte and the story loses its power. It becomes a lie. I call this the "sad but true" ending. Does your story need to end sadly? Does your happy ending have a false ring? If so, you may want to write a sad but true ending.

Changing Morals: Revising Fables

A fable is a teaching story that ends with a moral, which tells you exactly what to take away from the story. The most famous fables are those of Aesop, which came from Ancient Greece. If we change or add on to the story of a fable, we can change the moral. For example, in "the Tortoise and the Hare," an over-confident rabbit loses the race to a slow but consistent tortoise. The moral is: Slow and steady wins the race. But let's say we decide to extend the story beyond the finish line. The next week the tortoise challenged five more hares to a race. They knew about what happened to the first hare so they took the race more seriously. The tortoise lost to all five hares. The moral: Quit while you're ahead. Take a fable from a book or choose the one listed below. Revise it to change the moral. Have fun.

Once there were two seeds sitting in a barnyard. The first seed couldn't wait to put down roots and grow into a plant. The second seed was afraid. What would happen if he became a plant? His leaves might wither, his roots could dry up if it didn't rain, a child might pick his flowers. In time the first seed grew into a magnificent plant with orange flowers and a sweet scent. The second seed sat and watched, until one day a chicken came and ate him.

Moral: Only through risk can we grow and bloom.

2

Using the Binoculars

Turning the Knob

When I was in school I thought details were just extra words to add in a story to make it better. I thought detail was decoration or wallpaper, syrupy adjectives that stuck to nouns, adverbs that propped up flabby verbs ("He walked slowly" instead of "He slithered." "The gleaming sun shone" instead of "The sun scorched me like a hot iron.")

Details are not wallpaper; they are walls. When I describe a room I don't describe it; I build it. I create it.

Think of a pair of binoculars. You look through them at first and they are blurry. Here's a blurry sentence: "I walked into the McDonald's and there were people everywhere." You've been there before. All McDonalds' are the same, right? Wrong. Now take out your binoculars and turn that little knob. You turn the knob by asking questions. Questions that focus your own binoculars on all your senses. Here, I'll show you.

What did they look like? (Eyes)
What were they wearing? (Eyes)
What were they doing? (Eyes & ears)
What did it smell like? (Nose)
What was the air like? (Touch)
What was in your mouth? (Taste)

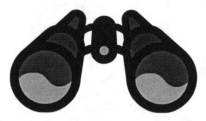

You don't need to ask these questions out loud, but you can. You can even pair up with a partner and turn the knob on each other's binoculars. Or you can just sit there and imagine your binoculars focusing. Then write your way past the blurry room and see, smell, hear, touch, and taste the details.

The workmen leaned on the stainless steel counters, bellies bursting out of stained tee shirts. An old man in the corner held an aluminum cane in one hand and a rolled-up newspaper in the other. He swatted at flies as the workers scurried behind the counters, stuffing bags with greasy burgers, rushing to the beeping fryolaters to scoop the golden greasy potato sticks, slinging steaming robot food into cardboard trays and paper bags. The smell of sizzling fat hung in the air and I could taste, swallow and digest that hamburger before the young girl could say,

"Have a nice day."

P

Information-Not Words

Jessie Yorko is a first grader whose teacher taught her the binoculars. Notice the difference between draft one and draft three. Jessie adds information, not extra words, to her story.

My Pig by Jessie   Draft 1 (before binoculars)

I made a pink pig. His name is Ham Yorko. He rolls in the mud. One day he ate a lot of food. He rolled down the hill. He couldn't walk so he didn't try to get up.

The next morning I got up to feed my pig. I didn't see him. Then I went to look for him. I couldn't find him so I went home.

When I got home, there he was, and he never ate a lot of food again.

My Pig  by Jessie   Draft 3 (after binoculars)

I made a pig out of garbage. His body was a milk carton. His ears were those tiny styrofoam "peanuts" they pack glass in. I made his tail out of string. I wrapped him in pink paper to make him be a pink pig.

His name is Ham Yorko. He rolls in the mud on the shady side of the house.

One day he ate a lot of food. His food was on the edge of the hill. He spilled a little water. He slipped and started rolling down the hill.

He got hurt a little. His leg got a cut. It hit a rock while he was rolling down.

He rolled down the hill into the woods at the bottom of the hill, and landed on his back out of breath. When he caught his breath, he tried to get up again because he was too fat. So then he just stayed there for the night.

The next morning I got up and went outside to feed my pig on the edge of the hill where I have a bowl for his food. I didn't see him.

I look around first on the other side of the house. I don't see him. Then I go looking in the wood. I see a pine tree. On the edge of the pine tree I see my pig's leg sticking out. He's on the other side of the pine tree. He's surprised to see me.

He just looked at me, kind of glad. And then I helped him get up. I carried him home. He was heavy. I was tired going up that hill. I let him go and stopped for a minute to take a rest. When we got to the top of the hill, he ate all his breakfast. I was happy he ate all his breakfast. He was happy to be back home. Then he rolled in the mud again.

P

Make a Zoom Book

Each turn of the binocular knob often brings surprising detail. Nowhere is this fact more evident than in Istvan Banyai's wordless picture book, *Zoom*, where we discover new worlds as the camera pulls back from a barnyard. Below, first grader Brendan makes his own Zoom book. Notice how we learn new information with each turn of the knob. Make your own Zoom book.

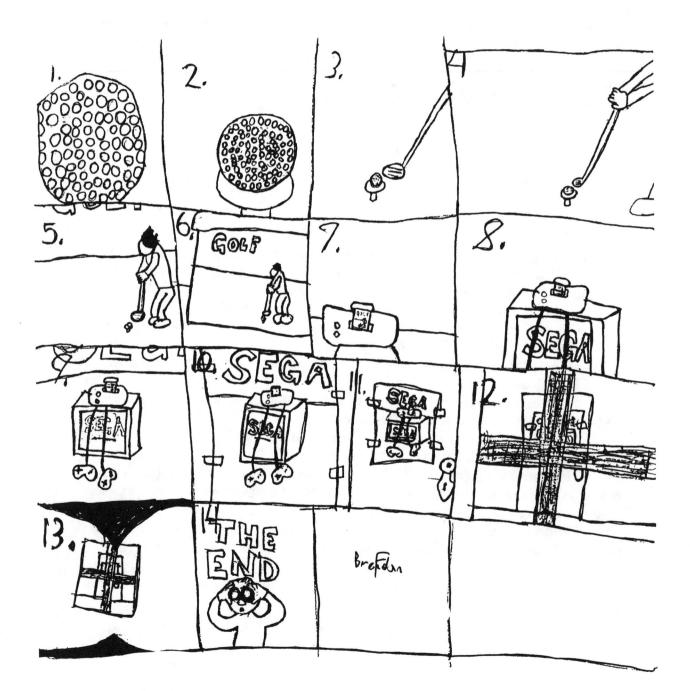

P

I Am a Camera

Below are two pictures I took in San Francisco, California. The first is the window of Underhill's Barbershop. In the second I zoomed in to look at the official hairstyles of men and boys. If I zoomed in one more time, I might focus on the figure in the upper left-hand corner of the poster: George Washington with a crew cut. The more we zoom, the more surprising detail we are apt to find. Try zooming with your own camera or with drawings. Keep your eyes open for surprising detail.

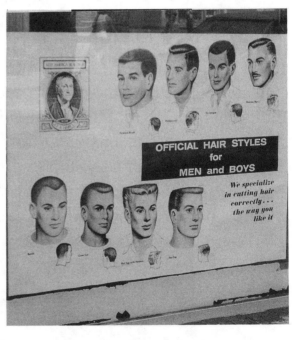

Zooming Fort Harrod

Below and on the following page are 5 photos of Fort Harrod in Harrodsburg Kentucky. At one time in American history, this was the furthest point west. When you stand in different places at Fort Harrod, you see different details.

When I first saw the fort, it was across a cemetery where many of the settlers were buried. I looked down at a grave of moss-covered stones. Some of the graves had only small stones. A sign told about the eight styles of grave markings. It said the small stones were the graves of children. One grave had a special sign. It said, "The First White child entombed in Kentucky." It seemed so absurd .to single out this one little stone from all the others. Are we not all made from the same dust?

When I walked up to the wall of the fort I thought of all the people who lived and died here. I put my hand on the fence and stared up at the chiseled wooden poles. They looked like teeth biting against the sky.

Can you see how the camera sees different things when it stands and points in different directions? These details spark thoughts and new directions. Try this: next time you go somewhere, bring a real camera or a sketch pad. Stop in different places and observe and record detail with your camera or sketch pad. Later look at your pictures and write about what you see and remember.

There are 8 types of grave markings visible in this graveyard.
1. Conventional type with headstone and engraving.
2. Concealed type which is flat on ground and originally covered by dirt and grass so that Indians would not desecrate them.
3. Skull and crossbone which means stark reality of death.
4. Religious type with cross engraved.
5. Coffin shaped stones.
6. Small stones for infants and children.
7. Stones with epitaph engraved.
8. Small crude rocks.

Fort Harrod

P

Living in the Specific

Read the following blurry sentences, pick one or two and make them come alive with specific details. Try working with a partner and asking each other questions to turn the knob on your binoculars. Make a list and star (*) your favorite details to share with your classmates. If you don't like any of the sentences below, make up one of your own.

I have a dragon.

Ms. Jones had a bizarre way of punishing her students.

It was a more awesome planet for kids than earth.

Americans care more about freedom than safety.

He/she was a disgusting eater.

Neil was getting the feeling all night that Elizabeth might not be interested in a second date.

When you have the "math curse" you see math problems everywhere.

P

Crazy Clothes Get Crazier

With a partner or two, list details on the left to make the blurry sentence below come alive. Remember, details are boxes inside boxes. If your first detail is polka dots, keep turning the knob on each other's binoculars to get pink and purple pear-shaped polka dots. Write your more specific and crazier details in the right column.

He/She liked crazy clothes.

1st Details	More specific
Red pants	Fire engine red polyester bell-bottoms

P

Clean Your Room

Is your room messy? Has it ever been messy? If so, how messy? Is there junk on the floor? What kind of junk? Are there toys? papers? underwear? Where are the toys? Where is the underwear? Zoom in on the details of your messy room and list them below. Star your best details and try doing a poem of the mess.

The Messy Room

Clothes wrestling on the floor,
the shirts and pants pinning the underwear,
the socks balled and stinky,
sprinkled like black olives over the furniture.

In one corner
the mangled Barbies gather.
Malibu Barbie surfs a sea of headless Ken
Naked Hawaiian Hair Barbie drowns
in a mass of matted grass skirt
wadded with the grape bubble gum
that you had tried to save.
A legless Skipper has skipped her last time.

Legos crunch beneath your feet as you
proceed to the unmade bed,
the bed you were supposed to make every day,
if you were the kind of child
that made her bed every day
that put her toys away,
and never drank milk from the carton

when no one was looking.   Barry Lane

P

What Are They Doing?

One way to use your binoculars is to zoom in on gestures and motions of your characters. It's difficult to describe faces in writing but easier to describe what people are doing with their hands, how they walk,
Mannerisms give readers a chance to see your characters. One way to practice is to go to a public place and record the
mannerisms of strangers. Here are some I did recently.

As he leaned across the table and reached for the salt his white sleeve dipped into the puddle of ketchup.

He ran his hand across his slicked back hair and pinched the end of his nose in lieu of a tissue.

He thrust a chocolate ice cream cone into the air like the Statue of Liberty and it melted in brown rivulets down his skinny forearm.

She sat on the plane with her hands folded reading her National Enquirer one page at a time as though the meaning of life might be hidden in its sacred pages.

The pilot held the clipboard in his lap and sipped from the white paper cup.

Grace pressed the brown bunny close to her chest and stared down at the twitching nose as though it might reveal the great mystery in its steady rhythm.

He dipped the net down into weeds, and as the dark fished floundered in the sunlight he wiped the sweat from his brow.

P

Write Small

Writing gets beautiful when it gets specific. It gets funny too.   Author Ralph Fletcher teaches us to write small, to zoom in on the little things, especially when big issues are at stake. Don't write about your fear of airplanes, write about the flight attendant pulling the yellow oxygen mask over her bored face and instructing all to breathe normally. Thinking small is a way of thinking that helps us to write more distinctly. You can practice beneath. For each idea find a specific image or object that gets to the idea without explaining it. Try it in your own writing next time you find yourself lost in a big idea or emotion.

Big Idea	Small Image
Birthday parties are fun.	Licking the pink frosting off the ends of the candles
School dances are strange.	Strobe lights flickering over laughing faces as the beat pounds on
The Holocaust was inhuman.	A mountain of children's shoes

Small Writing is Funny Writing

The writing gets funny when it gets small. In other words, humiliation is not funny, but noticing a certain zipper is down during a job interview and trying to correct the problem without the interviewer noticing is funny. Comedy writers know that no idea is proven till it gets specific. Here's something to try. In the left column write something that bugs you. In the right column write a specific example or image of the thing.

Funny concept   Funnier image

Funny concept	Funnier image
My brother doesn't clean the shower.	I hate hair on soap .
Snobby hotels	The toilet paper is folded to make you think nobody used it. Do they think we're that dumb?
Bored waiting in line at the supermarket	Being so bored at the supermarket, I I read all of Sister Fatima's predictions for the end of the world and Elvis's latest itinerary.
I hate big family weddings	Do I really want to catch up to date with Mom's second cousin Guido?

Verbs and Nouns

Strong writing is built on nouns and verbs, not adjectives and adverbs. In other words you can say, "I really, really hate school lunches because they are just so disgusting and gross," or you can say, "I don't eat stale cornbread, ravioli stuffed with gray mystery meat, powdered mashed potatoes, doughy pizza, beet cubes, army beans that look like they've been through one too many battles and yellowing vanilla pudding with gobs of cool whip, which coat the roof of your mouth like latex paint."

   Below is a description of Wilbur the pig's supper from *Charlotte's Web* by E. B. White and what Vietnam soldiers carry from Tim O'brien's book *The Things They Carried*. Notice how lists of nouns pull us in. Try writing your own lists of nouns to describe a meal, a place, a certain time, a classroom, or whatever else strikes you. If you want, write your list as a poem as I have done beneath. Keep lists in your toolbox.

At four would come supper. Skim milk, provender, leftover sandwich from Lurvy's lunchbox, prune skins, a morsel of this, a bit of that, fried potatoes, marmalade drippings, a little more of this, a little more of that, a piece of baked apple, a scrap of upside down cake.

Charlotte's Web   E.B. White

Henry Dobbins, who was a big man, carried extra rations; he was especially fond of canned peaches in heavy syrup over pound cake. Dave Jensen, who practiced field hygiene, carried a toothbrush, dental floss, and several hotel-sized bars of soap he'd stolen on R&R in Sydney, Australia. Ted Lavender, who was scared, carried tranquilizers until he was shot in the head outside the village of Than Khe in mid-April. By necessity, and because it was SOP, they all carried steel helmets that weighed 5 pounds including the liner and camouflage cover.

   The Things They Carried   Tim O'Brien

Binoculars Mine Memory

When we ask students to write a topic sentence and three supporting details we often get a list of details, but when a curious writer like Liz Mandrell, a teacher from Mt. Sterling, Kentucky, uses her binoculars, details emerge with each turn of the knob. When you read the following excerpt from an essay titled *"Trial by Error in the Halls of Ignorance,"* think of how your own binoculars can help you mine your memory.

Try writing about your own teachers and see which details miraculously emerge when the ink hits the paper.

Elementary school! I was completely terrorized by Mrs. Elwood Norton. Why did anyone name a girl Elwood? I queried from my seat in the back row. I wanted to be up front. I wanted to shine under Elwood's bifocaled stare but she put me in the back row with Gladys Dibble. Gladys Dibble who stood six feet tall in the first grade, Gladys Dibble whose dad was the only Hell's Angel in three counties, Gladys Dibble who critically injured Joey Taggart when he spit on me at recess, Gladys Dibble who sniffed 400 pounds of snot back into her sinuses every day. Blow it out, I wanted to scream. Blow it all out! Her condition seemed to accelerate at afternoon milk break when we as a class became a veritable symphony of plastic straw suckers, our straws like rosined fiddle bows scraping every resonant corner of the milk carton in search of the last drop of moo. Gladys out-sipped, out sniffed all of us with her sinus in B-minor concerto. To this day, I don't drink chocolate milk, but I did manage to struggle to second grade.

Mrs. Patterson wore no bra beneath her gauzy dashiki-blouses (this was the 1970's) and one day during reading...incidentally, I was in with the Wombats, which I thought was a really cool name for a reading group until I found out that Wombats were burrowing marsupials in the badger family...but one day during reading her left breast fell right out, practically planting itself on the table. The earth tilted, planets spun and we all stared, eyes big as skeet plates at the still jiggling dollop of humanity on our reading table. Mrs. Patterson reached down. "Excuzay Mwoi," she said and flopped herself discreetly back into the gauzy depths of her blouse. And there we were, six little wombats scarred forever.[1]

Binoculars on Prompted Tests

A first grade teacher handed me the following responses by her students to a prompted test. The directions were to imagine you planted a magic bean in your garden. Write a story about what happened to it in the garden. Remember to include a beginning, middle and end and tell your story in the order things happened.

   As you read the following responses notice how the kids who excel the most tend to ignore the directions and just write and write where the binoculars lead them. It is their sense of audience and story that guides them. Real organization grows out of having something to say and then trying to say it better.

One day a boy went to the store. On the way he saw magic beans. He looked at the price it was only 50 cents. He bought the beans and as soon as he got home he planted them. The next day he looked at his plant. It didn't look like a candy tree so he started to cry. But he looked around it he saw a piece of candy and now he always looks around before crying and you can still see that same tree with candy on it. **Tom**

Once there was a teenager named Chris. He was very poor. One day his mom said sell this horse today and get some money. On his way he met up with an old man. He said I'll trade you for that horse for magic beans. Sure he said. When he got home his mom said what do you have magic beans. So his mom went outside and planted them in the garden. During the night it grew into a giant beanstalk. Chris saw it and started to climb it. He climbed and he climbed to the top. He saw a path. He walked down the path. He saw a GIGANTIC castle. He knocked on the door and an old woman asked, what do you want? Some money I am poor. Come in. A giant gave him some money and Chris killed him. **Chris**

I put a magic bean in the garden. My mom said nothing will grow. I said something would grow too. And it grew I came to a castle. A giant lives there. **Emma**

Once there was a little girl named Julia. She had a magic bean. She decided to plant it in her garden and she did. She watered it every day. She did everything to it! Julia asked her mother when it was going to start growing. "Oh it will grow sooner or later. Her mom said. But Julia waited for two weeks and said Mommy when will my bean start growing. Oh said her mother. It will grow sooner or later. She said, But Mama you said that before and nothing happened. Well let it come up on it's own. A month went by, and Julia waited and waited and waited until one day her plant got a little sprout and she said. "I have a little sprout and as she said it the plant got bigger and bigger and bigger until it was a tree. Julia looked at the tree and said... "What kind of tree is this? It is a candy tree that looks very good! The next two months came her birthday and she did not have to buy candy for the goody bag she just took it off the tree. And you probably are thinking how does she get all the candy when it runs out! Well it just grows back and she always has it! And she never runs out isn't that amazing? Well it is to me! Julia loved this tree. She said to her mom one day it must have been a magic bean and it was....... **Julia**

When you really listen you hear questions.

Barry Lane

Prove It!

In expository writing, using the binoculars often times means zeroing in with facts to back up blurry opinions, but sometimes we have to look twice to tell the difference between a fact and an opinion.

Here's a chance to practice. Use the page below or draw a line down a page in your journal. On the left side of the page, write opinions. On the right side of the page, write facts that back up those opinions. You may have to go to the library to find a specific fact. For example:

Opinion (Don't believe me?)	**Fact** (I'll prove it.)
The earth is being poisoned by toxic chemicals.	An average of 21 toxic spills take place in the United states each year.
There are more black bears in New Hampshire today then there were in 1900.	There were an estimated 50 black bears in New Hampshire in 1900. The NH Fish and Game department estimates there are 2,500 today.
Nuclear power in the former Soviet-bloc countries is dangerous.	Between 1993 and 1998, there were 418 nuclear accidents in the Ukraine

Alien Eyes See Funny Detail

Attention students, the spaceship will be leaving for planet earth in ten minutes. We must prepare ourselves. Put on your foot sleeves, your skin slippers, your brain lids. Make sure your leg receptacles are full with metallic tender disks to ensure proper remuneration. Connect your anti—splat buckles...

If you were from another planet you would not know what to call things. You would stand outside everything that you know about human beings and have to guess at what you were seeing. Like a poet you would have to make up words for everything you see. In Jean Willis's children's book, *Earthlets*, aliens describe infants. A line like "the earthlet grandmother makes earthlet wrappers from fuzz of sheep" makes us smile because the words give fresh life to what we know already. Words are not simply a means of describing a world already there. Words create the world they describe. Try using your own alien eyes with the exercise below.

Warm up

1) Translate one or two of the following things into alien language. Give a brief definition as if you are writing an alien dictionary.

Toaster -- Interstate 95 -- Television -- A little brother/sister -- A sandwich
People smoking cigarettes -- Airplanes -- School cafeteria

2) You and your students are now ready to file your dispatches home. You may want to begin by brainstorming a list of events, places, people or things your alien can describe. Remember that your alien is by no means an expert on what he is describing. She may be trying to figure out the world. The uncertainty in your alien's voice may make it more fun to play with.

Tip: There is a tendency to write in longer words when you do this exercise. This works but sometimes leads to aliens who only talk like machines. Short words will give your aliens more soul and variety. In other words, a television could be an *humanoid reduction receptacle* or a *people shrinker box*. The second term has more life in it. You don't have to use big words to be an alien, you just have to see the world in a different way.

Light Eaters

The lifeforms are addicted to a particular form of entertainment activity. They sit in the life space on bloated reclining devices and ingest blue light rays from the cathode box, only leaving to spill fluid in the throne room or remove machine twisted food from the cold closet. Those unable to ingest the light rays stare at letter specks on bound paper. We have concluded this to be an ancient form of meaning construction, still popular, though no longer necessary. The lifeforms also have been seen making letter specks and attaching them to the cold closet. This is believed to be a way of circumventing decay in the thought organ.

P

Rhyming Detail

One way to find detail is to rhyme for it. The following is a group poem of rhymed couplets from a fourth grade class. It begins with a couplet from Walt Whitman and goes on from there. [2] Try adding some more rhymed couplets to the same poem, or make up your own.

America Right Now

4th grade

I hear America singing
I hear bells ringing
I hear teachers writing
I hear kids fighting
I hear cars running
I hear birds humming
I hear girls spelling
I hear boys yelling
I hear dreamers dreaming
I hear people screaming
I hear trumpets blowing
I hear people sewing
I hear dogs barking
I hear cars parking
I hear bullets flying
I hear people dying
I hear buildings burning
I hear revolvers turning
I hear newscasts blaring
I hear people swearing
I hear America crying
I hear politicians lying.

[2] *Teachers' and Writers' Guide to Walt Whitman* (Teachers and Writers Collaborative 1991)

Revising Basals

What happens when a 7th grader who loves to read and write finds an old basal reader? Revision happens. Below you'll find a simulated old basal story. On the next page you'll find what happened when Whitney Krohne, a 7th grader from Dowagiac, Michigan, got the idea of revising it from her teacher Paula Shaffer. Notice how much better the piece gets when we use the binoculars.

Revise a basal or any boring piece of writing today. You may want to begin by simply listing a few questions then using these questions as fuel for the story. When you're done, compare the two pieces of writing. How did you make it better? List some qualities of good writing.

Greg Jumped Up

Greg's mother came in.
She met Greg on the lawn.
"You need to go to bed," she said.
"You need to go to bed, so you can get up with the sun."
"Can Stan and I sleep on the lawn?" Greg said.
"No," Mother said, "you may not."
"The grass is damp."
"You can't sleep on damp grass."
"Then let me sleep on the floor with Stan," Greg said.
"Will you let me, please?"
"No, Greg. You will not sleep on the damp grass."
She went away.
But Greg was still standing on the lawn.
Greg laid on the wet grass and looked up at the sky.
Black clouds floated by.
Then Greg had a surprise..
A bright light came in the dark sky.
The light went very fast.
Do you know what it was?
The light which came and went was lightening.
The lightening made Greg jump up.

The Bath ("Greg Jumped Up" revised)
by Whitney Krohne

"Greg!" Mrs. Solomon called to her eleven-year-old son who at the moment happened to be racing his bike with his best friend Stan.

He came to a skidding stop, spraying loose gravel over the overworked, underpaid waitress's feet.

"Whaddaya want?" He asked, his top lip curled in a nasty snarl.

"Get in that house and take a bath! I'm not going to tell you again!" said the irritated mother.

"I don't wanna take a bath! Besides, Stan and I are gonna sleep in the yard tonight."

"Fine. Skip the bath. I don't care if you smell like a dead skunk, but you're not sleeping in the yard and that's final!" shouted his angry mother. "Now get in that house and go to bed!"

"Fine!" he shouted back at her. He then whispered to Stan, "Meet me here in an hour."

Greg let his mother lead him to his room. There he shut the door in her face and pretended to get into his pajamas. He waited until he heard her gentle snoring in the next room, then he sneaked outside to meet Stan.

"Did you bring a blanket to sleep on?" asked Stan.

"Of course I did, dumbhead!" Greg snapped.

So the two boys spread out their blankets on the wet grass.

After a while of talking, the two boys drifted off to sleep.

Around 2:00 a.m. Stan felt a drop of water hit him square between the eyes. He sat up and heard the pitter patter of raindrops hitting the sidewalk between them. He looked over where Greg was.

"Greg. Greg," Stan said groggily as he felt for his friend in the dark. "That jerkface! He left me out here to get soaked in the rain while he's inside sleeping in a warm, dry bed. I'll get him for this!" Stan swore, grabbed his jacket, and went toward his home next door.

"Whoa!" Stan said as he tripped over a pile of blankets wadded up in a careless heap. "That stupid poopface! He didn't even bother to take in his blankets! Well, he's in for a big surprise. I'll just take them."

Little did Stan know that his friend was still there but had been covered in the blankets that Stan had just taken. Since it was dark, Stan didn't see Greg when he took the blankets.

Being the sound sleeper that he was, Greg didn't even feel the rain. Then it started raining harder, tickling Greg.

"Ha, ha, ha, ha, ha!" Greg laughed in his sleep, waking his mother.

The Bath (continued)

Sleepily she climbed out of bed and peered out the window, brushing her tangled red hair from her eyes.

"What in the world?" she wondered out loud. Her eyes popped open the instant she realized what was happening.

She rushed to the bathroom, grabbed the shampoo and soap, and raced to the yard before her son woke up. She knew that she would never get another chance like this.

"Ha, ha, ha, ha!" Greg's high pitched, hyena laugh filled her ears as she neared the ticklish boy.

The mother, now almost completely soaked, knelt down by Greg's side and took off his shirt. She lathered the soap all over his upper body. She poured the shampoo over the mess of tangled knots he called hair.

She cleaned and scrubbed until she had blisters on her hands and her face was a light shade of blue. Then she went into the house, plopped down on the couch and was asleep instantly.

The next morning, Greg awoke to an unfamiliar smell. It wasn't a bad smell, but just new to him. "Why am I all wet?" he wondered aloud.

He walked inside (totally forgetting Stan) to see what was for breakfast. To his horror he saw his mother on the couch gripping a bar of soap that had been worn down to a stub.

A distorted look of hatred overtook his face as he realized what his mother had done.

"MOOOOOOMMMMM!" Greg yelled.

"What? Huh? What?" came the frantic cries of a tired mother. "Who are you?" asked the mother as she squinted her eyes to see him better.

"What? I'm your son! Don't you even know who I am?" the child asked in a worried voice.

"You can't be my son."

"Why not?"

"My son smells like a dead skunk."

"Don't try to change the subject," he replied sharply. "You cleaned me last night and you know who I am. You're not getting out of this one that easily."

"Go get my glasses from the bathroom. They're under the mirror, " said the clever mother who didn't wear glasses.

Greg stepped into the bathroom and flicked on the light. He flinched at the sudden brightness.

"I don't see any glasses. Whoa!" he said with a note of amazement in his voice when he saw his reflection in the mirror.

"Mom! I look cool! Can I take another bath tonight so that I'll look like this for school tomorrow?"

The Sad Man Revealed

Did you ever wonder the true story when you read a book like the one quoted beneath? Now is your chance. You see they left those big spaces between the lines so you could write your questions. Why was the sad man running? What was his name? Use your questions to revise the story. Keep turning the knob on your binoculars to make the story more interesting.

The Sad Man

The sad man ran.

The sad man ran to Fran.

Fran had a fan.

Fran can fan the sad man.

P

The Math Binoculars

In Jon Szeiska's *Math Curse*, the main character sees math problems everywhere. What about you? How many math problems can you think of between the time you got up this morning and the time you're reading this? Take out your mathematical binoculars and start turning the knob. In the left hand column write some math facts you've found in newspapers or books or in real life. On the right side list some math questions you could ask about that fact.

Example: Sylvester Stallone will get 60 million dollars for his next three movies. (Source: *USA Today*)

My question: Assuming he works 40-hour weeks for 156 weeks (3 years) what is his hourly wage?

I came up with $9,615.38 per hour.

Not a bad job.

Facts

A dragonfly eats an average
of 300 mosquitoes a day.

Questions

How many mosquitoes a week?
If you bring ten dragonflies
to your house, how many mosquitoes
will they eat a month?

P

Questioning Character

In fiction, characters develop the more we ask ourselves questions about them. The binoculars can help you build a character before you begin your story. Here are a few basic questions to ask about a character. Try pairing up and asking each other more. Make lists or webs about your character. Draw pictures too. Remember stories are about characters with real problems and real goals. Keep asking questions to help your character's problems and goals grow and change.

Name:_____ Age:____ Height:____ Weight:____

Family and friends:

Outstanding positive quality:

Outstanding negative quality:

Problem	Goal

P

The Problem and the Potato

Once your character has a problem the next question to ask is, what's the potato underneath the problem, the thing the story will dig at? For example, if your character's name is Matt and his problem is that he beats up people the next question you have to ask yourself is, why? Is it because his big brother beats up him? Is it because his father died and he is angry? Is it because he can't read well and it's frustrating? Maybe it's all these problems.

Write your character's problem on the left side and see if you can come up with some potatoes that grow beneath that problem on the right side. Remember, potatoes are not the problem but are the cause of the problem that often lies buried out of sight.

Problem	Potato

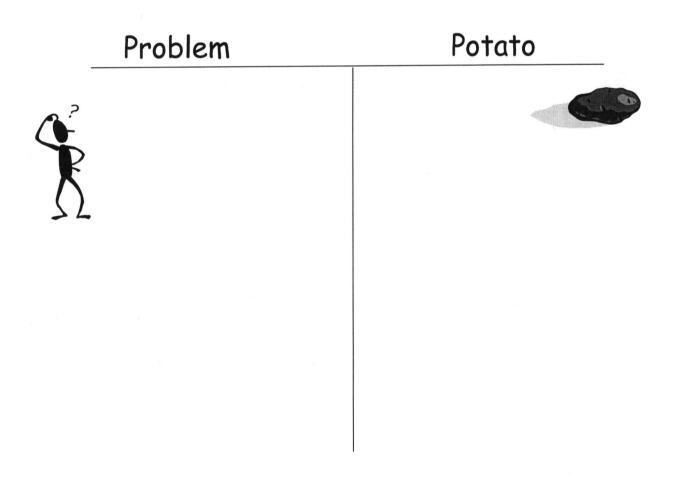

I Bet You'd Never Guess

Interesting characters often surprise us. The bank robber who we find is afraid of spiders, the nun who plays poker on Saturday nights, the four-star General who takes needlepoint classes, all are interesting people who we want to spend time with. Contradictions make for interesting people. Predictability is boring. Think about your characters. What makes them who they are? What surprising detail could you reveal about them? Practice on the characters and historical figures below. Try some of your own.

Person	Surprising Detail
George Washington	eats peas with his knife
Winnie the Pooh	would like to be Tigger
Susan B. Anthony	
Charlotte (the spider)	
A man works as a toll-booth attendant	
A woman who cleans rooms at a motel	

The Thoughts of Pocahontas

Below is a portrait of Pocahontas painted in England after her named was changed to Lady Rebecca. As you might know, she was an Indian princess who married a trader named John Rolfe and went to live in English society. What do you think is going on inside her head? Use your imaginary binoculars and zoom in on Pocahontas's thoughts.   Read the book *The Double Life of Pocahontos* by Jean Fritz for more ideas or do some research and write your own story.   . (photo: Library of Congress)

photo; Library of Congress

Walk the Neighborhood

When poet Charles Boyer remembered the lane that ran behind the house where he lived as a child, the memories flooded back rich and vivid. Try writing about your neighborhood. Begin by drawing a bird's eye view. Then label houses, buildings, stores and fields. See what memories flood you and start writing.

When I read Gogol I thought my childhood's lane
must have been straight out of Russia
but it was pure America

stretching between two frog-rich ditches
out past the tennis courts on the edge of town
through the flat Illinois corn fields.

They gathered the stalks in the fall
into teepee shapes we played about
that seemed like nests of giant birds.

The lane ran east to west
straight as a surveyor's rule
to three houses crouched in the shrubs.

That was where I was going that day,
eight years old with two quarters in my pocket,
sent by my mother to buy eggs

from the old lady who lived all alone
on the edge of my universe
with her ammoniacal-smelling chickens

herky-jerky about the gate,
the gate where I hesitated
and stepped back, unsure.

I walked away past the other houses
mouldering like toadstools
in the burdock and thistle.

The gravel ended, leaving just
a center row of dusty weeds between
two strips a little worn by tires.

Above me the endless cumulus tumbled on
in slow motion, with the sun blazing between,
and I felt watched, as children do, and somehow judged.

In one sway-backed shack there lived
the odd teen who ran traplines in the woods.

beyond the cornfield, beyond the cow
We'd see him—never riding, always striding
in his vehement, ramshackle way
up and down the lane toward high school

his trouser legs flapping.
Once he asked my sister out
and she was confused, aghast,

discussing the embarrassment with my mother,
both sitting side saddle on her bed.
Then in the dead of winter our cat disappeared

for three days, resurrected again in our garage
with one leg missing, blood smeared
over her white fur. She lived on for years.

We knew the kid had found her in his trap
and returned her quietly, guiltily,
at night while we slept,

and so we thought of him with anger
for his bloody trade, with gratitude
for his furtive decency.

The third house lay behind
a screen of scrub maples and thistles
along the fence row.

I walked past it one summer evening
wandering alone, feeling so safe
I didn't know I felt safe.

Beyond the screendoor my neighbor
watched the White Sox flickering
in black and white.

The buzz of play by play calls
blended with the myriad insects
and tossed a trembling net

over the night, capturing it
and letting it go, like memory.
That was when it started.

The angry voice.
A woman's shrill fear.
The sound of blows.
We were all such sealed mysteries moving
through the Illinois noons and nights—
yet some things we knew.

On that day though I passed that empty house
and turned by the black walnut tree
where fruit thunked down

like compact little bombs
and their Martian-green husks
rotted in the sun.

And so I circled back to where
the egg lady now stood in her yard
(she must have been looking)

and by the rusted gate I told her why I'd come
and followed her up the dusty walk
into her asphault-shingled, non-gingerbread house.

Her whitish eyes looked blind
behind the distorting lenses of her glasses.
She walked arthritically on bandaged legs,

and on her shoulders rode the hump of years.
Inside lay an uneven floor of plywood sheets,
belly-to-belly with the earth itself.

Her dead husband's concertina
hung from a hook on the door
and a canary stirred in a shaft of light.

No one had ever told her she was poor,
this little old lady who lived all alone
on the edge of the spinning prairie—

with wallpaper holding up the walls,
with night winds strumming the loose panes,
with time creeping like a vine,

without tv or son or books,
with that dignity we summon
as all else fades away.

She gave me a paper poke
full of her still-warm eggs
and her hands rustled like quick fire
as she plucked the warm coins from my palm

3

Snapshots and Thoughtshots

P

Snapshots at All Ages

My supper is always the same.
My sister won't eat. My parents
get upset. My other sister whines ,
but I just listen to the crickets.

             Delia   (2nd grade)

The ladies' dresses are made from milkwood or dandelion fluff, dyed with rose petals.
Their aprons are made from flower petals sewn together. Men's clothes are made
from leaves sewn together. Hats are made from fiddleheads. Buttons are made from
sunflower seeds. These are beginning to sound like fairies, but they aren't, because
grown ups are about one and a half feet high and instead of dwarves they are called
Pequenoes, (pe-cwain-yoze).

             Sarah Connor (5th grade)

She swiftly moves through the air tumbling and leaping. When she's finished with her
tricks she bends her back in an arch and has her hands perfectly positioned in a salute.
Her short, tiny body helps her glide in her flips. When she's completed doing a back-
walkover on the balance beam, she wipes away her anoying wisps of hair from her
face, preparing for her next move. When her hair is removed from her face you can
see her greenish eyes shining along with her cute, little troll-like nose and a smile that
seems never to fade. She is my nine year old sister, Annie.

             Sarah (6th grade)

Then I saw her, the queen of the Gypsy pack. She stood looking through the spaghetti
(gypsies always eat Italian food, I remembered.) She had long, black hair that was
twisted into a pigtail, which ran straight down her back. On her ears were two long
silver earrings with pearls on the ends. Her coat was old and tattered, stains covering
random portions of it. The large maroon pants she wore were partially tucked into her
boots.

   Her husband walked down the aisle toward her. He had a small pencil-thin
moustache that stood out on his chubby face. He was a stout little man, dressed in
workclothes that were decorated with splotches of paint. In a thickly accented voice
he told his wife to hurry up.   So the Gypsies must be working nearby, I thought. My
mouth fell open at the sight of the two of them. Where did they park their wagon? I
wondered. I didn't see it in the parking lot. I turned and ran through the entire store.
My mother wasn't leaving me with the Gypsies!

             David (college freshman)

Snapshots and Thoughtshots

Show, don't tell. Maybe you've heard this good advice from your teacher. Writing gets better the more we can zoom in on specific concrete details to make powerful feelings come alive. Don't write about how bad your day was at school. Describe the inky pen stain on your pants, the scab forming on your grass-stained knee, the smashed peanut butter sandwich which was supposed to be your lunch, the crumpled chemistry test in your back pocket. Strong writing blooms with physical detail, but it's not always that simple.

There is also a time in writing to **"tell, don't show,"** a time to go inside with thoughts of how you feel, what you're thinking, dreaming, imagining, a time to write thoughtshots, reflections, ideas. All writing moves from thoughts to physical detail and back again, sometimes in the same sentence, but sometimes writers get stuck in one place or another. Have you ever written a story and felt you were stuck in events as they happen (then this happened and then this happened)? Maybe this is the kind of story that might benefit from a few added thoughtshots. Maybe this is a time to "tell, don't show." "It was not the worst day of school I'd ever had, but it ranked right up there."

Snapshots and thoughtshots are simple tools to help shift gears as a writer. The point is not to write perfect snapshots or thoughtshots, but to hear the difference between the two, and to insert them into your writing

Attention! Revise this Book!
Please paste this page over the current page 75

Snapshots at All Ages

My supper is always the same.
My sister won't eat. My other
sister whines but I
just listen to
the crickets.

Delia   (2nd grade)

The ladies' dresses are made from milkwood or dandelion fluff, dyed with rose petals.
Their aprons are made from flower petals sewn together. Men's clothes are made
from leaves sewn together. Hats are made from fiddleheads. Buttons are made from
sunflower seeds. These are beginning to sound like fairies, but they aren't, because
grown ups are about one and a half feet high and instead of dwarves they are called
Pequenoes, (pe-cwàin-yoze).

Sarah Connor (5th grade)

She swiftly moves through the air tumbling and leaping. When she's finished with her
tricks she bends her back in an arch and has her hands perfectly positioned in a salute.
Her short, tiny body helps her glide in her flips. When she's completed doing a back-
walkover on the balance beam, she wipes away her anoying wisps of hair from her
face, preparing for her next move. When her hair is removed from her face you can
see her greenish eyes shining along with her cute, little troll-like nose and a smile that
seems never to fade. She is my nine year old sister, Annie.

Sarah   (6th grade)

Then I saw her, the queen of the Gypsy pack. She stood looking through the spaghetti
(gypsies always eat Italian food, I remembered.) She had long, black hair that was
twisted into a pigtail, which ran straight down her back. On her ears were two long
silver earrings with pearls on the ends. Her coat was old and tattered, stains covering
random portions of it. The large maroon pants she wore were partially tucked into her
boots.
   Her husband walked down the aisle toward her. He had a small pencil-thin
moustache that stood out on his chubby face. He was a stout little man, dressed in
workclothes that were decorated with splotches of paint. In a thickly accented voice
he told his wife to hurry up.   So the Gypsies must be working nearby, I thought. My
mouth fell open at the sight of the two of them. Where did they park their wagon? I
wondered. I didn't see it in the parking lot. I turned and ran through the entire store.
My mother wasn't leaving me with the Gypsies!

David (college freshman)

Sketch People

Writers often describe a character or a place with two or three quick sentences. This is called a thumbnail sketch, after the quick drawings artists make in their sketchbooks. Read a few that I've collected below and try writing a few yourself. Remember the goal with a thumbnail sketch is to say as much as possible about your subject with only a few well chosen details.

He was one of those men who can be a car salesman or a tourist from Syracuse or a hired assassin.
John D. MacDonald

John Viduary was six feet two inches in height and had the most perfect profile in Hollywood. He was dark, winsome, romantic, with an interesting touch of gray at the temples. His shoulders were wide, his hips narrow. He had the waist of an English guards officer, and his dinner clothes fit him so beautiful it hurt.
Raymond Chandler   *Pick up on Noon Street*

He thought he was the handsomest guy in the Western Hemisphere. He *was* pretty handsome too—I'll admit it. But he was mostly the kind of handsome guy that if your parents saw his picture in your Year Book, they'd right away say, "Who is this boy?" I mean he was mostly a Year Book kind of handsome guy.
J.D. Salinger   *Catcher in the Rye*

Some people had problems with Benjamin Franklin. They accused him of not having any gravity. Now that doesn't mean he floated around like a weightless space voyager. Gravity has another meaning, as in "grave." No. Not a place where you get buried, but you are getting closer. Someone who is grave is very serious, maybe a bit dull, and certainly not much fun. Ben Franklin did have a problem. He just couldn't stay serious. He was always playing jokes or having fun.
Joy Hakim   *Making Thirteen Colonies*

The man was an Indian—dressed in furs and leather, with moccasins that came all the way up to his knees. His skin was dark. His hair was dark, and he wore a dark coloured headband. His eyes sparkled in the sunlight, but the rest of his face was hard as stone.
John Reynolds Gardiner   *The Stone Fox*

Another reason I don't like Judd Travers is he spits tobacco out the corner of his mouth, and if he don't like you—and he sure don't like me—he sees just how close he can spit to where you're standing.   Phyllis Reynolds Naylor   *Shiloh*

Sketch Places

When writers introduce a setting they often paint a thumbnail sketch of a place. With a few quick brush strokes they evoke a mood, a personality, an aura that goes beyond just physically describing what's there. After you have read a few thumbnail sketches of places below, try writing one yourself. You may want to begin by listing a few details of the place, or your feelings about the place and what it reminds you of. You may want to just sit and think about that place for a while and not start writing till you have an idea, or you may want to just start writing and let the ideas come as you write. Try drawing a picture of your place before or after you write.

The great, dark trees of the Big Woods stood all around the house, and beyond them were other trees and beyond them were more trees. As far as a man could go north in a day, or a week, or a whole month, there was nothing but woods. There were no houses. There were no people. There were only trees and wild animals who had their homes among them.

Laura Ingalls Wilder The Little House in the Big Woods

I didn't see hardly anyone on the street. Now and then you just saw a man and a girl crossing the street, with their arms around each other's waist and all, or a bunch of hoodlumy-looking guys and their dates, all of them laughing like hyenas at something you could bet wasn't funny. New York's terrible when somebody laughs on the street late at night. You can hear it for miles.

J.D. Salinger Catcher in the Rye

Pieces of tree, pieces of metal, pieces of seat and wing gleamed in the moonlight. Some of the plane lights remained on, so what was left of the plane twinkled in a friendly way. The plane was immense. It seemed impossible that such a huge thing was ever airborne. It looked bigger and longer than a house, garages and stable. Like some incredibly large, white celestial cigar suddenly ripped in pieces and thrown to the ground.

Caroline B. Cooney Flight #116 Is Down

It was the kind of building you saw in some abstract painting. Sugar Cubism, Levin called the style: a series of long white rectangular buildings with dark sliding glass doors and windows shaped like TV screens. Each time he approached the lobby and the doors parted with a whisper he imagined he was entering heaven. The doctors and nurses became wingless angels examining the new arrivals who sat reading magazines in the patent leather lounge chairs.

Barry Lane Passion Play

P

Some Student Thumbnails

Here are some student thumbnail sketches across the grades. More are collected in Appendix C. Make a collection of your own or collect some of your favorites from literature you read.

My dad is sleeping on the white couch and my big white dog is on him. My dad is six feet tall. He is wearing blue jeans and square striped rainbow clothes with no buttons on it. He's dreaming. He has smooth black hair and a black spider is on his nose.
(2nd Grade)

The lady sits there on the couch, with a phone up to her ear. Wearing a plaid nightgown finishing smoking a cigarette. All you smell is the cigarette. A smile on her face. All you hear is a dog scratching at the door.
5th Grade

There was a very strange kid in my class. His name is Bert. We are learning about planets and he claims he is from the planet Zorbort, which he also claims is a planet that humans haven't discovered yet. He doesn't look much different than me or my friends although he has green nails. We are not sure if he paints them or maybe it's just fungus.
5th Grade

My mother is in the kitchen early Christmas morning. She is wearing red flannel pajamas and white slippers. She is singing "O Holy Night" while making French toast for my brother and I. While sitting in the family room, the smell of the cinnamon lingers towards me from the kitchen.
10th Grade

P

The Aunts

Here's a snapshot of the Aunts from *James and the Giant Peach* by Roald Dahl. Try drawing what Roald Dahl makes you see, then look at the illustrations from the book.

Aunt Sponge was enormously fat and very short. She had small piggy eyes, a sunken mouth, and one of those white flabby faces that looked exactly as though it had been boiled. She was like a great white soggy overboiled cabbage. Aunt Spiker, on the other hand, was lean and tall and bony, and she wore steel-rimmed spectacles that fixed onto the end of her nose with a clip.

The Barbarians

Near the start of Thomas Cahill's magnificent history book, *How the Irish Saved Civilization,* the author draws a snapshot of the barbarians as they prepared to cross the Danube river and sack the Roman Empire. Try drawing what Cahill makes you see.

Their bodies are discolored by paint. Some of men are huge and muscular to the point of deformity, their legs wrapped comically in garments called braccae—breeches. There is no discipline among them: they bellow at each other and race about in chaos. They are dirty and they stink. A crone in a filthy blanket stirs a cauldron, slicing roots and bits of rancid meat into the concoction from time to time.

P

Snapshot of _____

_____

_____

_____

_____

_____

_____

_____

_____

_____

Snapshots in Expository Writing

In expository non-fiction writing, a snapshot can be used as a tool to draw a reader into the "real world," so that abstract ideas and understandings sink in. As you read the snapshots below, notice how ideas bloom when we root them in what we all know.

In his book **Be Seated,** *James Cross Giblen gets us thinking about chairs through the seat of our own favorite chair.*

You probably have a favorite chair. It may be an easy chair with deep cushions, or a colonial-style rocking chair, or a modern chair with a canvas seat and a metal frame. In it, you like to read or watch television, talk on the phone, or maybe just sit back and snooze.

Whatever you do in the chair, you feel comfortable. That's why it's your favorite. And you probably assume that everyone has his or her favorite chair, too.

If you do, you're mistaken.

This essay, which traces the development of modern aviation to the invention of a tool that shows pilots which direction their wings are facing, begins with a snapshot which helps us understand that our own personal fears about flying have a basis in aviation history.

People who distrust the sensations of flight, who balk when an airplane banks and turns, are on to something big. I was reminded of this recently while riding in the back of a United Boeing 737 that was departing from San Francisco. Directly over the Golden Gate we rolled suddenly into a steep turn, dropping the left wing so far below the horizon that it appeared to pivot around the bridge's nearest tower. For a moment we exceeded the airline maximum of a thirty-degree bank, which is aerodynamically unimportant but is imposed for passengers' peace of mind. Our pilots may have thought we would enjoy a dramatic view of the famous bridge and the city beyond. But as the airplane turned, the startled passengers looked away from the windows. A collective gasp rippled through the cabin.

William Lange Wieshche   *The Turn*

Joy Hakim doesn't just tell us about the governor's palace at Colonial Williamsburg, she invites us in for a visit.

If you stand outside the governor's palace and look at the brick fence—with its stone British unicorn on top and fancy iron gates—you will be impressed. If you are lucky you might get invited in for a musical evening. You'll sit in the candlelit ballroom, where men in starched linen blouses and women in silk brocade gowns smile and nod at each other. A display of muskets and swords in the entry is intended to leave you awed with the Crown's military might.

Joy Hakim   *The Making of Thirteen Colonies*

Simile Making

Similes grow out of trying to describe something that's just too hard to describe on its own. It's like you're looking at a cloud and you're trying to describe it, but all you come up with is white and puffy. So you try again and you come up with it's white and really really puffy. So you look for a simile. I looked up at the sky and saw a white puffy cloud that looked like a marshmallow piano tap dancing on a pumpkin, but it's not right because it doesn't quite do justice to that cloud and your feeling about it so you keep trying. Below are some similes I've collected from literature. Collect some of your own from what you read and what you write. Try writing some yourself. ......

The sun was pasted like a wafer in the sky.
Stephen Crane

 Trying to get health information on the Internet is like trying to drink water from a fire-hose.

He was as nervous as a hemophiliac in a razor factory.

Measuring the richness of learning with a standardized test is like judging chili by counting the beans.
Daniel Ferri

Trying to create peace in the Middle-East is like trying to make whipped cream out of motor oil.

When my baby sister cries it's like the world is on fire and all I have to put it out is gasoline.

P

The Simile Factory (a game)

Ever played with a simile? Held one in your hand and tried to match it with something in the world of ideas? Here's how you can try and have some fun in the process. **1)** Gather some objects, at least five or ten. If you're at home make at least one trip to the refrigerator and include some food in your collection. **2)** Next look at the list of feelings or ideas I have collected beneath. Try adding some of your own. **3)** Match an idea to one of your real life similes using the sentence provided, then use your binoculars to zoom in on the match and add more specific detail. For example: *Truth is like a half empty carton of milk. You reach for it and when you pick it up you know it will help you today but you're never quite sure if there will be enough for tomorrow.* [Note: A metaphor is a simile without the "like" or "as". Try out the metaphor sentence too.]

Love   Truth   Joy   Sadness

Fear   Anger   Hope   Generosity

Winter   Summer   Spring   Autumn

People   Hate   Madness

_____

_____ is like a _____.

_____ is a _____.

P

My Soul is a Metaphor

A metaphor does the same thing as a simile without the use of the words "like" or "as." For example, "All the world is a stage and we are actors."

As writers we tend to get metaphorical when trying to describe things just beyond our grasp. Below you'll find poems by first graders about their souls. Begin a poem with the words " my soul is..." and see what metaphors spring onto your page.[1]

My soul is invisible.
You can't see it.
It's the wind
in the sky
when I die.
My soul will not be invisible at all
it will be so bright
that I could not tell the sun from it.

My soul is the wind
flying across the sky
seeing children play together
seeing birds fly by
make cool winds come
I love my soul.

My soul is a vacuum cleaner sucking up memories of yesterday
when I dropped my ice cream cone and my sister gave me
some of hers.

My soul is a bronco running out of control because he ate hot chilly peppers and his mouth is burning.

_____

[1] Adapted from *Poetry Now* by Jack Collum and Sheryl Noethe Teachers and Writers Collaborative NYC

Personify

In poetry, skies can cry, trees can scamper, love can sigh. When we give a voice to something that doesn't usually talk it's called personification. Read the following poem and circle places where the poet personifies things. Try putting personification into one of your poems as poet Verandah Porche does.

Solstice Spell

Watch: our shadows spill like ink over the milky field.
Time cracks and sprawls: Day breaks. Night falls.
Dip your pen in the dark and write

what syllables December spells: whooshh! fooshh!
Ice silvers the birches. Moon wants you to
watch our shadows spill like ink. Over the milky field

a barn owl curves his question like a scythe:
"Who next? Who's next of kin?" Listen:
dip your pen in the dark and write

about miracles: Courage blazes with breath of fuel;
and infant summons kings and cows as peers. Love, keep
watch. Our shadows spill like ink over the milky field.
Dip your pen in the dark and write.

Verandah Porche

Point and Shoot

When a writer describes a place, it's like a photographer slipping into a room with three loaded cameras around her neck. She points and shoots, and new details emerge from each angle and each click of the shutter. Below are a series of frames. Think of a place to describe, and draw details of that place in each frame. Put a caption under each detail you draw.

Inserting on the Test

Notice how by adding snapshots and thoughtshots this fifth grader from Sherri Masson's class in Michigan, improves a piece of writing on the state writing proficiency test.

WRITING Grade 5

DAYS 1 AND 2

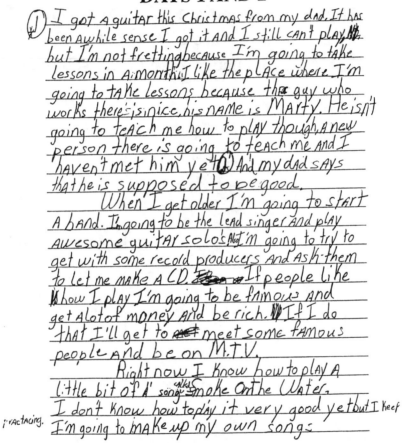

① I got a guitar this Christmas from my dad. It has been awhile sense I got it and I still can't play it, but I'm not fretting because I'm going to take lessons in a month. I like the place where I'm going to take lessons because the guy who works there is nice, his name is Marty. He isn't going to teach me how to play though, a new person there is going to teach me and I haven't met him yet ② And my dad says that he is supposed to be good.

When I get older I'm going to start a band. I'm going to be the lead singer and play awesome guitar solos. Also I'm going to try to get with some record producers and ask them to let me make a CD. If people like how I play I'm going to be famous and get a lot of money and be rich. If I do that I'll get to meet some famous people and be on M.T.V.

Right now I know how to play a little bit of a song Smoke On the Water. I don't know how to play it very good yet but I keep practicing. I'm going to make up my own songs

Page 5   24

① *s.s.* ─ the guitar that he gave me was black with a black pick gaurd and I didn't like it very well so I told him and we exchanged it for a better one.

② His name is scott

The Snapshot poem

A snapshot poem paints a picture with words by stringing one or several vivid images together. Below are two snapshot poems, one from a high school teacher/poet and the other a fourth grade student/poet. Try writing your own snapshot poem.

A Place in Winter

The hands on the clock face of night
Strike the eternal moment,
Shiver two brittle shadows
Like bones strewn upon starkness.

The old man and his old hound
Walk the icy fringe, again,
To the boy who sleeps
Among the wind-licked stones.

Stephen M. Holt

The Bird

Under a low sky
on this quiet morning
of red and yellow leaves
a bird disturbs no more than one branch
of a green-leafed peach tree

Melissa

New Thoughts

Pick a page in a book. Find an interesting character and give him
or her four extra thoughts.   (Thanks to Sherri Masson.)

Connect Thoughts to History

Below is a picture of a car used in the JFK presidential assassination limo tour parked on Dealy Plaza in Dallas, Texas. If you take the tour, you sit in the car and hear the shots go off when the car passes the Texas Book Depository. What do you think of the JFK Limousine tour? Would you go on it? What would it tell you about history? Could you design your own tour for a different period of history you have studied? Write your thoughts about tours or write about why we should all go on historical tours.

Mathematical Wondering

Mathematical thoughtshots can lead us to deep understandings about ideas and about life. In the world we live in, we are bombarded with statistics but the true meaning of numbers doesn't come about until we link numbers with real things.

In other words, I can tell you that the average american girl has 8 Barbie dolls and that's an interesting statistic, but if I can make that number real I could make you understand how many Barbies we are really talking about here. Let's see, an average Barbie is a foot long, that's eight feet per girl. Let's figure 50,000,000 girls give or take a few million. 8x50 is 400; that's 400,000,000 feet. There are 5280 feet in a mile. If we divide that into 400 million, that will give us the number of miles all the Barbies would stretch if laid end to end. Are you ready? 75,757.58 miles. That's almost three times around the circumference of the planet earth. Now do we know what we're talking about here?

Try making the numbers below more real by projecting them into real terms. For more inspiration read the book *Counting on Frank* by Rod Clement or *How Much is a Million* by David Schwartz. See the math bibliography for more books to get you mathematically wondering.

Numerical Fact	I Wonder
The average pen draws a line 7000 feet long.	How many pens would it take to draw a line to L.A. from Boston?
One acre of forest produces 942 hardcover books.	
6,000,000 Jews died in the Holocaust	
We spend 1/3 of our lives sleeping.	

What They Said: Collecting Quotes

In non-fiction writing, quotes from people more famous than you can give your writing more clout. You can find these quotations collected in reference books at the library or in books you read. Sometimes a quote placed as an epigraph at the beginning of a chapter can set the tone for what will follow. Try collecting quotes and pasting them like butterflies in your journal.

Without music life would be a mistake.
Nietzsche

Humor is the oil that keeps the engine of society from getting overheated.
Mary McNorton

Why does man kill? He kills for food. And not only food: frequently there must be a beverage.
Woody Allen

Play is often talked about as if it were relief from serious learning. But for children play *is* serious learning. Learning play is really the work of childhood.
Fred Rogers

The smile is the universal symbol for accepting others.
Susan Isaacs

My way of joking is to tell the truth; it's the funniest joke of all.
George Bernard Shaw

It's deja vu all over again,
Casey Stengel

You grow up the day you have your first real laugh—at yourself
Ethel Barrymore

Types of Thoughtshots

In fiction writing, thoughtshots can be divided into different
categories: Flashbacks, Flash forwards, and Internal dialogue[1].
Below you'll find some examples. Next time you write a story,
look for oppurtunities to explore these types of thoughtshots

Flashback:

She remembered the day he came for the first time. He was a little
boy then...

Flash-ahead:

She thought about her options. She could go there and pretend it
never happened. . She could tell him everything. She could buy a
plane ticket to Bermuda with the money...

Internal Dialogue:

There was no way she could do it. She knew that, but still her feet
kept moving, one step after another. She thought about why she
was doing this but there was no way she could make sense of it...

---

[1] The Writer's Toolbox by Laura Harper   See Page

Give a Picture a Thought

Below is a photo of Harriet Tubman, the famous leader of the underground railroad. What is she thinking?

Now imagine what Harriet is looking at. Place her anywhere in your life today. Bring her to a McDonalds or a K-mart. Have her describe what she sees through her life experience. Use your imagination and also research Harriet Tubman's life by reading a book like *Harriet Tubman, Conducter of the Underground Railroad* by Ann Petry. (photo: Library of Congress)

4

Playing with Time

Today the Boys were
chasing me and Fiona I got
Amber David Kot me and tost me
urawd and Pucht Me. I told
the Teacher she Put him on
the woll I wacd awy and
Staredid To cri

Time as a Writer

When you write, your whole life is a stretch of mountains and you choose where you want to hang out. You can write one sentence and describe twenty years of your life or write three pages about one tiny moment that only lasted a minute. This is the kind of moment you'd make in slow motion if you were making a movie. This is the big moment, the moment too important to just let slip by with a sentence or two. You need to make the reader feel what your character feels. You need to pull the reader into a place, a time, an event. You need to make the reader swim in your ocean of words.

There are many ways to explode moments over the page. You can write long descriptive snapshots or delve deeply into a character's thoughts or write down a dialogue mixed with snapshots and thoughtshots, or combine all three of these strategies. The trick is to use what works best for the particular moment you are describing. We'll be exploring these ideas in this chapter.

Along with slow motion is fast motion writing. That's when you compress large blocks of time into a paragraph or two. One great way to shrink time is to find specific examples from the period you are describing to make your ideas and opinions about it come alive. Another way is to simply talk about what makes that time significant or interesting to you now. The main thing to remember is that writing is not like living; you can skip the boring bits. When you write you control the hands of the clock

P

Explode a Moment

If you were a movie director making a film of your life, where would you use slow motion?

Think of happy moments, sad moments, joyful moments. Talk with friends and trigger each other with ideas.

When you are ready, fill a piece of paper with that one moment. Don't go to the next day or later that same day. Stick inside that moment. Don't write big or add extra words just to fill the paper. Instead, allow yourself to get stuck, then try out some of these ideas.

* Use your binoculars: zoom in with sights, sounds, smells, tastes.
* Read your last sentence. If it's a snapshot try switching to thoughtshots, or if it's all thoughtshots try switching gears and adding snapshots.
* If you finish half-way down the page, go back and insert (^) a snapshot or a thoughtshot.
* Close your eyes and imagine yourself there. Wait for words to come.

Here are a few quick suggestions of moments to explode. Make a list of your own while talking with your classmates.

- A time you got lost
- A time you lost something or someone
- Something painful happened
- Something happy happened
- The big moment in the game
- The time a skill paid off
- A time you almost forgot
- A moment funny now, not then
- A moment involving a pet
- A moment involving a sister or brother

Slow Motion Moments

Here are some slow motion moments from students in grades 2-12 and beyond.

The Wall

Today the boys were chasing me and Fiona. I got Amber. David caught me and tossed me around and punched me. I told the teacher. She put him on the wall. I walked away and started to cry.

2nd grade

Daydreaming

One day my teacher was asking us questions and I wasn't really paying attention to her. And then she called out my name and I was like oh now what am I gonna do. I don't even know why she called my name out for. What if I'm in big trouble for something I don't even know I did! I felt like I was gonna pass out. I felt like I was gonna have to wait in the hall and get yelled at. But then she told me to come up to the white board and fill in the answer to the question on the board. I felt like screaming. My face turned bright red when she told me I wasn't in trouble.

3rd grade

The Jump

I nervously boosted my body upon the giant animal. My hands were shaking as I took the soft leather reins. I could feel a drop of sweat trickle down my pale face. My parched throat seemed like a sandy desert. The ground beneath me began to quiver. My heart was in my throat. The wind seemed to be teasing and hissing. The dusty saddle beneath me jerked. I'd have to go through with it. The white painted rail seemed as tall as a building. I gave the giant a kick and one word came out of my mouth. "Canter!" The wind took my hair as I approached the jump rapidly. As my hands let go of the reins I clung to the saddle with my limp legs. I spread my arms like eagles' wings. I was flying. Suddenly I hit the ground. My hands immediately grasped the dusty mane. I did it! I clung to the horse's neck. Tears in my eyes formed! I love horses.

Sarah 5th grade

Dad

I went to my parents' bathroom where I found my dad. He was taking the shaving cream out and cologne even though he had already shaved. I thought he was going to shave again but after what seemed an hour he put them into a box. Everything for his hair and face was in that box and so were my thoughts. I looked at him but only saw his jeans because I was only as tall as his knees. Then I looked at him staring wide-eyed and asked, "What are you doing?" I was lied to when he said he was visiting a friend that afternoon. After he packed his box he put it with other boxes and went downstairs. After a while of peace I heard yelling and screaming from my mom and dad. Then my dad put the boxes and his suitcases in his car. He said goodbye and drove away.

4th grade

Mustard

"Squeak!" A bone chilling squeal comes from the guinea pig cage. Out comes Mustard, (my guinea pig) calm, cool, and incredibly subdued. She walks to her food bowl and chews a pellet. Two seconds later she grabs yet another. Her soft black and cream fur shines in the golden afternoon sunlight. Her two young pups (babies) nurse off her. Mustard never seems bothered by this. She goes on eating, never minding these two annoying attachments. She now moves towards the water bottle in a sort of waddle, her eyes set on something elsewhere. She reaches for some water and "click!" You hear her teeth click against the tube. The two annoying attachments cling to her as she walks to her nesting box. As soon as she reaches it, she begins to rearrange the cotton inside, (she can never have it just right!) and lays down her pups. The pups are so full you can see the milk inside their tummies. She watches over them carefully, her eyes glued to theirs.

Sarah Morton 6th grade

Powder

It was the day my sister came home from the hospital. She was tiny and small and helpless, I hated her so much. I didn't know her; I just hated her. She had taken what I had away, because now she was the littlest. She was the baby of the family, not me. So when we were supposed to take a picture I hid behind the door and I wouldn't hold her. She had a pink, red face. She had no hair, these pink little hands and little pink feet. She barely fit in any clothes. But something in my head said not to like her. So I did what any normal jealous kid would do. I stayed away till I couldn't take it any more seeing her sitting there and she gets whatever she wants.

do is grab it. It was right there. So I did. I took the powder and very quietly opened it up and

shook it all over her. I didn't know what good this would do but it seemed like a good idea at the time next thing I knew she was covered with powder and she was white as a ghost. She looked at me like "What did I do to you?"

   At that moment is when my mom woke up and saw me sitting with powder in my hand and my sister Casey sitting right next to me and the last thing I remember is going to my room for 10 minutes to think about what I had done.

Tiffany Tank (7th grade)

The Beach

I was in a daze as I stared out over the vast amount of water. The salty air surrounded my tense body and seemed to be pushing me towards the big blue ocean. I breathed in deeply, trying to get myself together before I attempted the long journey from the beach to the ocean. The wind picked up slightly, and the sand began whirling around my legs, stinging them. I closed my eyes and began walking forward. Images of sharks and whales began swimming through my mind. I could see their large canine teeth tearing me apart piece by piece. I came to a sudden stop as my bare feet came in contact with the cold, salty water. Chills were racing up my back, and I felt the need to turn and run back toward the safety of the beach towel. For some reason I took another unsure step. The water raced around my ankles now and waves kept rushing toward me. I started walking at a steady pace now. The water was up to my knees then my waist. The water felt so good, so refreshing. I soon forgot my fears and began enjoying my first trip to the ocean.

8th grade

The Yo Yo

It was a typical hot and humid afternoon in July. Having just returned from a visit to King's Island, my brother and I were full of energy. My father was working on the worn out Chevrolet and my mother was sitting under the not so shady locust tree reading the newspaper. I was marveling at a new toy I had coerced my parents to buy for me. It was a yo-yo, but not just any yo-yo. It had the great fortune of sporting the honorable Scooby Doo's vision on its red, plastic shell. I was elated. I had never owned a yo-yo, even though I was already eight years old, because my father was wary of any toy that could be slung/shot or used as a noose. I had no intention of using it for any of those purposes, but not yet having mastered the yo-yo's true use, I wanted to twirl it in ballet-like circles, letting centrifugal force do its mischief with the yoyo. Unfortunately for my brother, he had not noticed my new "skill." Being a typical four-year old, he managed to find his way into the path of destruction. I should have stopped when I saw his face repeated in several of my revolutions, but I was having too much fun. But when the soft thud conducted down the twine, I knew I had left my mark.

My brother lay on the ground, grasping his forehead, his eyes showing disbelief, letting out a wail that would embarrass the time-atomic bombshell. My father was a blur, as was my mother. My mother consoled my brother, but my father's agenda was much more violent. The yoyo was last seen circling my father's head and then soaring into the tree tops in the distant woods. I wasn't as lucky. I knew that the large, scared man on my left would soon be experiencing another strong evaluation that would redden his face and my bottom.

Aaron Psimer (10th Grade)

Suspenseful Moments

One reason to write in slow motion is to build suspense. Read the following piece by 9th grader Luis Dechtiar and try writing about your own suspenseful moment.

 ## The Animal

Sara stepped into the empty living room of the old house. The boards creaked under her feet. Dust covered the walls, the floor, the ceiling, everything. There was a window with pieces of broken glass sticking out. The fireplace was made of red bricks, which were black from years of use.

She walked down a dark hall. paint peeling off the walls, exposing the decaying wood boards. She came up to a heavy wooden door and reached down to the knob, but grabbed air. She looked down and saw only a hole where the door knob used to be. The door only needed a little push. It swung open with a squeaky sound, and banged against the wall. Sara stared into the bedroom. Dried leaves flew around the floor. Wood from the ceiling lay in pieces on the floor. She walked in and looked up at the dark hole. Hundreds of spider webs hung down from the inside. This room had a balcony instead of a window, with a beautiful view of the church and hills behind it. Sara imagined herself as an old woman, sitting in a rocking chair, admiring nature and letting time go by.

Walking out of that room, she headed down the stairs towards the basement. The stairway was dark, and she could barely see the steps, but there was sunlight in the basement. The more she went down, the colder it was getting. As she reached the bottom, she saw there was a small window on the wall, close to the ceiling, where the light came through. Sara stood for a few seconds on the cold cement floor, staring at the huge mess.

Then the smell caught her nose and mouth and she felt her stomach tighten and the sensation of nausea fill her chest. The smell was so strong she could taste it in her mouth. Sara looked around, looking for the source of the strange odor. She saw pieces of cracked wood and crumbling bricks spread all over. Ripped paper and cardboard boxes lay wet all around. Metal parts of machines or motors twisted awkwardly and covered with oily substance. There was a big puddle of dirty brown water in the middle of the basement room. A long crack on the ceiling was letting water drip in. Sara could see one spot on the floor that wasn't covered.

Suddenly, in the middle of the trash, she saw something moving. She backed up and picked up a piece of wood from the floor. There was a low scratching sound coming from under the wet cardboard. Sara tried to guess what was underneath. *If that's a rat, I'm outa here!* she thought. She hated disease-transmitting rodents, garbage –eating insects and fast crawling reptiles of any sort. She didn't just hate them, she feared them.

She was terrified of them.

She noticed then that she had been holding her breath for a while now. She let it all out with a whoosh, then covered her mouth and nose with her shirt. Using it as a kind of smell filter, she took another long breath and held it it.

And then she heard another noise. Squeaking. It sounded like a hurt animal. Now Sara started to wonder if it was a rat. Could it be what it was sounding like? A cat?

Sara took a step closer and listened harder. Yes, it sounded like a cat. Was it stuck underneath the trash covering or suffering wet and cold? Sara couldn't bare seeing a cat suffer. She took another step closer and reached the stick up to the cardboard. She slid the stick under it and slowly pushed it to the side...

With a violent movement the cardboard flew in her direction, and a deafening scream echoed through the basement. Sara jumped back and screamed as she saw the furry black animal leap up and grab the ceiling. It slid into the crack and was gone in a fraction of a second.

Time Stands Still

In Alan Lightman's novel, *Einstein's Dreams*, the author imagines different concepts of time that Einstein may have dreamed about. What if, for example, we lived an entire lifetime in each moment? Or what if each day we had the ability to rewind time at our own whim and relive happy moments like we might with a good video? Can you imagine time being different? Start by thinking how time will be different in your world. Then, if you want, draw a picture of that world or write a brief description of what it would be like. I've quoted 3 sentences from a chapter in Lightman's book can you finish it or make up your own time concepts like I've done beneath. Use your binoculars to zoom in and help the reader to see the strange new world you are creating.

There is a place where time stands still. Raindrops hang motionless in air. Pendulums of clocks float mid-swing. Dogs raise their muzzles in silent howls. Pedestrians are frozen on the dusty streets, their legs cocked as if held by strings....

_____

_____

_____

There is a world where time goes backwards. You are born old and each day your skin loses it's wrinkles, your body grows less stiff, your eyesight sharpens, your white hair blackens....

_____

_____

There is a world where time has no beginning or end. You know everything that has ever happened and ever will happen. Each day, when you get up you make a list of all the phone calls you will get and all the things you will do..._____

_____

_____

_____

Inventing a Slow Motion Moment

Chris, a seventh grader, wrote about a fictional moment, but he makes us believe it by zooming in with strong details and by writing believable dialogue. Read the piece beneath and try inventing your own slow motion moment. Remember to pull yourself and your reader into the piece with vivid details.

The Rat

My dad owns a motorcycle. It was shiny stream-like and sleek. It was colored a beautiful turquoise blue with those little sparkly things in the paint. Then something happened that I'll never forget. An innocent rat came out of the bushes. Its movements caught my eye. I watched closely as its fuzzy little body quickly scurries around then stops, looks around, then scurries around some more. I saw its little nose twitch, and its bare twig-like tail hover low to the ground. It quickly ran to my dad's motorcycle. It stopped and stared at its tail pipe. Then with one fluent movement leaped into the air and plugged its little body into the tail-pipe. As its body disappeared into the pipe you can hear its sharp claws scratching against the metal. Soon it was all the way in. Then I said, "Dad, a rat just crawled into your tailpipe!" "What?" my dad said in disbelief. "Yeah, it just jumped right in there!" Then he did something that wasn't very smart. He couldn't find a flashlight, so he used a lighter. "I don't think that's a good idea, Dad," I warned him, but it was too late. I watched cautiously. He lit the lighter and the flame ignited a gas pocket. All of a sudden, almost instantaneously, a large yellow ball of fire shot out and hit my Dad in the face and caught his beard on fire. Before he could even acknowledge that his beard was flaming a second fire ball came out. This time the fire ball had a tail! It shot out and hit my dad cold in the nose. I was shocked. It happened so fast. It seemed only 2.4 seconds, but so much happened. Then with a loud bellow my dad burst into a panic. I watched in amazement as he slapped his face over and over while screaming. Finally the human torch was out. The only thing I could do was laugh. Hysterically. I laughed for at least fifteen minutes. Then it got old. Then I said something I've been waiting for my whole life. "I told you so!"

Climb Inside a Head

Here's an interesting way to explode a moment. Stare at the photo below of Edwin Tennison, a Georgia private killed in action at Malvern Hill on July 1, 1862. Find another photo of a person from the past if this one does not intrigue you. Next, imagine you are in the mind of this person at the moment the photo was taken. Write a monologue of your thoughts. Use your research to make your monologue realistic. When you're done, you can try making a mini-documentary by reading your monologue into a video camera as the lens focuses on the picture.

Tinting Moments with a Feeling

Brian Honeker, a ninth grader from Stanford, Kentucky, exploded a fearful moment as he remembered it as a child. Notice how the surprise at the end of this moment works because of how well Brian wrote in slow motion. Remove three sentences and read it to your class. Notice how much weaker the piece gets.

Here's a fun exercise. Describe your room as if you had just won the lottery. Don't mention the lottery or how you feel. Just describe. Describe the same room as if you just witnessed a murder. Don't mention the murder. Just describe.

I stood motionless at the point where my road began. The nighttime air chilled me as I contemplated the first step. I looked ahead and saw the luminous moon in the sea of stars about me. The dim light shone against the pavement almost glowing. The baying of a hound in the distance inspired everything that could possibly happen tonight. My chest throbbed with the voice of the drum. Shadows danced before each one taking on its unique ghostly form. Trees became savage demons with razor teeth and grasping claws. The road became a snake beneath my feet that slithered up and down the hills before me.

I stepped faster. I heard my own footsteps as if they were someone else's. I turned to look behind me and saw nothing but cool night air. I continued to walk as visions of one-eyed freaks and monsters filled my mind. I looked into the distance. From what seemed miles away I could see a light that could only be my house. I broke into a run. Anything and everything that could exist was probably hot on my heels. A half-step closer would surely mean death. I ran with my hands grasping ahead for the doorknob. I found it and slowly turned it. It slammed shut behind me. I looked outside to see the moon full in the sky. Your first time walking home in the dark is a big deal when you're seven.

P

Building Scenes

Scenes are usually dialogue mixed with snapshots and thoughtshots. Here is the equation:

Snapshot + Thoughtshot + Dialogue = Scene

You can interchange any of these tools when you build a scene.
For example:
Replace a page of boring dialogue with a quick snapshot.

"Hi Joe. How's it going."

"Not bad, and you?"

"Not bad. Just waiting for the bus."

"Yeah. It's a little late."

"It always is."

Replace with: *They chit-chatted for a while until the bus came.*

Replace a snapshot with dialogue or a complete scene at a moment where the dialogue reveals character.
For example:

Replace: *When Charlene got home she found out her parents had already found out about the cheating incident and they grounded her for a month.*
Replace with:

"Charlene, is that you?" The voice came from the kitchen.
It was a firm voice. Not the voice she wanted to hear.

"Hi mom. I've got a lot of homework so I'm going straight to my room."
She bolted toward the stairway but the stairway wasn't there. A man stood there instead.

"Dad? What are you doing home?" But even as the words left her lips, *Charlene knew.*

Snapshot+Thoughtshot+Dialogue

Though some writers are able to write pages of dialogue without inserting snapshots or thoughtshots, most writers build scenes. Below is a scene from an essay by Jan Wilson stripped of snapshots and thoughtshots. At the bottom of the page is the same scene with snapshots and thoughtshots.

Bet he kisses mushy and wet!
Look—just finish your dinner and be quiet. He does not either.
Wet mushy kisses--wet mushy kisses--Janie loves David's wet, mushy kisses.
Stop it. You are one little smart aleck! Mom and Dad will get mad if they hear you!
Does he know you stuff your bra with Kleenex?
I do not you, little dummy! Take this. If you don't hush up and be quiet I'm going to pour this over your head! Every last drop!
You wouldn't dare. Dad would kill you.
You don't think so? I would, too. You're just asking for it.
You're chicken! You'd never do it.

"Bet he kisses mushy and wet!" my sister taunted me. I twisted around and looked at her, my elbows deep in dishwater.

"Look—just finish your dinner and be quiet. He does not either." I didn't want to discuss my boyfriend David with my blabbermouth little sister. What did she know about kissing anyway?

"Wet mushy kisses—wet mushy kisses—Janie loves David's wet mushy kisses," she singsonged to herself but clearly intended for my ears.

"Stop it. You are one little smart aleck! Mom and Dad will get mad if they hear you," I warned, trying to distract her. Actually, I admitted to myself, David's kissing wasn't any bargain but I couldn't stand her needling me.

"Does he know you stuff your bra with Kleenex?" she teased, with that smug, know-it-all, expression on her face.

"This was too much. My adolescent sensitivity burst with indignation. "I do not, you little dummy! Take this!" I scraped the soap suds off my arms and picked up a quart of milk, shoving it in her face. "If you don't hush up and be quiet I'm going to pour this right over your head." The quart was nearly full.

"You wouldn't dare," she glowered. "Dad would kill you."

"You don't think so? I would, too. You're just asking for it."

"You're chicken! You'd never do it," she said assuredly, her eyes sparkling with excitement.

Snatch and Clip

Good dialogue reveals character. It often surprises us as it reveals. Try clipping good dialogue from books, newspapers and life itself. Collect them in your writer's notebook or journal. Below you'll find some snippets of dialogue I have collected with ideas of where to get it.

Family lines (Do people in your family say things that everyone remembers? Write them down in your notebook.)

"The third helping's as good as the first." *Aunt Mabel*

"You think it's your life and then you wake up." *My mother talking about death*

"Your eats are on the table." *My mother talking about dinner*

"Slice mine paper thin." *Aunt Mary referring to the cheesecake*

Lines from books and magazines and radio

"Man, what I would have given for wheels like that."

Legendary baseball player Ted Williams
talking about Ricky Henderson's speed

"An archeologist is the best husband any woman can have: The older she gets, the more interested he is in her."

Agatha Christie

Little brothers and sisters (Try writing down what your little brother or sister says.)

'She repairs us for second grade."

First grader telling what his teacher does

"What that some 'whobody'?"

18- month old child
pointing to feet in a toilet stall

Capture Brief Exchanges

Sometimes brief exchanges between people reveal interesting and surprising dialogue. I was on a plane recently and we had a rough descent through the clouds on the way into Logan airport. I turned to the woman next to me and said,
  "We made it."
  She replied, "You didn't think we would make it? You were scared?"
  I nodded and then she said, "I'm not scared of dying with 300 other people. I'm scared of dying alone!"
  Write down brief snatches of dialogue. Try to write it down just as they said it. Here are some examples from my journal and the journal of Gretchen Bernabei.

Grace: Daddy? What's slumber
Daddy: It means to sleep.
Grace: You mean sleep on lumber.

Opa: That country ham? There are 3 or 4 slices of it left. Is it still good?
dd: I don't know.
Opa: I'd go on ahead and cook it.
dd: I've been trying to hold off because you don't much like it.
Opa: Well I like it better before it rots.

Ms. Bernabei: Andrew, wow. That's great! You are really talented.
Andrew: No, I'm not.
Ms. Bernabei: Yes you are.
Andrew: No, I'm not.
Mrs. Bernabei: You always argue.
Andrew: No, I don't.

A Secret Fuels a Scene

In the last chapter of Ralph Fletcher's novel, *Fig Pudding*, the Abernathy family has a secret. The narrator's little brother, Josh, has accidentally stepped in the fig pudding that was on the floor in the back seat of the car on the way over to the family reunion. After cleaning off the sneaker and smoothing over all evidence, they sit down to a family dinner. As you read the following scene from Fletcher's heart-warming novel, notice how the dark secret fuels the humor. Try writing a scene where characters have secrets from each other. Have them talk around the secret and notice how much of what we say becomes what gets left unsaid.

But as the plates were cleared away, and everyone started eyeing the sweet table, I started getting this funny feeling in the pit of my belly. Nate sneaked a smile at me. Cyn looked down at her fingernails. Teddy caught my eye; his face looked serious, almost too serious. Mom and Dad were sitting directly across from each other but they avoided eye contact when Aunt Pat put the bowl of fig pudding onto the table.

"Ah!" Uncle Billy said. He smacked his lips.

"My favorite!" Aunt Marilyn said.

"There are so many other great desserts," Dad was saying. "I think I'm going for Grandma's blueberry pie."

"Pass down that fig pudding!" Uncle Eddie cried. "I've been dying for that pudding all week!"

The bowl got passed down. Uncle Richie passed it to Nate who passed it to Aunt Marilyn who passed it to me who passed it to Mom who passed it to Uncle Eddie. Uncle Eddie weighed two hundred sixty if he weighed a pound, and he had a tremendous appetite. Out of the corner of my eye I watched him put two large dollops of pudding into his bowl. He took a bite. I tried not to look, but I couldn't help it. Suddenly, he sat up. Looked at Dad. Took another bite.

"Say!" Uncle Eddie said to my father. "This is dee-li-cious! I mean it! The best fig pudding you ever made. Did you add some new ingredient this year?"

"Not really—" Dad began, but he stopped as mom made a funny sound, half gulp and half choke. She put her napkin to her mouth, got up, and quickly rushed into the kitchen.

"Excuse me," Dad said, getting up to follow her.

"You really ought to try this fig pudding," Uncle Eddie was saying, digging in again. "Terrific stuff!"

"Scuse me," I mumbled, rising and pushing back my chair.

I found Mom and Dad at the small kitchen table, leaning against each other, eyes closed, tears running down their faces. Dad's shoulders were shaking. He grabbed his gut, as if in pain. Mom was red-faced, gasping for breath.

"Some new ingredient!" Mom choked, and they both let out a howl of laughter, almost a scream, a wild animal sound that startled me as it rang out and bounced off the walls and brought the other kids in our family running into the kitchen.

"Good job, Dad!" Cyn said with a huge grin.

"Couldn't have made it without Josh!" Dad said, cracking up again, falling against Mom. And suddenly I was laughing, too. We all were, laughing hard, mouths open, roaring, barely able to stand.

"Hey, what's going on here?" a voice boomed. Uncle Eddie's big face looked down sternly at us. The very sight of him made everybody laugh even harder.

"Some new ingredient!" Dad said, still red-faced and squeezing his belly. "I can't stand it!"

Uncle Eddie had a confused look on his face.

"Everything all right?" he asked. Behind him, Grandma Annie's face appeared.

"What on earth are you all laughing at?" she demanded.

"It's just...so...funny!" Dad said, shrugging and laughing some more. Uncle Eddie walked over and punched Dad lightly on the shoulder.

"Hey, nice pudding, Clifford," he said with a big smile. That cracked up everybody again. He shrugged and left. Grandma Annie stayed behind, a bemused look on her face, watching us gasp and belly laugh, with the tears running down our faces.

Excerpt from *Fig Pudding* reprinted by permission of Clarion Books (1995)

Shrink Poems

Poet Andrew Green shrinks the entire year of eighth grade into this one-page poem. Can you think of a block of time in your life that can be characterized by one word? If so, try writing your own poem, full of specific memories.

Eighth Grade   by Andrew Green

Nothing made sense in eighth grade
everything was stupid back then
the stupid man behind the candy counter at Carlton Market
where we stole stupid Reese's peanut butter cups,
stupid jaw breakers, and stupid packs of baseball cards
stupid Mr. Bensen who smoked Lucky Strikes
and made me stand in English class and read the stupid note
I had just passed to Victoria Higgins
stupid study hall
stupid Schwinn bicycle with a banana seat that someone stole
stupid locker whose combination only worked half the time
and where I hung my Rolling Stones poster, so that some stupid kid
could draw a mustache on Mick Jagger's stupid face
stupid Johnny Tremain
stupid school dances where the stupid girls would gaggle
by the windows in the back of the stupid cafeteria
while the stupid girls in their stupid saddle shoes would dance
stupidly with each other on the red and white flecked tile floor
stupid winter nights when I had to walk one stupid mile home after playing on the stupid
basketball team
where I never played much anyway
stupid blue gym shorts we had to wear in stupid gym class
when it was twenty stupid degrees outside
stupid friend Bill and his stupid bottle collection
stupid Bill's mom and her stupid rule
about taking off your stupid shoes before you walk into her stupid house
stupid nights with nothing better to do than talk on the phone
with stupid Jimmy about stupid things
stupid textbooks I found at the bottom of my locker
at the end of the year and which I had stupidly paid for
because I stupidly thought I had lost them
stupid ninth graders who thought they were so cool
stupid seventh graders who were nothing to us
stupid pimples all over my stupid face
stupid everyone's face
stupid skinny body growing in stupid ways
stupid voice getting deeper and deeper
stupid curly hair
stupid bell-bottoms I wore each stupid day
stupid, stupid, stupid eighth grade
who didn't love me

One-Page Novel

One way to shrink time is to write a one-page novel. The goal here is to have fun and tell a story that sweeps through at least one lifetime in one page. But though time passes quickly you can zoom in to specific moments as Kenny Torrey, a 4th grader, does below. Above all, have fun.

Mr. Ding

One day a mad scientist named Mr. Ding was making a potion that would make his head forty times bigger. The potion was made of pigtails, brain expander, fish guts, and pond scum, but he accidentally added brain shrinker instead of brain expander, but he drank it anyway. All of a sudden POP! He was transformed into a fat dumb brainless guy.

One day (one month later), Mr. Brainless was getting a tan when he saw the sun and said "GOLD!" so he started to build a rocket ship so he could get to the sun. When he tried the ship exploded and the police said it was suicide. So Mr. Brainless was gone for good. The town joked for years until one day a thirty-three foot tall green slime pile (Mr. Brainless's remains) swallowed the town. He got this way because when he died they threw him in a toxic waste dump so he was transformed. So Mr. Brainless lived in the Atlantic ocean for nine years eating ships off the coast of Florida.

Eighty-two years later a submarine saw Mr. Brainless they made an S.O.S. call when he attacked them. Before help arrived they were eaten alive. When help arrived they were eaten too. The news said MONSTER IN ATLANTIC!!!! So the city left and no one returned for two thousand years.

When someone finally went back they were never seen again, so the army sent some artillery and it was eaten too, so the whole world fought against Mr. Brainless and won. So the world was finally peaceful. Or was it?

THE END

Where Were You?

Below is a photo taken in Dealy Plaza in Dallas Texas in November of 1997, thirty-four years after President John F. Kennedy was assassinated there. I was standing in the exact spot where the limousine was when the first shots were fired. My camera is pointing up at the window. If you look closely at the corner window five floors up, you can see the cardboard book boxes which Lee Harvey Oswald propped his rifle on. When I visited the Museum and stood in the spot where Oswald stood, I found out the boxes were full of the same third grade primers we were using that day at Woodman Park School in Dover New Hampshire, when I found out.

I remember it clearly. We were singing the windshield washer song and we went into the hall to get a drink of water at the white porcelain fountain. That's when I saw Miss Foley, the fourth grade teacher, with her head in her hands sobbing. When we returned our teacher said, "I'm sorry, children, No more singing today. President Kennedy has been assassinated." I had never heard the word before but it did not sound good. I knew something terrible had happened, something so terrible, it stopped us from singing.

At the 6th Floor Museum at the Texas Book Depository, there is a large white book filled with blank paper. Over the book is a sign which says that we are all a part of history and some day all of us who experienced the death of President Kennedy will be gone. All that will be left will be is this book.

Have you been a part of history? Do you remember where you were when something big happened, something that caused the whole world to grieve, or rejoice, or laugh? Try exploding a moment from history as seen through your eyes.

It was the Best of Times....

In the opening of his novel about the French Revolution, Charles Dickens shrinks the French Revolution into a paragraph by reflecting about this crazy time of extremes. Read it below and see if you can't add some specific examples to breathe life into Dickens's sweeping generalizations. Try using the same sentence patterns as I do below, or shrink a period of time from your own life.

It was the best of times, it was the worst of times, it was the age of wisdom, it was the age of foolishness, it was the epoch of belief, it was the epoch of incredulity, it was the season of Light, it was the season of Darkness, it was the spring of hope, it was the winter of despair, we had everything before us, we had nothing before us, we were all going direct to Heaven, we were all going direct the other way--in short, the period was so far like the present period, that some of its noisiest authorities insisted on its being received, for good or for evil, in the superlative degree of comparison only.

It was a time when it was always recess, it was a time when it was always raining so you had to stay in. It was a time when you never got caught drinking from the milk bottle. It was a time when the milk was always sour. It was a time when your locker always opened. It was a time when the book you wanted wasn't in there. It was a time when buses never were late; it was a time when you were always too early...

You Are There

Below is photo taken during a woman's suffrage demonstration on a New York street in 1913. Stare at the photo for a while and pick a person inside the photo to be you. Then explode the moment from that person's point of view. Make sure you address the issue of woman's suffrage in your writing. When you are done go to the library or the Internet and find information on the struggle for women to get the vote. Go back and revise your writing or find other photos from other historical periods to write about.

Voice Lessons in Expository Writing

Jeff Fagan

Putting Sway Back into the Hips

My six year-old daughter Grace was in the Christmas show and all the teachers at her school kept telling me how I just had to see her dance. Now as a parent I know Grace loves to dance, because she often dresses up in a black evening gown and plays Ginger Rogers to her older sister Jessie's Fred Astaire. I have videotaped her twirling and dipping and kicking up her barefoot toe as Strauss waltzes waft from the stereo. But it's one thing to dance like Martha Graham at home and another to do it in school with all her friends and their parents watching. Up to this point, Grace was a very serious student, and like many "serious" students she saw school as a place to prove herself, not to be herself.

The morning of the performance, Carol-lee, my wife, went upstairs to get Grace ready for school and found her in tears, standing in front of her full-length mirror two-stepping side to side in robot-like fashion. When questioned Grace said she was trying to dance like everyone else because a certain girl in her class had told her that two of the sixth graders had said she didn't dance well.

In the car on the way to school we each tried to console her about the importance of being herself. I told her about the teachers I work with and how often the great ones are shunned by their less imaginative colleagues or by a system that would prefer that no one stand out. I gripped the steering wheel tighter as I spoke and watched for her reaction in the rear view mirror. She was still worried and Carol-lee and I both knew it was only her teachers who could reassure her in this matter.

At school, Grace's teachers heard our concerns and like true professionals not only listened, but swiftly moved to remedy the painful situation. That morning they called together the girls who allegedly made the remarks and found they had said nothing but that they liked Grace's dancing. It turns out another girl who told Gracie about the remarks had been lying. She apologized and all was well.

Now it was time to dance and Grace's teachers made sure through three rehearsals that Grace swayed her hips with full power. During the performance, one of Graces teachers sat up front, allegedly to take pictures but also to make eye contact and encourage Grace.

As teachers of writing, a big part of our job is to help our students to sway their hips, to find their own voice and experiment with forms. Many teachers seem to encourage this in what is called "creative writing" (fiction and poetry), but stop when it comes to "expository writing" (report writing). This is very ironic because in the real world boring informational writing demands a lively and creative presentation.

If your students' reports sound like the famous author C. D. Rom wrote them, you may want to experiment with ways to revise your assignments and your concept of what expository writing is and what it can do. This chapter will give you many ideas on where to begin along with suggestions to help along the way.

Myths about Expository Writing

1. Effective academic reports are factual with little or no voice.

Wrong!

As information becomes more available through the Internet and other sources, our ability to package information in a compelling way becomes even more crucial. Dumbing down encyclopedia writing so a teacher thinks you wrote it is not an important skill for the 21st century. Writing with curiosity and passion is.

2. Term papers should be objective and contain little or none of the author's point of view.

Wrong!

Most writers strive for objectivity for one reason and one reason only, to make their point better. The skill of being objective is the skill of stating the other side to develop a clear understanding of the truth, not to remain neutral.

3. Learning to write five--paragraph themes is a crucial skill that will help students their whole lives as writers.

Wrong!

The five-paragraph theme is a form that developed in late 19th century America to lessen the reading load of overworked college professors. Today, many colleges have abandoned the theme as an assignment, but knowing to write it can help a student succeed on college blue book tests where encapsulation is all. It is a limited form of writing and won't help in the real world.

Better Questions about Reports

What if you asked your teachers the same kind of questions that writers ask editors when given a boring assignment? When you are bored with an assignment, that's the time to start figuring out ways to make it more interesting. Can you think of more questions to ask? Here are a few ideas.

Think outside the box!

Instead of:

How long does it have to be?

Ask:

Would you mind if I wrote my report as a poem? Or a song? Or a newspaper article? Or a resume? Or an obituary? Or a play? Or a _____?

Instead of:

What do you want?

Ask:

Who is the audience for this report? Do I have to dress up in a tuxedo or can I wear a tee-shirt? May I use the pronoun "I," or do you want me to stay out of it? Would you mind if I used illustrations or pictures to highlight my report? May I present my report orally as well as written?

Instead of:

When is it due?

Ask:

After I hand it in and you grade it, may I continue to work on it for my portfolio?

P

Interrogative CPR

You can revive any boring topic by asking curious and passionate questions. Write your boring subject in the box below and bring it to life with questions.

[Write boring subject in this box]

Write intriguing questions below

Lively Questions

Look at how the questions revive and revise a boring subject. To help find interesting questions, try dividing them into different categories. For example: "Who were the first insurance salesmen?" is a historical question. "What's the difference between insurance and extortion?" is a half-silly question. "How do you compute the value of a life?" is a mathematical question.

Insurance:

Should insurance be illegal? Did Al Capone start it? Why did insurance companies become so vital in our society? Who were the first insurance companies? Why do we need coverage in so many aspects of our life? What does a fiduciary do? How is a fiduciary related to the economy? If a fiduciary marries an agent, what will the kids look like? What are the various kinds of insurance? Do insurance agents buy more or less insurance than the average person? Do insurance agents really understand the product they sell? Why are insurance agents so stereotyped? Why isn't prevention part of an insurance company? Is insurance really important to have anyway? What would we do without insurance besides have more money in our bank accounts? What jobs would insurance agents have if they didn't sell insurance? Is there a relationship between the growth of the legal profession and the growth of insurance companies?

Laundry:

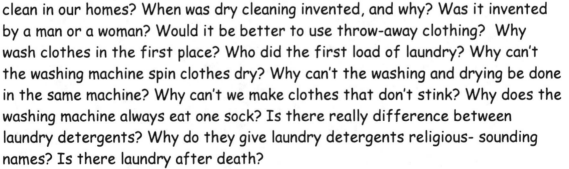

Why hasn't a better way to do it been invented?   Why can't we dry clean in our homes? When was dry cleaning invented, and why? Was it invented by a man or a woman? Would it be better to use throw-away clothing? Why wash clothes in the first place? Who did the first load of laundry? Why can't the washing machine spin clothes dry? Why can't the washing and drying be done in the same machine? Why can't we make clothes that don't stink? Why does the washing machine always eat one sock? Is there really difference between laundry detergents? Why do they give laundry detergents religious- sounding names? Is there laundry after death?

The 9 Minute Research Paper

It's time to get ready for college.

You went to the football game on Saturday, you went to the party on Saturday night. Now it's Sunday afternoon and you have to write your term paper. What are you going to do? Try this. Read through your notes and write a lead to your paper. Now you are ready to write. Set a timer for 9 minutes and find a comfortable chair. Write your paper from beginning to end. Write fast.

When the timer rings, stop. Look over what you wrote. Section off paragraphs and assign questions to them as the fifth grader does in the piece beneath. Go over your research and see how it can fit into the structure you have created.

Use what you've created to begin your paper.

WHAT TREES NEED

Do you know what a rain forest is? It is not a back yard and it is not a playground. A rain forest is a hot jungle near the equator. Rain forest's temperature goes up to 80 or 90 or more degrees. The places are very hot and sunny.

The layers of a rain forest are the Emergent, the Canopy, Tree trunks, Shade, and Forest floor. Many animals live in those parts.

The rain forests took around 70 to 100 millions years to evolve. Did you know that rain forest used to cover 14% of the earth? Today it covers less than 6% of the world. We have been chopping them down.

Trees need rain water just like us. But we don't need rain for ourselves. The rain forests get about 6 feet to more than 30 feet of rain a year. That is more than we get in some of our states. Trees need this water to help them grow. Some grow to about 250 feet (76m). Emergent's trees grow even higher. The Emergent trees are the most important trees because they have more room for animals. But they have their bad parts. They are most attractive to choppers.

Rain forest has between twenty five and over five hundred different trees growing in a single acre.

There are 7 different rain forest on the earth. Brazil is the one country that is most in trouble. Others are in Mexico, Australia and others.

Some trees don't need sun. Those trees exist in the forest floor. They just need water and soil and a little bit of sun, not much. Some big trees have to grow shallow roots because the soil has been going bad from the chopping of other trees. The roots are strong enough to steady the tree itself. Plants and moss grow on the trees because the tree's bottom does not get much sun.

WHAT ANIMALS NEED TREES

Lots and lots of animals need trees. There are over 100 different animals that need them. For instance there are the red orangutans. They eat fruit from the trees and they chew the leaves. They eat the bark and they steal eggs from birds' nests. They spend their life in the tree tops spying on prey birds so they could make notes how and what to eat and do in their life time. They are a rare type of monkey to find. This is because people chop their homes down and they die because they have no place to go. Scientists are still going against the chopping. For now the red orangutans are an endangered species...

Revising Point of View

The following passage was from a 1950's Home Economics textbook. It was trying to state a point of view objectively. Try revising it to fit a more modern point of view. Notice how shifting point of view helps us to see new details.

How to Be A Good wife

1) Have dinner ready. Plan ahead, even the night before, to have a delicious meal on time. This is a way of letting him know that you have been thinking about him and are concerned about his needs. Most men are hungry when they come home and the prospect of a good meal is part of the warm welcome needed.

2) Prepare yourself. Take fifteen minutes to rest so that you will be refreshed when he arrives. Touch up your makeup, put a ribbon in your hair and be fresh looking. He has just been with a lot of work-weary people. Be a little gay and a little more interesting. His boring day may need a lift.

3) Clear away the clutter. Make one last trip through the main part of the house just before your husband arrives, gathering up school books, toys, paper, etc. Then run a dust cloth over the tables. Your husband will feel he has reached a haven of rest and order, and it will give you a lift too!

4) Prepare the children. Take a few minutes to wash the children's hands too (if they are small), comb their hair, and if necessary change their clothes. They are little treasures and he would like to see them playing the part.

5) Minimize all noise. At the time of his arrival, eliminate all noise of the washer, dryer, dishwasher or vacuum. Try to encourage the children to be quiet. Be happy to see him. Greet him with a warm smile and be glad to see him.

6) Some don'ts: Don't greet him with problems or complaints. Don't complain if he is late for dinner. Count this as minor compared to what he might have gone through that day. Make him comfortable. Have him lean back in a comfortable chair or suggest that he lie down in the bedroom. Have a cool/warm drink ready for him. Arrange his pillow and offer to take off his shoes. Speak in a low, soft soothing and pleasant voice. Allow him to relax and unwind.

7) Listen to him: You may have dozens of things to tell him, but the moment of his arrival is not the time. Let him talk first.

8) Make the evening his: Never complain if he does not take you out to dinner or to other pleasant entertainment. Instead, try to understand his world of strain and pressure, his need to unwind and relax.

9) The goal: Try to make your home a place of peace and order where your husband can relax in body and spirit.

A New View

Here are a few revisions of the text on the preceding page. Notice how the details change when we get a new set of eyes.

How To Be A Good Husband

1) Be romantic
2) Give her the remote
3) Cook
4) Clean
5) Give random stacks of money to the wife

How to Be A Good Husband

1) We have to go 50/50 on dinner
2) If you could it would be nice to have a hot bath waiting for me when I get home.
3) Please sometimes clean up after yourself or the kids. Women sometimes need a break.
4) You could have the children's school clothes prepared and have them already in bed.
5) When I come home from work sometimes I do have a headache so keep the music down.
6) Don't complain all the time!!
7) Listen to me and I'll listen to you.
8) Give wife back massage when she is sore sometimes.
9) Tell each other you love one another.

Revising Hamlet

Here is a fun way to play with voice. I learned it from Vicki Spandel, co-author of *Creating Writers*. Below you'll find Hamlet's soliloquy. If you are not familiar with the play, let's just say Hamlet is having a rough time. His uncle and his mother have conspired to murder his father. He got the whole story from his father's ghost. Hamlet is a young man and must decide whether to do something or roll over and commit suicide. He is a young man and not great at decisions. Read Hamlet's soliloquy beneath and try revising it in a different voice. Begin by listing personalities whose voice you know well. Make sure you stick to the meaning and at least some of Hamlet's language, but don't be afraid to take wild departures in the name of voice. Turn to the next page for examples.

To be, or not to be, that is the question:
Whether 'tis nobler in the mind to suffer
The slings and arrows of outrageous fortune,
Or to take arms against a sea of troubles,
And by opposing end them. To die: to sleep;
No more; and by a sleep to say we end
The heart-ache and the thousand natural shocks
That flesh is heir to; 'tis a consumption
Devoutly to be wish'd. To die, to sleep;
To sleep; perchance to dream. Ay, there's the rub;
For in that sleep of death what dreams may come,
When we have shuffled off this mortal coil,
Must give us pause—there's the respect
That makes calamity of so long life.......

Some Little Known Hamlets

Preacher Hamlet

Todays sermon is going to be about
To be or not to be, that is
The question—
Is it better
Yesa, to suffer in the mind
(can I get an amen)
Are you gonna let the pain get to you
Or are you gonna face the struggle?
Somebody say, be strong.
Y'all don't hear me in here.
Should I die or should I rise?
I came to tell you that
You shall live (somebody say live)
And not die and declare the works
Of the Lord
Call on the blood of Jesus
(call him)
Resist the devil and he will flee.
Somebody say Amen.
            Shalana and Shakya 9th grade

Tupac Hamlet

To be dere or not to be dere
That's what I askin yo.
Whether yo mind get shot up
The gluks of keepin real, if we
Fight against the west side
killaz.
Then kill dem. Whether I get shot up
Or relax at da crib It don't matta
I'm goin down wit the hommies. Gang
fights and my honey cheatin on me
West side is mine. Man I wanna get shot up
and relax
In da crib—I be thinkin of riches,
But when I be in bed asleep I be realising
crap in my head. Yo!
            Birkleigh Foreman

Frosty Hamlet

To melt or not to melt,
that is the question...

Clueless Hamlet

Oh my god? Like to be or like—not to be.
That is the question PA ---leeeese.
Whatever? Noble to suffer in the mind? Uh?
Working slings and arrows???
 I don't think so. I'd be working with my
plastic sea of troubles? Mine is a day
without shopping. Uh, like I'd die without
that. Sleep? Hee-lloo? Beauty Sleep. Natural
shocks through the body? That'd give me
split ends! Tis a consumption. Yeah, I'm
watching my calories.

Jerry Hamlet

And then there's suicide. What a
hassle. You're depressed anyway
or you wouldn't be thinking about
it. Everyone says, "You're
depressed. Don't make any big
decisions till you snap out of it." But it's too
late. The idea has occurred. So now you
gotta decide. Do I do it? Do I wait? What
suicidal person has this kind of mental
energy.

Rocky Hamlet

Yo! To live or die. Do I go up against the
fighter or take a dive. It might be easier to
take the dive. I got to think about this one.

The Cat and the Hamlet

I may not want to die today,
 I may not, may not anyway.
I may not die neither here nor there,
I may not die anywhere.
I will not fight the slings and arrows
I will not fight, oh sorrow, sorrow.
I will not suffer the pain of man,
for sleep of death is in my hands.

Reading From the Inside Out

Here's a great way to begin finding the different points of view within a novel you've read, or a newspaper article, or a movie . It was taught to me by Gretchen Bernabei from San Antonio Texas. Below you'll find some definitions for forms on the following two pages. On the next page is a demonstration of the forms using Hamlet's soliloquy. On the following page is a newspaper article you can use.

Text is something someone says.

Paraphrasing is putting text into other, simpler words.

Subtext is what someone is thinking about.

Dramatic Analysis is what is happening around the person as he is saying the text; what the background action is; what he is doing. (This is written in the third person like stage directions.)

Imaginative Autobiography is the life story of the speaker of the text. You make up the details that you don't know, being guided by what you do know. This is written in the first person.

Reading Activity
1) Read a newspaper article
2) Label the 5 W's
3) Label all the spoken text both direct and indirect
4) Choose one quote to use as text
5) In cartoon form draw the speaker of the text (see next page)
6) In bubbles, write the text, paraphrase and subtext
7) Write the dramatic analysis
8) Write an imaginative autobiography

Responding to a Movie
1) Jot down some favorite lines from the film
2) Choose one
3) Draw a picture of the speaker of the text with a word bubble for text
4) Under the text, place a paraphrase in ( ), inside the bubble
5) In a thought bubble, write the subtext or the speaker's thoughts
6) Below that, write a one sentence dramatic analysis
7) Below that, write an imaginative autobiography

One-Liner from **Hamlet**

Dramatic Analysis: Hamlet is wondering if he should kill hemself.

Imaginative Autobiography: My name is Hamlet, prince of Denmark. My uncle knocked off my father so that he would become king and marry my mother. I am 19 years old and now that I have found this out I don't know what to do with myself.

Chipmunk Bites Toddler, Leads Police on Wild Chase

By HOPE ULLMAN
Union Leader Correspondent

FREMONT — Police were led on a foot pursuit with an unlikely suspect yesterday — a fleet-footed chipmunk that unlawfully entered a Main Street home and bit a toddler.

Police first responded to the home Wednesday night when the animal bit a 2-year-old girl on the foot. When they arrived, residents thought the chipmunk had left, so the search was called off.

The girl was taken to Exeter hospital where she was treated for rabies exposure and released Wednesday night, hospital spokesman Ron Goodspeed said.

Police received another call yesterday at 9 a.m. The chipmunk had reappeared, and was running through the home again.

While there is nothing funny about being bitten by a wild critter when it invades a home — or the rabies treatment that can be required as a consequence — the same can't be said for the efforts to capture one.

"We went there to apprehend the individual," Patrolman Shaun Marston said.

The suspect, however, was determined not to be taken by police. Marston and Animal Control Officer Reese Bassett raced around the living room and kitchen of the 572 Main Street home in hot pursuit.

"We went in the kids' bedroom, chased it around a few times, but it went out under the door," Bassett said. The officers then moved into the living room and sealed themselves in with the chipmunk.

"We captured it at approximately 9:25 a.m.," Marston said. "Once we had it under a clothes basket, we had to go for a sheet."

But victory was short-lived: The chipmunk seized the opportunity and fled.

"That was our critical mistake," Marston said. "We failed to secure the living room."

"It just came shooting right out the top," Bassett said. "It happened so fast, it was a blur."

With Marston on one side of the couch, Reese on the other, and the chipmunk poking its head out from underneath, the officers made their move.

"I gave officer Bassett the sign and I flipped the couch over," Marston said.

"That's when he charged me, but I protected myself with a basket," Reese said. "He was out of control. I think he snarled."

Marston described the critter as "a brown and black regular-sized chipmunk with little black-beady eyes."

A chipmunk was later spotted outside, but police could not tell whether it was the culprit since chipmunks tend to look alike. They said they'll likely place a Have-A-Heart trap in the kitchen in case it returns.

Chipmunks, raccoons, squirrels, bats, rats, mice and snakes are all possibilities when it comes to unwelcome summertime visitors, said wildlife damage control specialist Rob Calvert of the New Hampshire Department of Fish and Game.

"Common sense is the best way to deal with most problems," Calvert said. "If you have an animal running around in your home, the most important thing you can do is provide an escape route for the animal," preferably one that leads to the spot where it entered. One of best ways to keep wildlife from entering a home is to use hardware cloth screening bent in an L shape and attached to the foundation, Calvert said.

"Good sanitation eliminates an awful lot of problems," said Calvert, adding that it's best not to leave pets' food outside unless a re-creation of a "Wild Kingdom" special is the desired result.

"There's no simple cure on something like a chipmunk," he said, but noted that Have-A-Heart traps may help, particularly when used with corn mash bait. Always wear gloves when handling an animal, he advised. If you don't know what you're doing, call someone who does.

"We can help talk them through it," Calvert said.

For a list of nearby nuisance wildlife control operators who remove animals from homes, call the New Hampshire Fish and Game office in your region.

Calvert said that some residents may be coming across more chipmunks than usual this. "Some parts of the state have seen real spikes," he said. "This is time of year when they're running around. It really gives you the idea the ground's moving with chipmunks. There's so many around."

Chipmunks are driven by their food base, Calvert said. "In areas that have had good acorn crops, the chipmunk population is on rise," he said. "Chipmunks respond to a good acorn crop. The Seacoast had a gypsy moth problem with oak trees, and those trees have tried to compensate for that by having abundant nut crops."

Calvert said there has been a spike in calls involving woodchucks and bats.

When bitten by a chipmunk or any other type of critter, call a doctor immediately to find out whether rabies shots are in order, he said. The animal's symptoms may include a strange appearance, a head that droops or tips, mucus coming from the animal's mouth, nose or eyes, and impaired locomotion such as walking around in a circular motion. However, the only sure way to tell whether an animal has rabies is through a post-mortem exam.

Pick and explore a point of view in my story using the form on the next page.

Reprinted from the Manchester Union Leader with permission of the author

One Line Exploration:

Dramatic Analysis:

Imaginative
Autobiography: _____

_____

_____

_____

_____

Text
(Paraphrase)

Subtext

adapted by Gretchen Bernabei from Performing Literature, by Beverly Whitaker and Mary Frances Hopkins (1982) Prentice Hall

The Art of Subvertising

The Media Foundation in British Columbia, Canada, believes that the best way to make a point about oppressive advertising is to use the same language as the oppressor. They call it culture jamming, and when we teach it to students we give them critical thinking tools to evaluate the thousands of messages they receive each day through the media. We also teach them how to have a good time at the expense of multi-national corporations who can afford it.

1) Define the audience.

Begin by showing the class real ads. Let them bring them in from home. Talk about the audience for the ad in specific terms; in other words, not just young people, but young boys who want to look macho.

2) What is the message?

All ads have a specific message for their audience. To find the message begin your sentence with the name of your product and the verb "will:" for example, cigarettes will....... make you tough.

3) Make a list of what you know about the Product: Real research

Cigarettes give you cancer, emphysema, heart disease, birth defects. They smell bad and cost a lot.

4) Put what you know about the product into the image

In other words you are going to put a drunk in a beer commercial, a cancer patient in a cigarette ad. Make a list of what you know about cigarettes.

Image + Reality = Satire

Subvertising Assignment

1) Find an ad that seems false or only half true. Now list all the real truth not reflected in the ad.

> Example: "Coke is the Real Thing."
> Reality: 11 marshmallows plus carbonated water, caffeine and flavoring, that's the real "real thing."

2) Put the reality into the image. Do it with words or do it with thought bubbles or do it with new glued-in images. Ask them questions like: What would this football player in this Budweiser ad act like if he had just drunk a 6 pack? Would he catch the pass?

Send your best subvertisments to:
The Media Foundation
1243 West 7th Avenue
Vancouver, BC Canada v6h-1b7
for information about Adbusters magazine call 1-800-663-1243 www.adbusters.com

Some Subvertisements

Notice how the reality of cigarettes blasts apart the image advertisers have created to sell the products. Remember that advertisements don't sell products—they create products. You and I are the products they create. When we change words we change worlds.

This billboard is part of the California Department of Health's $22-million anti-smoking campaign.

The Classifying Voice

One favorite voice in expository writing is the classifier. This voice labels and constructs meaning by classifying information. Read the following piece by high school freshman Ben Barnes, then make a list of things you can classify, things like homework, teachers who get mad, football games, hand shakers....

Take your Pick

For anyone to deny they pick their nose would be bordering on hypocrisy. While it is not an act that people proudly boast of, its almost as common a function as brushing your teeth or taking a bath. Some people could make a living at it, and some seldom pick, but everyone has done it at least one time or other. When a tissue won't finish the job, one must take the situation into his or her own hands, if you would pardon the expression.

One type of nose picker is every grade school janitor's nightmare, commonly referred to as the wiper, predominantly seen in juveniles and young adolescents. This type will pick and then wipe anywhere inconspicuous. Swiftness of disposal is the key for them. Bottoms of school desks and chairs seem to be a popular place of concealment, leaving janitors with a situation that only determination, a strong stomach and perhaps a chisel will eliminate. Though often regarded as a child's designation, it is certainly not limited to the younger set. Adults lacking in certain social graces and/or tissues could easily fall into this category.

Another group would be the "pick and roll" crowd. Not to be confused with the pick and roll in basketball, these people pick with their index finger and after finding their desired goal, transfer the buger to the thumb where it is aggressively rolled with the middle finger. They continue to roll till the buger falls off their fingers, nowhere to be found. On occasion, the aforementioned process is repeated until satisfaction is complete.

Similar to the pick and roll is a sadistic group know as "the flickers." They use the same retrieval process as the pick and roll, but after rolling, they flick the solid nasal secretions instead of allowing them to quietly fall to the floor. Certain sects of this group flick for the sport of it, trying to get as much distance behind their flick as possible, while others take great pleasure out of taking aim at other people.

Still another classification is the pick and ponder group. This group can be seen performing their ritual most often while behind the wheel of a motor driven vehicle or behind the desk of a slow-paced office or classroom. Using their index or middle fingers, they pick and then proudly stare at their prize procreation, judging it for size, texture and color before disposing of it in the proper manner. Traveling salesmen and truck drivers seem to dominate this category.

The final group is the "Rambo" picker. This is a group with a mission, refusing to come out till they get what they came for. This group is easy to spot as they usually have their index finger buried one or two knuckles deep in their nostril at any given time. Rambo pickers have frequent nosebleeds.

You might fall into one or more of these categories or perhaps you find that there might be sub-groups in the five major categories. The important point to note, however is that there is a group for each and every one of us, so take your pick.

Ben Barnes 9th grade

The Persuading Story

Can persuasive essays be written as stories? Sure can, especially if the author makes an analogy between the thing they are writing about and the subject. This type of distance allows the author persuade through comparison. People know more about buying cars than they do education. Michael Dearborn brilliantly exploits the flaws in Californias prop 227.

By Michael Dearborn
Napa, Ca

"I had been hearing so much about this new model of education, the 227, that thought I'd head down to the dealership to check one out. Let me tell you what an eye-opening experience that was I was greeted at the dealership by Ron, the ever-smiling salesman. Dressed smartly in a jacket and tie, he called "Hello, and welcome!" from acrossthe parking lot. "How can I be of assistance today?"
 "Well," I said, "I've come to see the new 227. I hear it's fast and economical, the answer to our education prayers." With a wave of his hand Ron bid "Follow me into the showroom, and let me show you this little beauty." We entered the tidy showroom where I was immediately struck by its neatness: straight rows of desks, chalkboards cleaned, not a pencil out of place on the teacher's  desk. Looked like a smooth operation to me. "So, where's this 227 I've been hearing about?" I asked.
 "Well, truth be told, I don't have any in stock. We don't even have a working model, yet. But take a look at this brochure. Everything you need to know is right in here." Ron handed me a slick flyer. The 227 sure looked sleek. "It looks pretty sporty. You say it will be economical, too?" "You betcha," Ron purred. "This is the only education system you'll ever need. It will meet the needs of every student, regardless of age, background, language ability -- you name it, the 227 can do it. Why don'tyou come on into the office and I can get you signed-up for one."
"Uh-oh," I thought. I sensed the 'hard sell'. If the 227 was so great, why the need for the pressure? I wanted to know a little more before I made a commitment. We headed into Ron's office, and he closed the door behind us. "Have a seat," he said as he handed me a contract to by the 227. "All you have todo is punch the spot marked 'Yes' and you'll be all set to go." He handed me the stylette and inched the ballot box closer. "Sure, Ron. I'd just like to read the contract first. Is that OK with you?" I asked. "Well, it's utterly, utterly unnecessary but, if you must . . . ." He was clearly put-off by the delay. But I was too busy slogging through the fine print to care. After reading the fine print, I was still interested in buying one of these 227s, and I had some questions for Ron. But something didn't feel right. Although he tried to hide it, the perspiration on his forehead betrayed his nervousness. The hairs on the back of my neck were at attention now. What did this guy have to hide? "Well, Ron," I began, "I'm sure it's just anoversight, but I noticed that your brochure doesn't have a list of options.What options are available on the 227?" He loosened his tie. "The 227 won't come with any options," he told me flatly. "None?" I was incredulous.
 "But surely you've accounted for the different age groups and learning abilitiesthat this education will be applied to, haven't you? People like options, Ron." Wiping his forehead, Ron

got up and filled a Dixie cup at the water cooler. "That's the beauty of it," he said. "This is the perfect education for everyone. No one should want anything more." That struck me as odd. I thought that there were plenty of people around who might want more than the 'basic model'. And why did Ron think he knew what I 'should' want in an education? "You know, Ron, when you say that this is the perfect educationfor everyone, what you are really saying is that all children learn the same way -- that all kids are identical, right?" He took a second to answer. And then, "Well, if they're not, they should be. It would sure make things easier, wouldn't it?" He nudged the ballot box forward again. "Don't you agree?" Again with the pressure.

I tried to ignore Ron's obvious lack of knowledge about children and education. After all, this 227 was supposed to be pretty economical. The 227 still sounded like a good proposition, even if all it did was save money. I decided to pursue that angle. "I read in the contract, Ron, that all of the funding we currently spend on education will stay the same, but that the 227 requires an additional $50 million for each of the next ten years, and that the money won't go into the kids' classrooms. How is that going to save me any money?" Ron was taking his coat off now. "Obviously you don't understand financial matters. Even though you will spend more money, you'll actually be saving money. Really. Trust me." Trust him? Uh-oh. This was getting confusing. But Ron was the expert on the 227, so I asked him about his credentials. "So just how long have you been in the education business, Ron?" Ron was pacing now, stopping frequently to refill his Dixie cup. "Well, funny you should ask," he stammered. "Actually, I'm not in the education business per se, I just sell it. I haven't actually studied how it works, and in fact I've never even been in a classroom, I'm proud to say. Education isn't something you need any training to do. It's just common sense. That's why I've designed the 227 without any requirements for teachers or silly 'standards' that students should have to meet before they move on." I was baffled now. "Wait a second Ron," I said. "Are telling me that you're selling the 227, even though there's nothing in it to make sure that the students learn anything at all? No tests? And that the teachers don't need to have any training in how to use the 227?" "That's right." He was smiling nervously now. "That's the beauty of it. If we all just use the 227, then everyone will learn the same way. It's like magic."

"So what's in this for you, Ron? Do you get a commission on every 227 you sell?" I asked. He became indignant, and his trembling had spilled a little water from the well-worn paper cup.

"Commission? Me? No, no, no. You see, I'm doing this because I love children. Education these days costs too much and doesn't get the job done. And I think that parents should have more choice in education. Just as long as their choice is the same as mine, of course."

"So let me get this straight. You think that education is costly, ineffective and limits choice. And you are selling a model which costs more, has no options and nothing under the hood. And you want voters to buy the227 before you even have a model of it that works. Have I got it so far?" Ron was draining the remains of the water cooler.

 "Yeah, that just about covers it," he said. "But the brochure sure is nice, isn't it?"

Leaving the dealership that day, I was relieved that I had done a little checking of the 227 before I made the mistake of buying one. You should take a look at the contract, too. It's on page 75 of your California Voter Information Guide Ballot Pamphlet. I think once you read the fine print, you'll also want avoid buyer's remorse. You can do it by voting no on Prop.227 on June 2.

Keep the Eye on the Ball

Write a persuasive essay about something you don't care about.

Question: When would you ever have to do that in life unless you were to become a lawyer or a sociopath?

Answer: On the state expository writing test.

Betty Riley, a feisty reading teacher from Connecticut, helped raise scores 30 percentage points in one school by organizing "fake writing week" the week before the test was given. She acknowledged that prompted tests don't often test your ability to write with meaning and purpose, but rather test your ability to fake it.

Gretchen Bernabei, a teacher from Texas, has her students practice delivering their persuasive essays as speeches. They have to pound their fist on the desk in their writing and in real life. When it's test time, she reminds them to not just state an opinion, but to get the fist pounding. She has grasped the theatrical aspect of state testing, and her students score highest as a result.

On the following page you'll find some tips for revising test day into fake writing day. Read them to your class before test day and remember that fake writing day is only a day, not a year or a month. Your best preparation for the test is to let your kids write and read every day.

Sometimes after a writing workshop a teacher will come up to me and say, "This was wonderful, I used to teach this way before the TAAS or the MEAP, or the PEEP." This teacher was suckered into believing that test writing was the only important writing. They replaced thoughtful inquiry with nifty formulas and graphic organizers. The irony, of course, is that most tests are created to improve instruction and encourage best practice, not to promote mediocrity.

The good news is that I find teachers all over the country whose kids have scored the highest on the state test, and when you look at their classroom you find kids who love to read and write. They do very little to teach the test directly but encourage their students to see themselves as writers. Your best preparation for the state test is to keep it in perspective and keep your eye on the real ball, a lifelong love for literacy.

P

Fake Writing Day

For reasons beyond your control you are sometimes asked to write about things you don't care about. This more often than not occurs on state tests which tell the world how well you write. If this seems dumb to you, perhaps one day when you grow up you will join a state department of education and set them straight. Until then you need a few tricks to survive this strange world. If you see the test day as fake writing day you won't be shocked or bored with the prompts they give you. Rather, like skilled magicians you will learn to fake out the audience by pretending to have an opinion when you don't, or reinventing totally boring writing prompts with your imagination. Here are some tips for surviving Fake Writing day:

1) They don't usually care if it's true or not. In other words, they want you to write about a new piece of playground equipment you would like to see. You don't really care about this prompt, but what if you could invent a 200 foot dragon-powered turbo swing with special hyper-pumping wings installed on either side. Let your imagination go wild. The worst that can happen to you is , after you pass the test with flying colors, they may ask you to speak with the school counselor for an evaluation.

2) Specific reasons and examples are the oxygen of any opinions.
Practice making any opinion breathe by listing examples. Here are a few tough ones to warm up with.

Why I Love Homework! -- The Joy of Little Sisters and Brothers.
Summer Should be Shorter.

3) The first and the last sentence are the MOST important on any test. If you don't believe me, ask your teacher to read you some average test samples. They will all begin: "In this paper...." Boooooooring. Write five leads before you start your essay and pick the one that makes you want to write most, or better yet, leave the first page blank and go back to write your beginning after you know about the end.

Look at your ending and make sure it ties up with the beginning somehow. If it doesn't, add more or cut back to a place that does.

4) Loosen up

If you are not having a good time, your writing will sound as exciting as rain on a tin roof. You have to find ways to release your voice as a writer. Here are a few suggestions. Wear funny clothes on test day. Tell jokes the hour before the test. Have a party with plenty of good snacks on test day. Imagine you are not writing your test to the State Department of Education but to a close friend. Skip lines so you can go back and add extra thoughts. Don't be afraid to stop and stare. You don't have to write fast to succeed. You need to breathe deeply and think clearly.

5) Don't fake it. Be honest

If you don't feel like faking it, try honesty. Write about why you think it's a dumb test or what you think would be a better prompt, but back up your opinion with details and passion. Remember, the test should be about evaluating your ability to express your ideas, not to make you write lies to get a good score. **Caution:** Honesty will not work on all state tests. Consult your teachers or the State Department of Education.

Take a Management Role

State departments of education are like poorly run hotels. If you've ever stayed at a poorly run hotel you'll know what I mean. Nobody takes responsibility for your problems. Nobody really works there. They all tell you to wait for someone else in another department who will solve your problem. I have a method that works well at these establishments. I pretend I own the place. Instead of asking if anyone can help me find a dolly, I say, "I need the dolly. I think it's in that closet but I don't have a key. Could you let me in there?" No problem. People respond and are very glad to be told what to do. Your state department of education is dying to be managed by you. If you only knew how clueless bureaucracies are, you would write them every day and tell them exactly what to do.

Consider this. In today's corporate world they judge the health of an organization by how fast information flows from the lowest tier to the highest. In a company this would be from the factory floor to the CEO's corner office. In a school it would be from the classroom to the State Commissioner of Education's office. You make the whole system healthier when you contact the state department.

If your best writer scored low on the state test because he didn't write a formula essay, you need to let the assessment coordinator know about it. There could be a serious problem on how the tests are scored, and your input could help the test evolve in its next incarnation. The test won't improve if you keep its failures a secret.

In Appendix IV, you'll find the address of the state department of education in all 50 states. Address your faxes, e-mails and letters to the Assessment Coordinator/Director or send it right to the Commissioner and let them pass it on. Remember, you are in charge. Tell them what you want and you will be surprised. E-mail your miraculous stories to Discover Writing Press and we will publish them in a later version of the Reviser's Toolbox

6

15 Wacky Research Reports

World's thinnest books

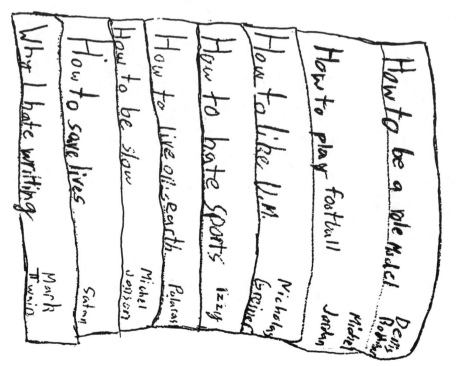

Nicholas Greiner

1-The Tabloid Research Paper

A tabloid research paper begins with a shocking headline and reveals an intriguing "believe-it-or-not" type angle on whatever subject you are researching. With younger students snappy headlines and pictures might be enough, but with older students an entire article like this one can be a wonderful way to find a focus and point of view in a sea of research. The next page gives a form to begin your paper tomorrow.

IN REAL LIFE, SNOW WHITE WAS MURDERED...

FRACTURED FAIRY TALE!

By RICHARD SERBER / *Weekly World News*

Snow White was a real person! But unlike the fairy tale, she didn't live happily ever after — she was killed to stop her from marrying a king.

Even more horrifying, the dwarfs were really child slaves who were forced to work in copper mines.

German teacher Eckhard Sander uncovered the shocking truth behind the Grimm Brothers' fairy tale that became a popular Disney movie.

After four years of research, Sander learned that the model for Snow White was the German Countess Margarethe von Waldeck, a 16th-century beauty from Bad Wildungen.

Like the fairy tale character, the Countess had a wicked stepmother. But the stepmother wasn't the one who wanted her killed. The bad guys were the Spanish secret police.

"Margarethe fell in love with King Philip II of Spain and was poisoned by the secret police because they decided the marriage would be a political disaster," said Sander, who wrote the book *Snow White: Myth or Reality*. And the dwarfs who rescued Snow White in the fairy tale were based on real children — who worked 12 hours a day in a mine owned by Margarethe's brother in Bad Wildungen.

"The children grew bent and crippled because of the work, the terrible conditions and because they were permanently undernourished," said Sander. "They went prematurely gray and rarely lived beyond the age of 20.

"As for the poisoned apple, I discovered that Bad Wildungen had a man who did know how to poison apples — or at least make them very bitter.

"It appears that he handed

... and the dwarfs were child slaves!

them out to children to stop them from raiding his fruit trees."

Over time, these details were told and retold until they became the fairy tale that we know today, according to the researcher. He concluded, "I don't believe the Grimm Brothers had any idea of the real story."

SNOW WHITE and the seven dwarfs lived happily ever after in the Disney movie based on the fairy tale — but not in real life.

(adapted from 51 Wacky We-search reports
Discover Writing Press ©1999)

Classroom Star

All the shocking news that's fit to print!

2-Want Ads

Try writing a want ad for someone or something out of history, science or math or any subject. Begin by listing some facts about the subject of your ad. Then construct your ad from the central pieces of information.

Wanted:
One Abraham Lincoln. Must be 6' 4" tall, have beard and high silk hat. Must hate slavery and be very honest. Religious attitude toward war and suffering a must. No shrimps or rebels. Call 775-6754; ask for Union Powers.

Wanted:
One Rain Forest. Must be able to produce mass quantities of oxygen from carbon dioxide. Must be able to grow 1/3 of the plant species on the planet earth and provide the world with medicine. Don't miss this exciting opportunity to grow in a new field. Call 1-800-223-9008 ask for Scorched Earth

Wanted:

Wanted:

Wanted:

₃-Truth Telling

Here is an ad for the Pony Express written over a hundred years ago. What I love about it is how honest it is. You can tell the writer really did the job and wasn't afraid to tell the truth. Try writing a brutally honest ad about a job that you know. Use your research to make the ad believable.

Example: Wanted

One Artery Clogger.

must have experience dispensing high cholesterol foods

to unsuspecting public.

Must be able to perform like good-natured robot.

Have Nice Day.

PONY EXPRESS

St. JOSEPH, MISSOURI to CALIFORNIA

in 10 days or less.

☞ **WANTED** ☜

YOUNG, SKINNY, WIRY FELLOWS

not over eighteen. Must be expert riders, willing to risk death daily.

Orphans preferred.

Wages $25 per week.

APPLY **PONY EXPRESS STABLES**

St. JOSEPH, MISSOURI

(adapted from 51 Wacky We-search reports
Discover Writing Press ©1999)

4-Build your Own Cell

One way to learn a subject is to create an entirely new species of the thing you are studying, using your knowledge to make your new species accurate to the tiniest detail. Below you'll find seventh grader Jessie's rendition of HKISSES, a new breed of cell.

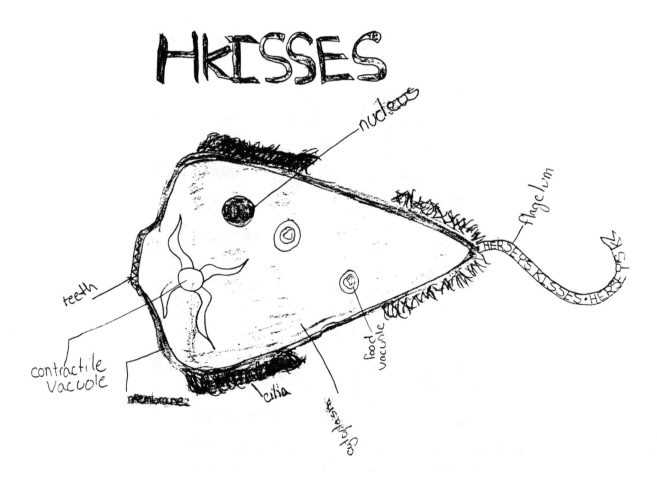

P

5 - World's Thinnest Books

A thin book is a book the author has no authority to write. To make a thin book you must start with research about your subject and then make the person an expert on something your research shows they know nothing about. For example, if I research Susan B. Anthony and find she is the woman who worked her whole life to secure the right to vote for women my thin book might be **Who Needs the Vote When You Have the Kitchen** by Susan B. Anthony. Look at the thin books below and fill in or make your own shelf.

P

6-The "How to" Poem

A "How To" poem is a list poem form which can be used effectively to play around with specific facts we have researched. Start by making lists about your subjects, then order them for best effect.

(Tip: Jokes come in threes. Try putting your surprising fact 3rd.)

How to be Thomas Jefferson

Write like an angel.
Live in your mind.
Have your heart broken many times.
Declare all men equal,
and never release your 200 slaves.
Buy lots of real estate from Frenchmen
without looking at it.
Live beyond your means
and owe lots of money.
Never finish the house
that years later will appear
on the back side of a nickel.

Barry Lane

How to be a Heart (1st grade)

Pump blood
Be the strongest muscles in the body
Don't stop
Have love in you
Beat fast in rats and slow in elephants
Don't stop...
Don't stop...
Don't stop...

Unreliable "How to" Narrators

It's fun to write "how to" poems where the narrators are self-serving. They pretend to be telling the truth but they are really just telling us to do what works for them. Here are some examples. After you've read them try using your research to write "how to" poems like "How to be a Zebra" by A. Lion, or "How to be an Arawak" by Christopher Columbus.

How to be a Bird

by A. Cat

Sit still on a low branch
Smile as furry friends approach
Never fly away from friendly felines
Wait till you are greeted with a love embrace
Sleep soundly.

How to be a Good Slave

by Harriett Tubman

Do what Master tells you,
Never share what you feel in your heart.
Know that freedom is only for folks with white skin
Never even think of running away
Never look north
Never peer through the tears
Don't listen to train whistles

Use the Language

> As you read the following mathematical and scientific "how to" poems, notice how the authors use specific language and research to make their poems stronger.

How to be a Fraction

Be ½ of what you are
Realise your lifespan will never be greater than one
When trying to be equal
treat your top the same as your bottom.
Multiply with other fractions
Spend 1/3 of your time being improper.
Simplify
Only be mixed if you are of the proper religion.
Be careful when you cross-multiply
Convert to decimalism.
Know that if you've had ½ as much fun as I've had
I've had twice as much fun as you.

Frank Youngman

How to be an Amoeba

Date yourself
Never eat out
Look in the mirror
if you don't like what you see
SPLIT!

Barry Lane

(adapted from 51 Wacky We-search reports
Discover Writing Press ©1999)

7-Lunes

A lune is a wonderful short form of poetry that can be a great way to play with research and other facts.

> **Here's what lunes**
> **look like when you write**
> **one real quick**

The first line is 3 words. The second line in 5 words. The third line is 3 words. You don't have to count syllables. A strong lune does something surprising in the last line. Here's one I wrote for the 1996 presidential election:

Dole and Clinton
sitting in the same tree
Get the saw!

Barry Lane

See how the last line does something unexpected. Even funny. Here's one a 4th grader wrote after studying Eleanor Roosevelt:

Can you see
Eleanor Roosevelt being very mean
to poor people?

> Now you write
> a lune and see if
> it breaks hearts.

(adapted from 51 Wacky We-search reports   **152**
Discover Writing Press ©1999)

8-_____ Ways of Looking at _____.

If you know the poem by Wallace Stevens called "Thirteen Ways of Looking at a Blackbird," you may enjoy writing similar poems to the ones shown below. Start by collecting facts about your subject then ask yourself what your subject might look like from different points of view. Make each line a new point of view.

3 Ways of Looking at Columbus

1 Great explorer
2 Bad map reader
3 Mass murderer

6 Ways of Looking at the Rain Forest

1   1/3 of the earth's surface
2   Giant medicine chest
3   Something to save
4   Oxygen factory
5   Lumberyard
6   Dreams up in smoke

4 Ways of looking at a Fraction

1 Common denominators
2 Decimals in disguise
3 I want the big half

(adapted from 51 Wacky We-search reports
Discover Writing Press ©1999)

9) Top Ten Lists

Comedian David Letterman has perfected the top ten list as a funny form. You can use your research to make your own top ten lists. Here are some examples of titles: *"Top Ten Reasons Why You Wouldn't Want to be a Christian in Roman Times"*; *"Top Ten reasons I'd Rather Be a One-Celled organism"*; *"Top Reasons the World Could Not be Round"*....etc.

The trick is to write a funny title then use your facts to bring the joke to life.

Tip; Jokes are funnier when they are stated indirectly. For example, lets say my poem was *"Top ten reasons I don't want to be a cat."* One reason could be my friend is a dog. But that's not as funny as me writing, "My best friend's name is Fido." Be a little indirect and your audience will find the laugh. Also move from 10 to 1, stacking your better reasons near the end. Try mixing some straight facts with your funny ones.

Top Ten Reasons Why Columbus Discovered America

10 - He needed a job

9 His compass had the eastern needle snapped off

8 Heard a rumor the Iroquois were going to invade Spain.

7 He tried to discover Portugal but someone beat him to it

6 He knew the state capital of Ohio would need a name

5 He didn't. His boats did.

4 Queen Isabella had a passion for new continents

3 He was sick of discovering his dirty apartment

2 He wanted to prove the earth was fat

1 He needed some gold to fill a tooth

(adapted from 51 Wacky We-search reports
Discover Writing Press ©1999)

10- **Research Recipes**

Recipe poems are a fun way to share your research in a tasty way. After gathering 10 specific facts about a specific subject, begin collecting recipes. Then list a bunch of recipe verbs on the board, verbs like, mash, beat, whip, fold, stir, bake, cream--good strong recipe verbs. Next list nouns like cake, cookies, soufflés, brownies etc. Now look at how recipes are set up. They start with a list of numbered ingredients and they end with instructions. Now you are ready to make your recipe. Get your index card and get to work.

(Tip: The more specific research you include, the better your poem will be.)

Constitution Stew

1 Teaspoon First Amendment
27 cups of amendments
Sliced hatred for King George
1 Cup of Preamble
13-15oz. of African-American Rights
16 cups voters' rights
Cook President for four years then remove
Strain out obsolete amendments
Mince and throw away leftover racism
Boil on high for three years
Preserve in freezer for hundreds of years
7th grade

(adapted from 51 Wacky We-search reports
Discover Writing Press ©1999)

P

11-Tee Shirt Time

What kind of tee-shirt would Henry the Eighth wear? What kind of tee-shirt would an hummingbird wear? a paramecium? Use your research to come up with a short slogan for what you are studying.

12-For Sale: One America.

Have you ever tried to sell something? The first question you ask yourself is, "Who the heck would want this?" Then you come up with details that would appeal to that person. The act of writing an ad involves imagining an audience and then establishing a point of view: good practice for researchers lost in a swamp of objective facts.

Ads can get funny when we ask funny questions and collect funny facts. Look at the ad below. Try selling something that you are studying. Begin by reading all kinds of ads from newspapers: ads for appliances, ads for cars. Begin by asking yourself who the audience is. Use some of your research to sell the product. Begin by defining the audience. Who are you selling to? Get specific. If you say people, what age? What gender? What is this product going to do for them?
Below is my attempt to sell America back to it's original inhabitants.

For Sale: One America

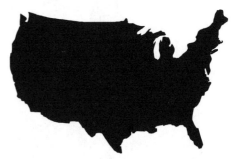

This 200+ year old country could be just what the medicine man ordered!

Nestled between 2 major oceans and bordered on the north and south by 2 friendly countries, the United States of a America has already been subdivided into 48 convenient parcels plus a vast track of land near the Arctic Circle and a few heavenly islands in the Pacific.

Though no longer containing huge herds of buffalo to hunt and crystal clear streams and lakes to fish in, native peoples will still enjoy the vast tracts of farmland and those with Visa cards will be able to buy food and manufactured items to help them forget the pristine beauty which was lost. You can also watch nature documentaries on TV.

Call 1-800-BUY-IT-BACK today for a free appointment

13- Haiku-ing Everything

What if your computer wrote error messages in Haiku? What if flight attendants read safety warnings in Haiku form? What if you wrote your research report as a series of Haiku? A Japanese form of poetry, Haiku uses 5 syllables, 7 syllables and 5 syllables. When Haikus work they exude a haunting image or idea that helps you to see something in a new light.

Play with your research to write some of your own.

First snow, then quiet.
This thousand dollar screen
dies so beautifully.
internet

Windows 95 crashed.
I am the Blue Screen of Death.
No one hears your cries.
internet

Columbus stands tall
with empty boats and dreams
Conquer, King, Killer.
Barry Lane

Arawak people
Watch the man in the big boat
Run the other way!
Barry Lane

(adapted from 51 Wacky We-search reports
Discover Writing Press ©1999)

P

14-The Profile Poster

A profile is a great way to display your most revealing information in a manner that is immediately understood. Travel to any museum or zoo and you're apt to find profile posters everywhere. Begin by collecting vital information about your subject. Next, take the most striking information and place it into a poster form. Make sure to include categories beyond the standard name—age etc.

The Amazon Rain Forest

Name: Rain Forest

Height: 50 feet

Weight: More than you can imagine

Favorite food: Sunlight

Favorite drink: Water

Hobby: Providing rich canopy of life for more than $\frac{1}{2}$ of the world's species.

Favorite saying: Burn me up and you will gag

(adapted from 51 Wacky We-search reports
Discover Writing Press ©1999)

15- The Comic Analogy

One great way to make a point in a persuasive essay is to compare your subject to something else. I heard consumer advocate Ralph Nader once compare the federal budget to a family's budget. "Imagine this," he said, "I go to your house and there is not enough food in the fridge to feed half of your family, but the first two floors are filled with every weapon imaginable. When I ask you, 'What's with all the guns,' you respond, 'You never know.' "

Begin a comic analogy by comparing your subject to something else. Next take out your binoculars and make the comparison come alive with research. Below you'll find a few comic analogies. Try making some of your own.

Automatic weapons   to   Teddy bears

No federal safety
standards

Four broad types
of federal standards

In 1993 guns killed
37,483 people in the US

Teddy killed no one.

Corporate Welfare to Aid to dependent children

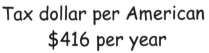

Tax dollars per American
$1388 per year

Tax dollar per American
$416 per year

©1999 Discover Writing Press- 1-800-613-8055 - www.discoverwriting.com
(adapted from 51 Wacky We-search reports
Discover Writing Press ©1999)

Forging Tools for Good Critics

Good Critics Make You Want to Write More

Peer writing conferences can be frustrating to both teachers and students. Students don't always know what to say about a piece of writing beyond, "I liked it." Other students attack a piece and send the unsuspecting writer into a retreat: "It wasn't that bad. I'm not changing a thing. Get lost!"

The first step in creating better peer conferences is to step back and look at what it takes to be a good critic. The words don't even sound like they go together. That's because we don't think of criticism as anything positive. We need to learn ways to value criticism and seek it out. We also need to realize that there are no easy answers. Writing is an art. Each piece has its own shape and it is the critic's and writer's job to find that shape.

This chapter is packed with tools and training wheels to make good critics. Try them out one at a time and remember beyond everything what Donald Murray says, "A good writing conference is when you walk away and you want to write more."

Good Critics:

*Listen

*Start Positively

*Praise Specifically

*Ask Curious ????

*Ask Helpful ????

* Make You Want
To Write More

Tell Me More

A class where writers listen to each other is a class where ideas grow and expand naturally. As you read this excerpt from an essay by Brenda Ueland, think of ways to encourage more listening in your class.

I want to write about the great and powerful thing that listening is. And how we forget it. And how we don't listen to our children, or those we love. And least of all—which is so important—to those we do not love. But we should. Because listening is a magnetic and strange thing, a creative force. Think how the friends that really listen to us are the ones we move toward, and we want to sit in their radius as though it did us good, like ultraviolet rays.

This is the reason: when we are listened to, it creates us, makes us unfold and expand. Ideas actually begin to grow within us and come to life. You know how if a person laughs at your jokes you become funnier and funnier, and if he does not, every tiny little joke in you weakens up and dies. Well, that is the principle of it. It makes people happy and free when they are listened to. And if you are a listener, it is the secret of having a good time in society (because everybody around you becomes lively and interesting), of comforting people, of doing them good.

Who are the people, for example, to whom you go for advice? Not to the hard, practical ones who can tell you exactly what to do, but to the listeners; that is, the kindest, least censorious, least bossy people that you know. It is because by pouring out your problem to them, you then know what to do about it yourself.

When we listen to people there is an alternating current, and this recharges us so that we never get tired of each other. We are constantly being re-created. Now there are brilliant people who cannot listen much. They have no ingoing wires on their apparatus. They are entertaining, but exhausting, too. I think it is because these lecturers, these brilliant performers, by not giving us a chance to talk, do not let us express our thoughts and expand; and it is this little creative fountain inside us that begins to spring and cast up new thoughts and unexpected laughter and wisdom. That is why, when someone has listened to you, you go home rested and lighthearted.

Now this little creative fountain is in us all. It is the spirit, or the intelligence, or the imagination—whatever you want to call it. If you are very tired, strained, have no solitude, run too many errands, talk to too many people, drink too many cocktails, this little fountain is muddied over and covered with a lot of debris. The result is you stop living from the center, the creative fountain, and you live from the periphery, from externals. That is, you go along on mere will power without imagination.

It is when people really listen to us, with quiet fascinated attention, that the little fountain begins to work again, to accelerate in the most surprising way.

Brenda Ueland

From the book <u>Strength to Your Sword Arm: Selected Writings</u> by Brenda Ueland. Copyright 1992 by the Estate of Brenda Ueland. Reprinted by permission of Holy Cow! Press. The book is available for $16.70 from Holy Cow! Press, Box 3170, Mt. Royal Station, Duluth, MN 55803; 218-724-1653.

Train a Critic Today

None of us are born good critics. We blame each other; we get defensive; we don't want to hurt each other's feelings so we wimp out and say helpful stuff like, "I liked it." Below are some ideas to train your conference partner.

When they say:	You say:
I liked it!	What part?
It was okay.	Tell me what's okay and what's not.
It was boring.	Tell me what places were the most boring.
I could identify with it.	Why? In what places?
I loved it.	Could you repeat that?

P

Title_____ Draft#_____ Writer_____

Date_____ Reader _____

What sticks?

I wonder…

One thing writer will do:

P

I Want More

Title_____ Draft#____ Writer_____

Date_____ Reader _____

I want more about…

I want less about…

Writer's plan:

Steps one and two are filled out by the reader. Step three is filled out by the writer after the conference.

The Do-it-yourself Teacher Conference

Your teacher is too busy to meet with you today but you really need a conference. What will you do? Easy, pretend you are meeting. Write a dialogue of what you will say to each other about your writing.

Title_____ Draft#_____ Writer_____

Date_____ Fictional teacher_____

Writer:

Ms./Mr._____:

Writer:

Ms./Mr._____:

One thing I will work on:

My Inside Critic

Your inside critic nods when it hears ideas that make sense. Before a conference write down what your inside critic tells you about the piece. Then write down what your inside critic thinks after the conference. How did your ideas change?

Title_____ Draft#_____ Writer_____

Date_____ Reader _____

Thoughts from my Inside Critic before:

Thoughts from my Inside Critic after:

How did my ideas about the writing change?

Teacher Conference Ticket

Title_____ Draft#_____ Writer_____

Date_____

1_____date_____

2_____date_____

3_____date_____

4_____date_____

How has the writing changed?

P

Writing Goals for this Week

Name:_____ Week starting_____

Monday:

_____

Tuesday:

_____

Wednesday:

_____

Thursday:

_____

Friday:

"Get black on white."   Guy de Maupassant

Graphing Interest in a Story

Title_____ Draft# _____ Writer_____

Date_____ Reader _____

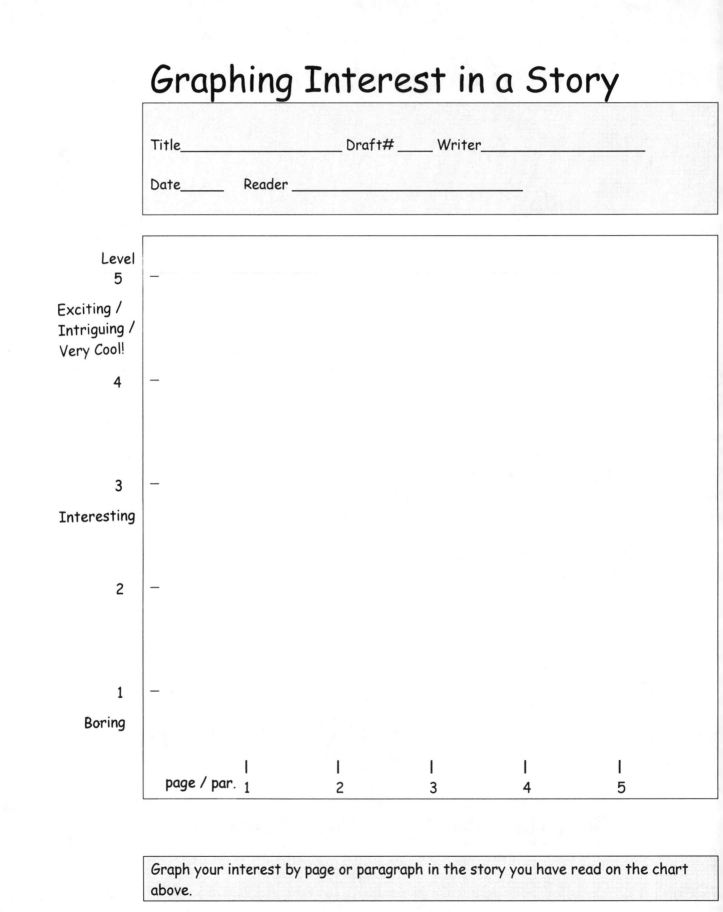

Level
5

Exciting /
Intriguing /
Very Cool!

4

3

Interesting

2

1

Boring

page / par.   1   2   3   4   5

Graph your interest by page or paragraph in the story you have read on the chart above.

Build Your Own EKG

Here's a way to get a unique look at your writing. Graph a story you have written on one quality of your choice.

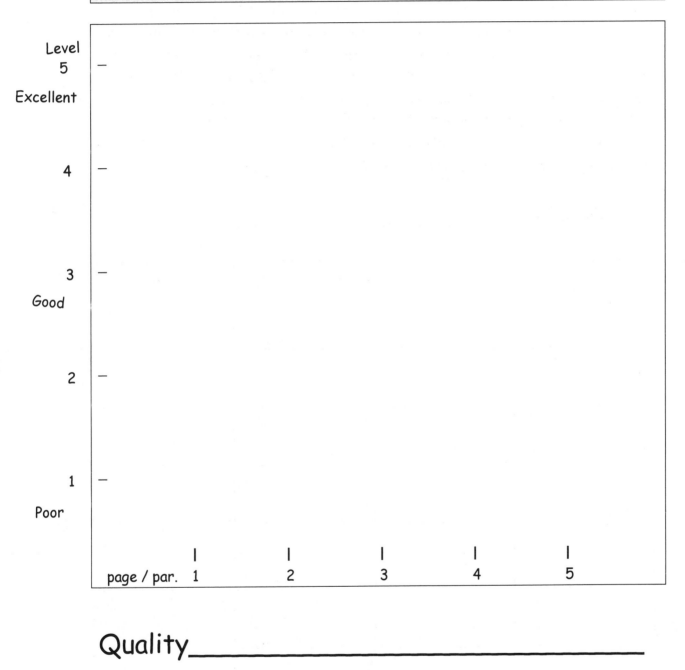

Quality_____

FUNNY RUBRICS

The word "assess" comes from the Latin verb assidire (to sit beside). A rubric is a describing tool that helps us to see qualities or criteria in anything you decide to assess, be it bubble-gum, potato chips, school lunches or even writing. In the space below, write the thing you want to assess. On the left define the 6 criteria. For example, if I picked potato chips for my thing, my criteria might be salty, crispy, unbreakable, cheap. In the 3 boxes across, define the three levels of each criteria. The third is highest. For example, 1 might be barely salted, 2 might be lightly salted, 3 would be very salty. Now you're ready to start assessing. Get the dip.

Assessing_____

Criteria	1	2	3

The Ancient Art of Assessment

As you can see from the cartoon beneath, assessment has been around much longer than we might care to admit. The following few pages contain my favorite assessment rubrics.

The Horserace of Criteria

Pick 4 criteria to slip into the starting gates beneath. Criteria can be anything you can describe about a piece of writing, details, grammar, focus, etc.... These are the horses. Now draw a crayon line across the page for each criteria. Which is in the lead? Which have fallen behind?   Look at the race of criteria and comment on the piece.

Which Horse is in the Lead?

Starting Gate	

Idea Development

5 The writing is clear, well-supported or developed, and enhanced by the kind of detail that keeps readers reading.

- The writer selectively chooses *just* the right information to make the paper understandable, enlightening and interesting—without bogging down in trivia.
- Details work together to expand the main topic or develop a story, giving the whole piece a strong sense of focus.
- The writer's knowledge, experience, insight or unique perspective lends the writing a satisfying ring of authenticity.
- The amount of detail is just right—not skimpy, not overwhelming.

3 The writer has made a solid beginning in defining a topic or mapping out a story line. It is easy to see where the paper is headed, though more expansion is needed to complete the picture.

- General, global information, provides the big picture—and makes the reader long for specifics.
- Well-focused information blends with repetitive points, trivia or meanderings.
- The writer draws on *some* personal experience—but too often settles for generalities or clichéd thinking.
- Unneeded information may eat up space that should have gone to important details. Where's the balance?

1 Sketchy, loosely focused information forces the reader to make inferences. Readers will likely notice *more than one of these problems*—

- The main topic is still unclear, out of focus—or not yet known, even to the writer.
- Missing, limited or unrelated details require the reader to fill in many blanks.
- Lists of "factlets" may be substituted for true development or expansion.
- Everything seems as important as everything else. What *is* the main point?

Adapted from *Creating Writers*, Spandel and Stiggins, New York: Longman, 1997, pp. 51-57. Used with permission.

Organization

5 The order, presentation, or internal structure of the piece is compelling and guides the reader purposefully through the text.

- The entire piece has a strong sense of direction and balance. Main ideas or key points stand out clearly.
- An inviting lead draws the reader in; a satisfying conclusion ties up loose ends.
- Details seem to fit right where they are placed, making the text easy to follow and understand.
- Transitions are strong but natural.
- Pacing feels natural and effective; the writer knows just when to linger over details and when to get moving.
- Organization flows so smoothly the reader does not need to think about it.

3 The organizational structure allows the reader to move through the text without undue confusion.

- Sequencing of main ideas seems reasonably appropriate; the reader rarely, if ever, feels lost.
- The introduction and conclusion are recognizable and functional.
- Transitions are usually present, but sometimes a little too obvious or too structured.
- Structure may be *so* dominant or predictable that it literally smothers the ideas and voice.
- Information is *mostly* presented in an orderly if not quite compelling fashion.

1 Ideas, details, or events seem loosely strung together. Readers will likely notice *more than one of these problems*—

- As yet, there is no clear sense of direction to carry the reader from point to point.
- No real lead sets up what follows.
- No real conclusion wraps things up.
- Missing or unclear transitions force the reader to make giant leaps.
- Sequencing feels more random than purposeful, often leaving the reader with a sense of being adrift.
- The writing does not move purposefully toward any main message or turning point.

Voice

5 The writer's energy and passion for the subject drive the writing, making the text lively, expressive, and engaging.

- The tone and flavor of the piece fit the topic, purpose, and audience well.
- The writing bears the clear imprint of this writer.
- The writer seems to know his/her audience, and shows a strong concern for their informational needs and interests.
- Narrative text is open and honest.
- Expository or persuasive text is provocative, lively, and designed to hold a reader's attention.

3 The writer seems sincere and willing to communicate with the reader on a functional, if distant, level.

- The tone and flavor of the piece could be altered slightly to better fit the topic, purpose, or audience.
- The writer has not quite found his or her voice but is experimenting—and the result is pleasant or intriguing, if not unique.
- Though clearly aware of an audience, the writer only occasionally speaks right to that audience.
- The writer often seems reluctant to "let go" and thus holds individuality, passion, and spontaneity in check. Nevertheless, voice pops out on occasion.
- The writer is "there"—then gone.

1 The writer seems definitely distanced from topic, audience, or both; as a result, the text may lack life, spirit, or energy. Readers are likely to notice *one or more of these problems*—

- The tone and flavor of the piece are inappropriate for the topic, purpose, and/or audience.
- The writer does not seem to reach out to the audience or to anticipate their interests and needs.
- Though it may communicate on a functional level, the writing takes no risks and does not engage, energize or move the reader.
- The writing does not project enough personal enthusiasm for the topic to make it come alive for the reader.

Word Choice

5 Precise, vivid, natural language paints a strong, clear, and complete picture in the reader's mind.

- The writer's message is remarkably clear and easy to interpret.
- Phrasing is original—even memorable—yet the language is never overdone.
- Lively verbs lend the writing power.
- Striking words or phrases linger in the writer's memory, often prompting connections, memories, reflective thoughts, or insights.

3 The language communicates in a routine, workable manner; it gets the job done.

- Most words are correct and adequate, even if not striking.
- A memorable phrase here or there strikes a spark, leaving the reader hungry for more.
- Familiar words and phrases give the text an "old couch" kid of feel.
- Attempts at colorful language are full of promise, even when they lack restraint or control. Jargon may be mildly annoying, but it does not impede readability.
- General meaning is clear, but the brush is too broad to convey subtleties.

1 The writer struggles with a limited vocabulary—or uses language that simply does not speak to the intended audience. Readers are likely to notice *more than one* of these problems—

- Vague words and phrases (She was *nice* . . . *It was wonderful* . . . The new budget *had impact*) convey only the most general sorts of messages.
- Clichés or redundant phrases encourage the reader to skim, not linger.
- Words are used incorrectly ("The bus *impelled* into the hotel").
- Inflated or jargonistic language makes the text ponderous and hard to read.
- The reader has trouble grasping the writer's intended message.

Adapted from *Creating Writers*, Spandel and Stiggins, New York: Longman, 1997, pp. 51-57. Used with permission.

Sentence Fluency

5 An easy flow and rhythm combined with sentence sense make this text a delight to read aloud.

- Sentences are well crafted, with a strong and varied structure that invites expressive oral reading.
- Purposeful sentence beginnings show how each sentence relates to and builds on the one before.
- The writing has cadence, as if the writer hears the beat in his or her head.
- Sentences vary in both structure and length, making the reading pleasant and natural, never monotonous.
- Fragments, if used, add style.

3 The text hums along with a steady beat.

- Sentences are mostly grammatical and fairly easy to read aloud, given a little rehearsal.
- Graceful, natural phrasing intermingles with more mechanical structure.
- Some variation in length and structure enhances fluency.
- Some purposeful sentence beginnings aid the reader's interpretation of the text.
- Fragments may be present; some are stylistically effective.

1 A fair interpretive oral reading of this text takes practice. The reader is likely to notice *more than one* of these problems—

- Irregular or unusual word patterns make it hard to tell where sentences begin and end.
- Ideas are hooked together by numerous connectives (*and . . . but . . . so then*) to create one gangly, endless "sentence."
- Short, choppy sentences bump the reader through the text.
- Repetitive sentence patterns put the reader to sleep.
- Transitions are either missing or so overdone they become distracting.
- The reader must often pause and reread for meaning.
- Fragments, if used, seem accidental; they do not work.

Conventions

5 The writer shows excellent control over a wide range of standard writing conventions and uses them with accuracy and (when appropriate) creativity and style to enhance meaning.

- Errors are so few and so minor that a reader can easily overlook them unless searching for them specifically.
- The text appears clean, edited, and polished.
- Older writers (grade 6 and up) create text of sufficient length and complexity to demonstrate control of conventions appropriate for their age and experience.
- The text is easy to mentally process; there is nothing to distract or confuse a reader.
- Only light touch-ups would be required to polish the text for publication.

3 The writer shows reasonable control over the most widely used writing conventions and applies them with fair consistency to create text that is adequately readable.

- There are enough errors to distract an attentive reader somewhat; however, errors do not seriously impair readability or obscure meaning.
- It is easy enough for an experienced reader to get through the text, but the writing clearly needs polishing.
- The paper reads much like a second rough draft—readable, but lacking close attention to conventions.
- Moderate editing would be required to get the text ready for publication.

1 The writer demonstrates limited control even over widely used writing conventions. The reader is likely to notice *more than one* of the following problems—

- Errors are sufficiently frequent and/or serious enough to be distracting; it is hard for the reader to focus on ideas, organization, or voice.
- The reader may need to read once to decode, then again to interpret and respond to the text.
- The paper reads like a first rough draft, scribbled hastily without thought for conventions.
- Extensive editing would be required to prepare the text for publication.

P

Kid Friendly Rubric

Teachers at Atkinson Elementary School in Louisville, KY wanted to put the States rubric into language their students would embrace. The result is one of my all time favorite rubrics.

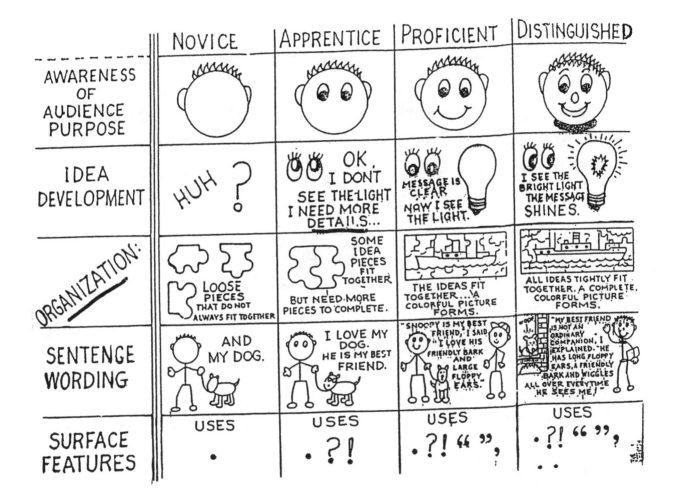

Snapshot Conference

In a snapshot conference, the reader looks for a few places in a draft where she wants more physical detail. Such places are marked with this symbol: The writer can decide which places make sense and write a snapshot to insert into those places. A snapshot can be just an extra phrase or sentence or even a whole paragraph or two. Length is not important. What's important is what the writer has to say and how to say it better. Here are a few ideas that can help. For more help see chapters 2 and 3.

- Show a character's movements and gestures.
- Paint a setting with a description of a place.
- Listen to sounds and speech.
- Zoom in close with physical detail of a person or place.
- Try to use more than one of the five senses.
- Paint a feeling in a setting without saying what the feeling is.

The Snapshot Conference

1. Begin by looking for places to add snapshots.
2. On a separate piece of paper, the writer writes a snapshot to add.
3. Read over the piece with the snapshot, then read it without it. Ask the reader, "Is it better?"
4. Repeat these steps. Remember, writing is an art like photography, and all art works by trial and error.

Thoughtshot Conference

In a thoughtshot conference the reader might look for places to add thoughts, reflections, flashbacks, flash-forwards, and internal debates into a piece of writing. Look for moments when the story seems too rooted in the physical, moments when your character would benefit by some thinking. For example:

- An important decision is coming up and your character needs to weigh the options.
- A character is lying and thinks of the consequences
- A song triggers a memory.
- A character says something he or she doesn't mean and thinks about it.
- A matter of conscience weighs heavy.
- Something must be figured out.

The Thoughtshot Conference

1. Read draft aloud.
2. Look for some places to add thoughtshots
3. Writer writes a thoughtshot or two on a blank piece of paper and inserts them into the piece.
4. Read the piece with and without the additions. Do they help?

Time Conferences

In a time conference the reader and the writer look for places to manipulate time within a piece of writing. We can slow down time by exploding moments or adding scenes. We can shrink time by cutting dialogue or skimming over events instead of writing in great detail about them (see chapter 4). Here are a few things to look for when reading for a sense of time.

- Does the piece move in real time? If so, does it start late enough in the day or can we shrink the morning and get to the good part sooner?
- Is there too much dialogue? Does the dialogue reveal character or could it be replaced with a sentence like "They talked for a while" and not leave a hole?
- Is there a big moment that just slipped by real fast, a line like "Then he robbed the bank and went home?"
- Are there more important moments in the story? If so, is there more time given to the more important moments?

The Time Conference

1) Read the story aloud. Pay attention to the exciting parts and also to the boring parts.
2) Mark the good parts and look for ways to expand them with more details, snapshots, thoughtshots, or dialogue.
3) Reader picks at least one slow part that the writer could cut or shrink.
4) Writer takes best suggestions and rewrites. Is it better?

Curious Question Conference

In a curious question conference the writer reads his piece as the reader listens and writes curious questions on a piece of paper. Curious questions can't be answered yes or no and they grow out of the reader's interest in the story. They don't try to fix the story. When writing curious questions you may want to consider the following.

- What do I want to know more about?
- What do I wonder about?
- What gets left unsaid?
- What do I want to know about the character?
- What confuses me?
- Where was I glued to my seat and where was I bored?
- Who did I want to get to know better in the piece?
- Which opinions needed more fact to back them up?
- Which ideas puzzled me?

The Curious Question Conference

1) Writer reads the piece aloud while partners listen and scribble questions during or after.
2) Writer collects the questions, then goes back to the paper to the places where the questions lead.
3) Writer tries answering the most interesting questions and adding the answers in the form or snapshots, thoughtshots, dialogue, etc. in the text.
4) Writer reads the piece with and without the rewrites. Does it get better?

Editing Conference

Come to an editing conference ready to look for one or two particular editing points. These points can be defined by the writer or the teacher. For example: If I've been working on starting sentences with capitals, or writing strong paragraphs, I might ask the reader to look in those two areas and search for errors or circle some places where I do it well. Here are some grammatical places to focus on.

Capitals: Do all sentences start with capitals?
Are names capitalized?

Sentences: Are all the sentences complete?
Do the sentence rhythms vary?

Paragraph: Is the piece written in paragraphs?
Does a new paragraph start with a new speaker?

Voice: Is the voice consistent?
Does it sound like the author?

Comma: Are commas used after the salutation of a letter, in a series list, and to divide a subordinate clause from an independent clause?

My Grammatical Report Card

Here's a way to keep track of what you know about grammar and what you need to work on. Fill out the grammatical report card below. Attach a piece of your writing to the card. Circle and number places that show what you know and what you are working on.

1) What I know:

2) What I am working on:

The Sentence Wringer

Gretchen Bernabei, an amazing middle school teacher from Texas has developed a wonderful way to teach her students an inner understanding of what sentences are . It's called the sentence wringer and if you teach it to your students, they will learn a language of how to work with each other to revise sentences. To ask Gretchen questions or to invite her to your school contact her directly by e-mail--bernabei@aol.com

So you think you've written a sentence.
PROVE IT!

1) Begin by giving your statement the Tim test or the Sarah test. Turn to anybody in the class, look them right in the eye and go, PSSSST then read the sentence. If they reply, "Huh?" it's probably not a statement. If yes proceed to part 2.

2) The verb hunt. Chances are there is there a verb in the statement, if it is a statement. Check for verbs by conjugating. For example, let's say my trial statement was, The sky falling. I can test words for verbs with this model

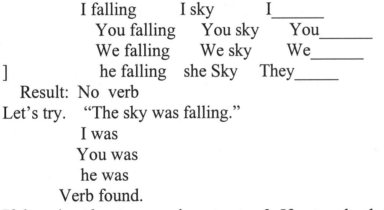

          I falling   I sky   I_____
             You falling   You sky   You_____
             We falling   We sky   We_____
]   he falling   she Sky   They_____

   Result: No verb
Let's try.   "The sky was falling."
        I was
        You was
         he was
       Verb found.

If there is at least one verb go to step 3. If not go back to stage one and write a sentence.

3) How many verbs? How many statements? If there are 2 or more statements they can be joined by a conjunction like and/ or/ but/ etc. a semi-colon or a dash. Never, Never, Never, are statements joined with a comma. Never, never, never.

These 3 simple steps will help you to find sentences and overhaul paragraphs.

Name_____date_____

The Paragraph Overhaul

Name_____date_____

1) Copy the original paragraph to overhaul.

_____
_____
_____
_____
_____
_____

2) The sentences (before)

1_____
2_____
3_____
4_____
5_____
6_____
7_____

3) The sentences (after)

1_____
2_____
3_____
4_____
5_____
6_____
7_____

4) Revised: Copy your fixed sentences into a new paragraph

_____
_____
_____
_____
_____
_____

Let's Talk Sentences

This scripted dialogue portrays Gretchen Bernabei's middle school students discussing their sentences in a piece of writing using the sentence wringer as their guide.

A: Read the first sentence.
B: I woke up one morning, I grabbed a slice of bread.
A: Is it a sentence? Statement?
B: Yeah.
A: Prove that.
B: I woke up one morning. (pause)
A: You didn't look in my eyes.
B: Jason!
A: I grabbed a slice of bread.   Did that make a statement?
B: Yep.
A: Ok, what's next?
B: Verb.
A: Does it have a verb.
B: Woke.
A: Prove it!
B: I woke, you woke, they woke.
A: That'll work.
B: What else?
A: How many statements?
B: Two.
A: Prove it.
B: I woke up one morning. I grabbed a slice of bread.
A: How are they joined.?
B: With a comma.
A: Is that enough.
B: Never, never, never.
A: So it's a run-on sentence?
B: Yeah.
A: So what are you gonna do about it?
B: I guess put an 'and.'
A: Very good.
B: Jason, don't be a nerd.
A: Read the next sentence.

© 1999 Discover Writing Press-- 1-800-613-8055--www.discoverwriting.com

Verbs and Nouns Rule

If verbs are the engines of sentences, nouns are the body. All other words are just passengers. Strong writing has strong specific verbs and nouns. Weak writing is often cluttered with blurry adjectives and adverbs. Try rewriting some of the sentences beneath to build stronger verbs and nouns. You can add extra words and ideas from your own imagination. Look at your own writing and search for places where a stronger verb or noun will help.

Example:

Before: The scared boy walked slowly into the old falling down house.

After: The boy crept one step at a time up the rotting stairs onto the porch of the mansion.

1) Jane was very happy to see her favorite cousin Jimmy when he showed up in her living room that day.

2) Sally walked quickly down the stairs on Christmas morning to find a gigantic stuffed bear sitting under the tree.

3) War is a terrible thing, Brad thought as a chill ran up his spine and he went onto the battlefield.

4) Abraham Lincoln became so religious near the end of the Civil War that he was often seen reading a Bible whenever he had a spare moment.

5) I just killed a President, John Wilkes Book thought as he hopped onto the stage of Ford's Theatre holding his hurt leg.

The Editing Alphabet

The standard copyediting symbols will help you to change your work so that even editors in New York City will know what your correction marks mean. Learn them and use them.

Symbol	What it means	Example
∧	Insert/add something	I need you. really
ℒ	Delete something	I ~~really~~ need you.
/	Add space here	I really need you
⌣	No space here/close gap	I really need you
¶	New Paragraph	¶ "Why?" I asked.) "Because...
⌒	No paragraph	I really need to know. Will you tell me?
∼	Reverse order	Will you tell me. I really need to know.
≡	Make this a Capital letter	Dear bob,
/	Make this a small letter	What Are you doing?
⊙	Insert a period	They went to the park She
⌄⌄	Insert quotation marks	Hello, she said
⌄	Insert apostrophe	Sharons clothes were on...

Reviser's Checklist

✔

- Do I like the lead or can I find or write a better one?

- Where can I use the  ?

- Where can I insert 📷☁ ?

- Is there a moment to ✦ ?

- Where can I build a scene?

- Where can I shrink 🕐 ?

Editing Checklist

- Circle words I am unsure of.
- Check "there," "their," and "they're."
- Check "know" and "no."
- Replace "a lot" with "much" or "many."
- Check paragraphing. Break long ones or meld short ones.
- Use apostrophes to show possession.
- Use capitals at the beginnings of sentences.
- Use a colon to begin a list.
- Put a comma after the salutation of a letter.
- Start a new paragraph when I have a new speaker.
- Keep the voice consistent (1st, 2nd, or 3rd person).
- Check verb tenses.
- Softly read each word out loud
- Watch for typos.

10 Ways to Re-enter a Draft

- Cross out "THE END" and write some unanswered questions. Turn one into a new lead.
- Insert a snapshot.
- Insert dialogue or replace boring dialogue with snapshots.
- Break story into chapters.
- Chunk story into illustratable sections.
- Write the story as a poem. Write the poem as a story.
- Find a better lead.
- Cut anything.
- Read the paper aloud and listen to your voice. Where do you speed up? Where do you slow down? Mark places you'd like to change.
- Write a new title.
- Add a scene.

Things I Don't Have to do Today

1) I don't need to read every draft of a student piece.
2) I don't need to correct every grammatical error\ my students make.
2) I don't need to pick topics for my students to write about.
3) I DON'T NEED TO BE THE EXPERT WHO FIXES MY STUDENTS' WORK!!!

Things to do today:

1) I will build a class of good critics, give them guidelines and model, model, model.
2) I will give students the editing pen and proofreading symbols. I will show them patterns of errors and places to focus. I will remember who needs more editing practice.
3) I will create a class culture of questioning. I will encourage and inspire students to dig potatoes daily. I will find tools to have THEM keep track of their work.
4) If I have 120 students, I will have 120 teacher's aides. I will train students to assess and reflect on their own work daily and take charge of their learning.

8

Talking Shop

In the 1980's International Paper Company interviewed writers , entertainers and business people and asked them for practical advice about writing. What follows are several of the most interesting pieces. Read them and try some of the suggestions and maybe you will begin revising your view of writing and reading.

How to write a personal letter

by Garrison Keillor

International Paper asked Garrison Keillor, author of the best-selling books, Happy to Be Here and Lake Wobegon Days, to tell you how to write a letter that will bring joy into the life of someone you love.

We shy persons need to write a letter now and then, or else we'll dry up and blow away. It's true. And I speak as one who loves to reach for the phone, dial the number, and talk. I say, "Big Bopper here — what's shakin', babes?" The telephone is to shyness what Hawaii is to February, it's a way out of the woods, *and yet:* a letter is better.

Such a sweet gift

Such a sweet gift — a piece of handmade writing, in an envelope that is not a bill, sitting in our friend's path when she trudges home from a long day spent among wahoos and savages, a day our words will help repair. They don't need to be immortal, just sincere. She can read them twice and again tomorrow: *You're someone I care about, Corinne, and think of often*

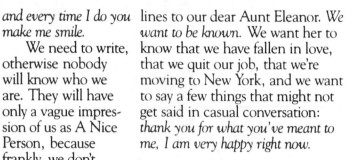

and every time I do you make me smile.

We need to write, otherwise nobody will know who we are. They will have only a vague impression of us as A Nice Person, because frankly, we don't shine at conversation, we lack the confidence to thrust our faces forward and say, "Hi, I'm Heather Hooten, let me tell you about my week." Mostly we say "Uh-huh" and "Oh really." People smile and look over our shoulder, looking for someone else to talk to.

So a shy person sits down and writes a letter. To be known by another person — to meet and talk freely on the page — to be close despite distance. To escape from anonymity and be our own sweet selves and express the music of our souls.

Same thing that moves a giant rock star to sing his heart out in front of 123,000 people moves us to take ballpoint in hand and write a few

"If you like to receive mail as much as I do, here's one infallible rule: To get a letter, you've got to send a letter."

lines to our dear Aunt Eleanor. *We want to be known.* We want her to know that we have fallen in love, that we quit our job, that we're moving to New York, and we want to say a few things that might not get said in casual conversation: *thank you for what you've meant to me, I am very happy right now.*

Skip the guilt

The first step in writing letters is to get over the guilt of *not* writing. You don't "owe" anybody a letter. Letters are a gift. The burning shame you feel when you see unanswered mail makes it harder to pick up a pen and makes for a cheerless letter when you finally do. *I feel bad about not writing, but I've been so busy,* etc. Skip this. Few letters are obligatory, and they are *Thanks for the wonderful gift and I am terribly sorry to hear about George's death* and *Yes, you're welcome to stay with us next month,* and not many more than that. Write those promptly if you want to keep your friends. Don't worry about the others, except love letters, of course. When your true love writes *Dear Light of My Life, Joy of My Heart, O Lovely Pulsating Core of My Sensate Life,* some response is called for. Some of the best letters are tossed off in a burst of inspiration, so keep your writing stuff in one place where you can sit down for a few minutes and *Dear Roy,*

I am in the middle of an essay for International Paper but thought I'd drop you a line. Hi to your sweetie too dash off a note to a pal. Envelopes, stamps, address book, everything in a drawer so you can write fast when the pen is hot.

A blank white 8″ x 11″ sheet can look as big as Montana if the pen's not so hot — try a smaller page and write boldly. Or use a note card with a piece of fine art on the front; if your letter ain't good, at least they get the Matisse. Get a pen that makes a sensuous line, get a comfortable typewriter, a friendly word processor — whichever feels

ment: *I'm sitting at the kitchen table on a rainy Saturday morning. Everyone is gone and the house is quiet.* Let your simple description of the present moment lead to something else, let the letter drift gently along.

Take it easy

The toughest letter to crank out is one that is meant to impress, as we all know from writing job applications; if it's hard work to slip off a letter to a friend, maybe you're trying too hard to be terrific. A letter is only a report to someone who already likes you for reasons other than your brilliance. Take it easy.

write to, a *compadre*, a soul sibling, then it's like driving a car down a country road, you just get behind the keyboard and press on the gas.

Don't tear up the page and start over when you write a bad line — try to write your way out of it. Make mistakes and plunge on. Let the letter cook along and let yourself be bold. Outrage, confusion, love — whatever is in your mind, let it find a way to the page. Writing is a means of discovery, always, and when you come to the end and write *Yours ever* or *Hugs and Kisses*, you'll know something you didn't when you wrote *Dear Pal*.

An object of art

Probably your friend will put your letter away, and it'll be read again a few years from now — and it will improve with age.

"Outrage, confusion, love — whatever is in your mind, let it find a way to the page."

easy to the hand.

Sit for a few minutes with the blank sheet in front of you, and meditate on the person you will write to, let your friend come to mind until you can almost see her or him in the room with you. Remember the last time you saw each other and how your friend looked and what you said and what perhaps was unsaid between you, and when your friend becomes real to you, start to write.

Tell us what you're doing

Write the salutation — *Dear* You — and take a deep breath and plunge in. A simple declarative sentence will do, followed by another and another and another. Tell us what you're doing and tell it like you were talking to us. Don't think about grammar, don't think about lit'ry style, don't try to write dramatically, just give us your news. Where did you go, who did you see, what did they say, what do you think?

If you don't know where to begin, start with the present mo-

Don't worry about form. It's not a term paper. When you come to the end of one episode, just start a new paragraph. You can go from a few lines about the sad state of rock 'n roll to the fight with your mother to your fond memories of Mexico to your cat's urinary tract infection to a few thoughts on personal indebtedness to the kitchen sink and what's in it. The more you write, the easier it gets, and when you have a True True Friend to

And forty years from now, your friend's grandkids will dig it out of the attic and read it, a sweet and precious relic of the ancient Eighties that gives them a sudden clear glimpse of you and her and the world we old-timers knew. You will then have created an object of art. Your simple lines about where you went, who you saw, what they said, will speak to those children and they will feel in their hearts the humanity of our times.

You can't pick up a phone and call the future and tell them about our times. You have to pick up a piece of paper.

Garrison Keillor

Don't you feel like writing a letter just about now? Decide who you want to write to. It may be an old friend, a parent, a grandparent, a famous person, a dead person. Like Keillor says, forget the excuses about why you haven't written before and just dive in. Allow your words to flow from your heart. The only thing better than writing a great letter is getting one in the mail!

How to read a newspaper.

by Walter Cronkite

International Paper asked Walter Cronkite, for years television's foremost news anchor and advocate of the need for a free people to keep fully informed, to tell you how your newspaper can help you cope better with your world.

If you're like most Americans, you use TV to keep up with the news. That's how 72% of us get 100% of our news.

The problem is that unless something really special happens, we in TV news have to put severe time limitations on every story, even the most complicated and important ones.

Get more than headlines.

So what we bring you is primarily a front-page headline service. To get all you need to know, you have to flesh out those headlines with a *complete account* of the news from a well-edited and thorough newspaper.

Newspeople have a responsibility. And so do *you*. *Ours* is to report the news fairly, accurately, completely. *Yours* is to keep yourself informed every day. As Thoreau said: "It takes two to speak the truth – one to speak and one to hear."

Take a three-minute overview.

Here's how I tackle a paper. For starters, I take a three-minute overview of the news. First, I scan the front-page headlines, look at the

pictures and read the captions. I do the same thing page by page, front to back. Only *then* do I go back for the whole feast.

The way the front page is "made up" tells you plenty. For one thing, headline type size will tell you how the paper's editor ranks the stories in relative importance. A major crop failure in Russia should get larger type than an overturned truckload of wheat on the interstate, for example.

Which is the main story?

You'll always find the main or lead story in the farthest upper right-hand column. Why? Tradition. Newspapers used to appear on newsstands folded and displayed with their top right-hand quarter showing. They made up the front page with the lead story there to entice readers.

You'll always find the second most important story at the top far left, unless it's related to the lead

story. Do you have to read *all* the stories in the paper? Gosh, no. But you should *check* them all. Maybe the one that appears at first to be the least appealing will be the one that will most affect your life.

News is information, period.

A good newspaper provides four basic ingredients to help you wrap your mind around the news: *information, background, analysis and interpretation*.

Rule #1 of American journalism is: "*News columns are reserved only for news.*"

What *is* news? It is *information* only. You can tell a good newspaper story. It just reports the news. It doesn't try to slant it. And it gives you *both* sides of the story.

Look out for a lot of adjectives and adverbs. They don't belong in an objective news story. They tend to color and slant it so you may come to a wrong conclusion.

Do look for bylines, datelines and the news service sources of articles. These will also help you judge a story's importance and its facts.

As you read a story you can weigh its truthfulness by asking, "Who said so?" Look out for "facts" that come from unnamed sources, such as "a highly placed government official." This could tip you off that the story is not quite true, or that someone – usually in Washington – is sending up a "trial balloon" to see if the idea gets a good reception.

Another tip: Check for "Corrections" items. A good newspaper will straighten out false or wrong information as soon as it discovers its error.

An upside-down pyramid.

Reporters write news stories in a special way called the "inverted pyramid" style. That means they start with the end, the *climax* of the story, with the most important facts first, then build in more details in order of importance. This is unlike telling stories, where you usually start at the beginning and save the climax for last. Knowing about the newspaper's "inverted pyramid" style will help you sift the facts.

A well-reported story will tell you "who," "what," "when," "where" and "how." The best newspapers will go on to tell you "why." "Why" is

often missing. And that may be the key ingredient.

Many important stories are flanked by "sidebars." These are supporting stories that offer not news, but the "why" – *background* and *analysis* – to help you understand and evaluate it.

Background offers helpful facts. *Analysis* frequently includes opinion. So it should be – and usually is – carefully labeled as such. It's generally bylined by an expert on the subject who explains the causes of the news and its possible consequences to you.

No good newspaper will mix *interpretation* with "hard" news, either. Interpretation goes beyond analysis and tells you not just what will probably happen, but what *ought* to happen. This should be clearly labeled, or at best, reserved for the editorial page or "op-ed" (opposite the editorial) page.

Form your own opinion first.

I form my own opinion before I turn to the editorial page for the pundits' views. I don't want them to tell me how to think until I've drawn my own conclusion. Once I have, I'm open to other reasoning. *Resist the temptation to let them do your thinking for you.*

Here's an idea I believe in and act on. When you read something that motivates you, do something about it. Learn more about it. Join a cause. Write a letter. Vote on issues by writing letters, particularly to your *representatives*.

Pick a TV story and follow it.

Now that I've told you about the basics of getting under the skin of a newspaper, let newspapers get under your skin.

Tonight, pick an important story that interests you on the TV news. Dig into the story – in your newspaper. Follow it, and *continue* to follow it closely in print. See if you don't find yourself with far more understanding of the event, even down to how it will affect you – and maybe even what should be done about it.

Keep up with the news the way my colleagues and I do – on TV *and* in the newspapers.

Learn to sift it for yourself, to heft it, to value it, to question it, to ask for it *all*. You'll be in better control of your life and your fortunes.

And that's the way it is.

Here's one way to follow Walter Cronkite's advice and revise the way you read the newspaper. Find or buy several different daily newspapers. Read the same news story in each paper and notice the differences in how the story is reported. Follow Cronkite's advice and ask questions like "Who said so" when opinions are reported as fact. Notice how some newspapers are better at showing more than one side of a story.

Try revising a slanted news article by including the other point of view.

How to spell

By John Irving

International Paper asked John Irving, author of "The World According to Garp," "The Hotel New Hampshire," and "Setting Free the Bears," among other novels— and once a hopelessly bad speller himself— to teach you how to improve your spelling.

Let's begin with the bad news.

If you're a bad speller, you probably think you always will be. There are exceptions to every spelling rule, and the rules themselves are easy to forget. George Bernard Shaw demonstrated how ridiculous some spelling rules are. By following the rules, he said, we could spell <u>fish</u> this way: <u>ghoti</u>. The "f" as it sounds in enou<u>gh</u>, the "i" as it sounds in w<u>o</u>men, and the "sh" as it sounds in fic<u>ti</u>on.

With such rules to follow, no one should feel stupid for being a bad speller. But there are ways to improve. Start by acknowledging the mess that English spelling is in—but have sympathy: English spelling changed with foreign influences. Chaucer wrote "gesse," but "guess," imported earlier by the Norman invaders, finally replaced it. Most early printers in England came from Holland; they brought "ghost" and "gherkin" with them.

If you'd like to intimidate yourself—and remain a bad speller forever—just try to remember the 13 different ways the sound "sh" can be written:

<u>sh</u>oe	suspi<u>ci</u>on
<u>s</u>ugar	nau<u>se</u>ous
o<u>ce</u>an	con<u>sci</u>ous
i<u>ss</u>ue	<u>ch</u>aperone
na<u>ti</u>on	man<u>si</u>on
<u>sch</u>ist	fu<u>chs</u>ia
<u>p</u>shaw	

Now the good news

The good news is that 90 percent of all writing consists of 1,000 basic words. There is, also, a method to most English spelling and a great number of how-to-spell books. Remarkably, all these books propose learning the same rules! Not surprisingly, most of these books are humorless.

Just keep this in mind: If you're familiar with the words you use, you'll probably spell them correctly—and you shouldn't be writing words you're unfamiliar with anyway. USE a word—out loud, and more than once—before you try writing it, and make sure (with a new word) that you know what it means before you use it. This means you'll have to look it up in a dictionary, where you'll not only learn what it means, but you'll see how it's spelled. Choose a dictionary you enjoy browsing in, and guard it as you would a diary. You wouldn't lend a diary, would you?

A tip on looking it up

Beside every word I look up in my dictionary, I make a mark.

"Love your dictionary."

Beside every word I look up more than once, I write a note to myself —about WHY I looked it up. I have looked up "strictly" 14 times since 1964. I prefer to spell it with a <u>k</u>— as in "strick<u>tl</u>y." I have looked up "ubiquitous" a dozen times. I can't remember what it means.

Another good way to use your dictionary: When you have to look up a word, for any reason, learn— and learn to *spell*—a *new* word at the same time. It can be any useful word on the same page as the word you looked up. Put the date beside this new word and see how quickly, or in what way, you forget it. Eventually, you'll learn it.

Almost as important as knowing what a word means (in order to spell it) is knowing how it's pronounced. It's gov<u>ern</u>ment, not goverment. It's Feb<u>ru</u>ary, not Febuary. And if you know that <u>anti</u>- means against, you should know how to spell <u>anti</u>dote and <u>anti</u>biotic and <u>anti</u>freeze. If you know that <u>ante</u>- means before, you shouldn't have trouble spelling <u>ante</u>chamber or <u>ante</u>cedent.

Some rules, exceptions, and two tricks

I don't have room to touch on <u>all</u> the rules here. It would take a book to do that. But I can share a few that help me most:

What about -<u>ary</u> or -<u>ery</u>? When a word has a primary accent on the first syllable and a secondary accent on the next-to-last syllable (sec're-tar'y), it usually ends in -<u>ary</u>. Only six important words like this end in -<u>ery</u>:

cemetery monastery
millinery confectionery
distillery stationery
(as in pap_e_r)

Here's another easy rule. Only four words end in -_efy_. Most people misspell them–with -_ify_, which is usually correct. Just memorize these, too, and use -_ify_ for all the rest.

stupefy putrefy
liquefy rarefy

As a former bad speller, I have learned a few valuable tricks. Any good how-to-spell book will teach you more than these two, but these two are my favorites. Of the 800,000 words in the English language, the most frequently misspelled is _alright_; just remember that _alright_ is _all_ _wrong_. You wouldn't write _alwrong_, would you? That's how you know you should write _all_ _right_.

The other trick is for the truly _worst_ spellers. I mean those of you who spell so badly that you can't get close enough to the right way to spell a word in order to even FIND it in the dictionary. The word you're looking for is there, of course, but you won't find it the way you're trying to spell it. What to do is look up a synonym–another word that means the same thing. Chances are good that you'll find the word you're looking for under the definition of the synonym.

Demon words and bugbears

Everyone has a few demon words–they never look right, even when they're spelled correctly. Three of my demons are _medieval_, _ecstasy_, and _rhythm_. I have learned to hate these words, but I have not learned to spell them; I have to look them up every time.

And everyone has a spelling rule that's a bugbear–it's either too difficult to learn or it's impossible to remember. My personal bugbear among the rules is the one governing whether you add -_able_ or -_ible_. I can teach it to you, but I can't

remember it myself.

You add -_able_ to a full word: adapt, adaptable; work, workable. You add -_able_ to words that end in _e_– just remember to drop the final _e_: love, lovable. But if the word ends in two _e_'s, like agree, you keep them both: agreeable.

You add -_ible_ if the base is not a full word that can stand on its own: credible, tangible, horrible, terrible. You add -_ible_ if the root word ends in -_ns_: responsible. You add -_ible_ if the root word ends in -miss: permissible. You add -_ible_ if the root word ends in a soft _c_

"This is one of the longest English words in common use. But don't let the length of a word frighten you. There's a rule for how to spell this one, and you can learn it."

(but remember to drop the final _e_!): force, forcible.

Got that? I don't have it, and I was introduced to that rule in prep school; with that rule, I still learn one word at a time.

Poor President Jackson

You must remember that it is permiss_ible_ for spelling to drive you crazy. Spelling had this effect on Andrew Jackson, who once blew his stack while trying to write a Presidential paper. "It's a damn poor mind that can think of only one way to spell a word!" the President cried.

When you have trouble, think of poor Andrew Jackson and know that you're not alone.

What's really important

And remember what's really important about good writing is not good spelling. If you spell badly but write well, you should hold your head up. As the poet T.S. Eliot recommended, "Write for as large and miscellaneous an audience as possible"–and don't be overly concerned if you can't spell "miscellaneous." Also remember that you can spell correctly and write well and still be misunderstood. Hold your head up about that, too.

As good old G.C. Lichtenberg said, "A book is a mirror: if an ass peers into it, you can't expect an apostle to look out"– whether you spell "apostle" correctly or not.

John Irving

With the advent of computer spell check John Irving's strategies for becoming a better speller may seem a little outdated. Not entirely so. Behind Irving's spelling strategies lies a fascination and a love for words (even difficult to spell words) which many writer's share.

Make a list of your own demon words—words you always spell wrong. Your computer can help. Now write the word correctly and write five mispellings beneath it. Put each spelling on a separate index card and see if your classmates can pick the right spelling. You may find your friends share spelling problems. Build a class list of tough words to spell. Instead of pushing a button to spell check, push the edit function and give it a try.

How to punctuate

By Russell Baker

International Paper asked Russell Baker, winner of the Pulitzer Prize for his book, Growing Up, and for his essays in The New York Times (the latest collection in book form is called The Rescue of Miss Yaskell and Other Pipe Dreams), to help you make better use of punctuation, one of the printed word's most valuable tools.

When you write, you make a sound in the reader's head. It can be a dull mumble—that's why so much government prose makes you sleepy—or it can be a joyful noise, a sly whisper, a throb of passion.

Listen to a voice trembling in a haunted room:

"And the silken, sad, uncertain rustling of each purple curtain thrilled me—filled me with fantastic terrors never felt before . . . "

That's Edgar Allan Poe, a master. Few of us can make paper speak as vividly as Poe could, but even beginners will write better once they start listening to the sound their writing makes.

One of the most important tools for making paper speak in your own voice is punctuation.

When speaking aloud, you punctuate constantly—with body language. Your listener hears commas, dashes, question marks, exclamation points, quotation marks as you shout, whisper, pause, wave your arms, roll your eyes, wrinkle your brow.

In writing, punctuation plays

"My tools of the trade should be your tools, too. Good use of punctuation can help you build a more solid, more readable sentence."

the role of body language. It helps readers hear you the way you want to be heard.

"Gee, Dad, have I got to learn all them rules?"

Don't let the rules scare you. For they aren't hard and fast. Think of them as guidelines.

Am I saying, "Go ahead and punctuate as you please"? Absolutely not. Use your own common sense, remembering that you can't expect readers to work to decipher what you're trying to say.

There are two basic systems of punctuation:

1. The loose or open system, which tries to capture the way body language punctuates talk.

2. The tight, closed structural system, which hews closely to the sentence's grammatical structure.

Most writers use a little of both. In any case, we use much less punctuation than they used 200 or even 50 years ago. (Glance into Edward Gibbon's "Decline and Fall of the Roman Empire," first published in 1776, for an example of the tight structural system at its most elegant.)

No matter which system you prefer, be warned: punctuation marks cannot save a sentence that is badly put together. If you have to struggle over commas, semicolons and dashes, you've probably built a sentence that's never going to fly, no matter how you tinker with it. Throw it away and build a new one to a simpler design. The better your sentence, the easier it is to punctuate.

Choosing the right tool

There are 30 main punctuation marks, but you'll need fewer than a dozen for most writing.

I can't show you in this small space how they all work, so I'll stick to the ten most important—and even then can only hit highlights. For more details, check your dictionary or a good grammar.

Comma [,]

This is the most widely used mark of all. It's also the toughest and most controversial. I've seen aging editors almost come to blows over the comma. If you can handle it without sweating, the others will be easy. Here's my policy:

1. Use a comma after a long introductory phrase or clause: *After stealing the crown jewels from the Tower of London, I went home for tea.*

2. If the introductory material is short, forget the comma: *After the theft I went home for tea.*

3. But use it if the sentence would be confusing without it, like this: *The day before I'd robbed the Bank of England.*

4. Use a comma to separate elements in a series: *I robbed the*

Denver Mint, *the Bank of England, the Tower of London and my piggy bank.*

Notice there is no comma before *and* in the series. This is common style nowadays, but some publishers use a comma there, too.

5. Use a comma to separate independent clauses that are joined by a conjunction like *and, but, for, or, nor, because* or *so*: *I shall return the crown jewels, for they are too heavy to wear.*

6. Use a comma to set off a mildly parenthetical word grouping that isn't essential to the sentence: *Girls, who have always interested me, usually differ from boys.*

Do not use commas if the word grouping *is* essential to the sentence's meaning: *Girls who interest me know how to tango.*

7. Use a comma in direct address: *Your majesty, please hand over the crown.*

8. And between proper names and titles: *Montague Sneed, Director of Scotland Yard, was assigned the case.*

9. And to separate elements of geographical address: *Director Sneed comes from Chicago, Illinois, and now lives in London, England.*

Generally speaking, use a comma where you'd pause briefly in speech. For a long pause or completion of thought, use a period.

If you confuse the comma with the period, you'll get a run-on sentence: *The Bank of England is located in London, I rushed right over to rob it.*

Semicolon [;]

A more sophisticated mark than the comma, the semicolon separates two main clauses, but it keeps those two thoughts more tightly linked than a period can: *I steal crown jewels; she steals hearts.*

Dash [—] and Parentheses [( )]

Warning! Use sparingly. The dash SHOUTS. Parentheses whisper. Shout too often, people stop listening; whisper too much, people become suspicious of you. The dash creates a dramatic pause

to prepare for an expression needing strong emphasis: *I'll marry you —if you'll rob Topkapi with me.*

Parentheses help you pause quietly to drop in some chatty information not vital to your story: *Despite Betty's daring spirit ("I love robbing your piggy bank," she often said), she was a terrible dancer.*

"Punctuation puts body language on the printed page. Show bewilderment with a question mark, a whisper with parentheses, emphasis with an exclamation point."

Quotation marks [" "]

These tell the reader you're reciting the exact words someone said or wrote: *Betty said, "I can't tango."* Or: *"I can't tango," Betty said.*

Notice the comma comes before the quote marks in the first example, but comes inside them in the second. Not logical? Never mind. Do it that way anyhow.

Colon [:]

A colon is a tip-off to get ready for what's next: a list, a long quotation or an explanation. This article is riddled with colons. Too many,

maybe, but the message is: "Stay on your toes; it's coming at you."

Apostrophe [']

The big headache is with possessive nouns. If the noun is singular, add *'s: I hated Betty's tango.*

If the noun is plural, simply add an apostrophe after the *s: Those are the girls' coats.*

The same applies for singular nouns ending in *s,* like Dickens: *This is Dickens's best book.*

And in plural: *This is the Dickenses' cottage.*

The possessive pronouns *hers* and *its* have no apostrophe.

If you write *it's,* you are saying *it is.*

Keep cool

You know about ending a sentence with a period (.) or a question mark (?). Do it. Sure, you can also end with an exclamation point (!), but must you? Usually it just makes you sound breathless and silly. Make your writing generate its own excitement. Filling the paper with !!!! won't make up for what your writing has failed to do.

Too many exclamation points make me think the writer is talking about the panic in his own head.

Don't sound panicky. End with a period. I am serious. A period. Understand?

Well . . . sometimes a question mark is okay.

Russell Baker

Here's a fun way to remember some of the simple grammar Russell Baker discusses. Make your own book of grammatical rules for each mark of punctuation in the article. If this doesn't sound like fun, you're right. That's why we are going to include a misuse of the punctuation as we make the book. For example, **Never use a comma to separate two independent clauses, it's just not the way it's done.**

See if you can make your mistakes as eloquent as your rules.

How to improve your vocabulary

By Tony Randall

International Paper asked Tony Randall—who is on The American Heritage Dictionary Usage Panel, and loves words almost as much as acting—to tell how he has acquired his enormous vocabulary.

Words can make us laugh, cry, go to war, fall in love.

Rudyard Kipling called words the most powerful drug of mankind. If they are, I'm a hopeless addict— and I hope to get you hooked, too!

Whether you're still in school or you head up a corporation, the better command you have of words, the better chance you have of saying exactly what you mean, of understanding what others mean—and of getting what you want in the world.

English is the richest language —with the largest vocabulary on earth. Over 1,000,000 words!

You can express shades of meaning that aren't even *possible* in other languages. (For example, you can differentiate between "sky" and "heaven." The French, Italians and Spanish cannot.)

Yet, the average adult has a vocabulary of only 30,000 to 60,000 words. Imagine what we're missing!

Here are five pointers that help me learn—and remember— whole *families* of words at a time.

They may not *look* easy—and won't be at first. But if you stick with them you'll find they *work!*

What's the first thing to do when you see a word you don't know?

1. Try to guess the meaning of the word from the way it's used

You can often get at least *part* of a word's meaning—just from how it's used in a sentence.

That's why it's so important to read as much as you can— different *kinds* of things: magazines, books, newspapers you don't normally read. The more you *expose* yourself to new words, the more words you'll pick up *just by seeing how they're used.*

For instance, say you run across the word "manacle":

"The manacles had been on John's wrists for 30 years. Only one person had a key— his wife."

You have a good *idea* of what "manacles" are—just from the context of the sentence.

But let's find out *exactly* what the word means and where it comes from. The only way to do this, and to build an extensive vocabulary *fast,* is to go to the dictionary. (How lucky, you *can*— Shakespeare *couldn't.* There *wasn't* an English dictionary in his day!)

So you go to the dictionary. (NOTE: Don't let dictionary abbreviations put you off. The front tells you what they mean, and even has a guide to pronunciation.)

2. Look it up

Here's the definition for "manacle" in *The American Heritage Dictionary of the English Language.*

man-a-cle (mân'ə-kəl) *n.* Usually plural. **1.** A device for confining the hands, usually consisting of two metal rings that are fastened about the wrists and joined by a metal chain; a handcuff. **2.** Anything that confines or restrains.—*tr. v.* **manacled, -cling, -cles. 1.** To restrain with manacles. **2.** To confine or restrain as if with manacles; shackle; fetter. [Middle English *manicle,* from Old French, from Latin *manicula,* little hand, handle, diminutive of *manus,* hand. See **man-²** in Appendix.*]

The first definition fits here: A device for confining the hands, usually consisting of two metal rings that are fastened about the wrists and joined by a metal chain; a handcuff.

Well, that's what you *thought* it meant. But what's the idea *behind* the word? What are its *roots*? To really understand a word, you need to know.

Here's where the detective work—and the *fun*—begins.

3. Dig the meaning out by the roots

The root is the basic part of the word—its heritage, its origin. (Most of our roots come from

"Your main clue to remembering a word is its root—its origin."

204

"'Emancipate' has a Latin root. Learn it and you'll know other words at a glance."

Latin and Greek words at least 2,000 years old—which come from even earlier Indo-European tongues!)

Learning the roots: 1) Helps us *remember* words. 2) Gives us a deeper understanding of the words we *already* know. And 3) allows us to pick up whole families of *new* words at a time. That's why learning the root is the *most important part of going to the dictionary.*

Notice the root of "manacle" is *manus* (Latin) meaning "hand."

Well, that makes sense. Now, other words with this root, <u>man</u>, start to make sense, too.

Take <u>man</u>ual—something done "by hand" (<u>man</u>ual labor) or a "handbook." And <u>man</u>age—to "handle" something (as a <u>man</u>ager). When you e<u>man</u>cipate someone, you're taking him "from the hands of" someone else.

When you <u>man</u>ufacture something, you "make it by hand" (in its original meaning).

And when you finish your first novel, your publisher will see your—originally "handwritten"—<u>man</u>uscript.

Imagine! A whole new world of words opens up—just from one simple root!

The root gives the *basic* clue to the meaning of a word. But there's another important clue that runs a close second—the *prefix.*

4. Get the powerful prefixes under your belt

A prefix is the part that's sometimes attached to the front of a word. Like—well, *prefix!* There aren't many—less than 100 major prefixes—and you'll learn them in no time at all just by becoming more aware of the meanings of words you already know.

Here are a few. (Some of the "How-to" vocabulary-building books will give you the others.)

PREFIX		MEANING	EXAMPLES	
(Lat.)	(Gk.)			(Literal sense)
com, con, co, col, cor	sym, syn, syl	with, very, together	conform sympathy	(form with) (feeling with)
in, im, il, ir	a, an	not, without	innocent amorphous	(not wicked) (without form)
contra, counter	anti, ant	against, opposite	contravene antidote	(come against) (give against)

Now, see how the *prefix* (along with the context) helps you get the meaning of the italicized words:

• "If you're going to be my witness, your story must <u>corroborate</u> my story." (The literal meaning of *corroborate* is "strength together.")

• "You told me one thing—now you tell me another. Don't <u>contradict</u> yourself." (The literal meaning of *contradict* is "say against.")

• "Oh, that snake's not poisonous. It's a completely <u>innocuous</u> little garden snake." (The literal meaning of *innocuous* is "not harmful.")

Now, you've got some new words. What are you going to do with them?

5. Put your new words to work at once

Use them several times the first day you learn them. Say them out loud! Write them in sentences.

Should you "use" them on *friends*? Careful—you don't want them to think you're a stuffed shirt. (It depends on the situation. You *know* when a word sounds natural—and when it sounds stuffy.)

How about your *enemies*? You have my blessing. Ask one of them if he's read that article on pneumonoultramicroscopicsilicovolcanoconiosis. (You really can find it in the dictionary.) Now, you're one up on him.

So what do you do to improve your vocabulary?

Remember: 1) Try to guess the meaning of the word from the way it's used. 2) Look it up. 3) Dig the meaning out by the roots. 4) Get the powerful prefixes under your belt. 5) Put your new words to work at once.

That's all there is to it—you're off on your treasure hunt.

Now, do you see why I love words so much?

Aristophanes said, "By words, the mind is excited and the spirit elated." It's as true today as it was

"The more words you know, the more you can use. What does 'corroborate' really mean? See the text."

when he said it in Athens—*2,400 years ago!*

I hope you're now like me—hooked on words forever.

Tony Randall

My favorite vocabulary game is called **Fictionary**. If you've never played it before, I'll tell you how. You begin by getting a thick dictionary. Each person gets a turn to find a word that nobody knows. Then he or she writes 3 fictional definitions of the word on a piece of paper. The other players vote on which is the correct definition. If you fool someone you get a point. If you fool two, you get two. It can be great fun and an even greater way to get familiar with the hidden treasures inside your dictionary.

How to write with style

By Kurt Vonnegut

International Paper asked Kurt Vonnegut, author of such novels as "Slaughterhouse-Five," "Jailbird" and "Cat's Cradle," to tell you how to put your style and personality into everything you write.

Newspaper reporters and technical writers are trained to reveal almost nothing about themselves in their writings. This makes them freaks in the world of writers, since almost all of the other ink-stained wretches in that world reveal a lot about themselves to readers. We call these revelations, accidental and intentional, elements of style.

These revelations tell us as readers what sort of person it is with whom we are spending time. Does the writer sound ignorant or informed, stupid or bright, crooked or honest, humorless or playful –? And on and on.

Why should you examine your writing style with the idea of improving it? Do so as a mark of respect for your readers, whatever you're writing. If you scribble your thoughts any which way, your readers will surely feel that you care nothing about them. They will mark you down as an egomaniac or a chowderhead – or, worse, they will stop reading you.

The most damning revelation you can make about yourself is that you do not know what is interesting and what is not. Don't you yourself like or dislike writers mainly for what they choose to show you or make you think about? Did you ever admire an empty-headed writer for his or her mastery of the language? No.

So your own winning style must begin with ideas in your head.

1. Find a subject you care about

Find a subject you care about and which you in your heart feel others should care about. It is this genuine caring, and not your games with language, which will be the most compelling and seductive element in your style.

I am not urging you to write a novel, by the way – although I would not be sorry if you wrote one, provided you genuinely cared about something. A petition to the mayor about a pothole in front of your house or a love letter to the girl next door will do.

2. Do not ramble, though

I won't ramble on about that.

3. Keep it simple

As for your use of language: Remember that two great masters of language, William Shakespeare and James Joyce, wrote sentences which were almost childlike when their subjects were most profound. "To be or not to be?" asks Shakespeare's Hamlet. The longest word is three letters long. Joyce, when he was frisky, could put together a sentence as intricate and as glittering as a necklace for Cleopatra, but my favorite sentence in his short story "Eveline" is this one: "She was tired." At that point in the story, no other words could break the heart of a reader as those three words do.

Simplicity of language is not only reputable, but perhaps even sacred. The *Bible* opens with a sentence well within the writing skills of a lively fourteen-year-old: "In the beginning God created the heaven and the earth."

4. Have the guts to cut

It may be that you, too, are capable of making necklaces for Cleopatra, so to speak. But your eloquence should be the servant of the ideas in your head. Your rule might be this: If a sentence, no matter how excellent, does not illuminate your subject in some new and useful way, scratch it out.

5. Sound like yourself

The writing style which is most natural for you is bound to echo the speech you heard when a child. English was the novelist Joseph Conrad's third language, and much that seems piquant in his use of English was no doubt colored by his first language, which was Polish. And lucky indeed is the writer who has grown up in Ireland, for the English spoken there is so amusing and musical. I myself grew up in Indianapolis, where common speech sounds like a band saw cutting galvanized tin,

"Keep it simple. Shakespeare did, with Hamlet's famous soliloquy."

206

"Be merciless on yourself. If a sentence does not illuminate your subject in some new and useful way, scratch it out."

and employs a vocabulary as unornamental as a monkey wrench.

In some of the more remote hollows of Appalachia, children still grow up hearing songs and locutions of Elizabethan times. Yes, and many Americans grow up hearing a language other than English, or an English dialect a majority of Americans cannot understand.

All these varieties of speech are beautiful, just as the varieties of butterflies are beautiful. No matter what your first language, you should treasure it all your life. If it happens not to be standard English, and if it shows itself when you write standard English, the result is usually delightful, like a very pretty girl with one eye that is green and one that is blue.

I myself find that I trust my own writing most, and others seem to trust it most, too, when I sound most like a person from Indianapolis, which is what I am. What alternatives do I have? The one most vehemently recommended by teachers has no doubt been pressed on you, as well: to write like cultivated Englishmen of a century or more ago.

6. Say what you mean to say

I used to be exasperated by such teachers, but am no more. I understand now that all those antique essays and stories with which I was to compare my own work were not magnificent for their datedness or foreignness, but for saying precisely what their authors meant them to say. My teachers wished me to write accurately, always selecting the most effective words, and relating the words to one another unambiguously, rigidly, like parts of a machine. The teachers did not want to turn me into an Englishman after all. They hoped that I would become understandable – and therefore understood. And there went my dream of doing with words what Pablo Picasso did with paint or what any number of jazz idols did with music. If I broke all the rules of punctuation, had words mean whatever I wanted them to mean, and strung them together higgledy-piggledy, I would simply not be understood. So you, too, had better avoid Picasso-style or jazz-style writing, if you have something worth saying and wish to be understood.

Readers want our pages to look very much like pages they have seen before. Why? This is because they themselves have a tough job to do, and they need all the help they can get from us.

7. Pity the readers

They have to identify thousands of little marks on paper, and make sense of them immediately. They have to *read*, an art so difficult that most people don't really master it even after having studied it all through grade school and high school – twelve long years.

"Pick a subject you care so deeply about that you'd speak on a soapbox about it."

So this discussion must finally acknowledge that our stylistic options as writers are neither numerous nor glamorous, since our readers are bound to be such imperfect artists. Our audience requires us to be sympathetic and patient teachers, ever willing to simplify and clarify – whereas we would rather soar high above the crowd, singing like nightingales.

That is the bad news. The good news is that we Americans are governed under a unique Constitution, which allows us to write whatever we please without fear of punishment. So the most meaningful aspect of our styles, which is what we choose to write about, is utterly unlimited.

8. For really detailed advice

For a discussion of literary style in a narrower sense, in a more technical sense, I commend to your attention *The Elements of Style*, by William Strunk, Jr., and E.B. White (Macmillan, 1979). E.B. White is, of course, one of the most admirable literary stylists this country has so far produced.

You should realize, too, that no one would care how well or badly Mr. White expressed himself, if he did not have perfectly enchanting things to say.

Ok. Here's a challenge. Find a piece of your writing that just doesn't sound like you. It can be that report on acid rain, that paper on Hamlet, that description of the mountains you were forced to write. Dig it out and read it over. Now take the Kurt challenge.

Spend ten minutes and start it over in your own voice. You may wish to begin with words like, "Do you really want to know what I think about acid rain?" Let your voice spill through.

How to make a speech

By George Plimpton

International Paper asked George Plimpton, who writes books about facing the sports pros (like "Paper Lion" and "Shadow Box"), and who's in demand to speak about it, to tell you how to face the fear of making a speech.

One of life's terrors for the uninitiated is to be asked to make a speech.

"Why me?" will probably be your first reaction. "I don't have anything to say." It should be reassuring (though it rarely is) that since you were asked, somebody must think you do. The fact is that each one of us has a store of material which should be of interest to others. There is no reason why it should not be adapted to a speech.

Why know how to speak?

Scary as it is, it's important for anyone to be able to speak in front of others, whether twenty around a conference table or a hall filled with a thousand faces.

Being able to speak can mean better grades in any class. It can mean talking the town council out of increasing your property taxes. It can mean talking top management into buying your plan.

How to pick a topic

You were probably asked to speak in the first place in the hope that you would be able to articulate a topic that you know something about. Still, it helps to find out about your audience first. Who are they? Why are they there? What are they

interested in? How much do they already know about your subject? One kind of talk would be appropriate for the Women's Club of Columbus, Ohio, and quite another for the guests at the Vince Lombardi dinner.

How to plan what to say

Here is where you must do your homework.

The more you sweat in advance, the less you'll have to sweat once you appear on stage. Research your topic thoroughly. Check the library for facts, quotes, books and timely magazine and newspaper articles on your subject. Get in touch with experts. Write to them, make phone calls, get interviews to help round out your material.

In short, gather—and learn—far more than you'll ever use. You can't imagine how much confidence that knowledge will inspire.

Now start organizing and writing. Most authorities suggest that a good speech breaks down into three basic parts—an introduction, the body of the speech, and the summation.

Introduction: An audience makes up its mind very quickly. Once the mood of an audience is set, it is difficult to change it, which is why introductions are important. If the speech is to be lighthearted in tone, the speaker can start off by telling a good-natured story about the subject or himself.

But be careful of jokes, especially the shaggy-dog

"What am I doing wrong? Taking refuge behind the lectern, looking scared to death, shuffling pages, and reading my speech. Relax. Come out in the open, gesture, talk to your audience!"

variety. For some reason, the joke that convulses guests in a living room tends to suffer as it emerges through the amplifying system into a public gathering place.

Main body: There are four main intents in the body of the well-made speech. These are 1) to entertain, which is probably the hardest; 2) to instruct, which is the easiest if the speaker has done the research and knows the subject; 3) to persuade, which one does at a sales presentation, a political rally, or a town meeting; and finally, 4) to inspire, which is what the speaker emphasizes at a sales meeting, in a sermon, or at a pep rally. (Hurry-Up Yost, the onetime Michigan football coach, gave such an inspiration-filled half-time talk that he got carried away and at the final exhortation led his team on the run through the wrong locker-room door into the swimming pool.)

Summation:

This is where you should "ask for the order." An ending should probably incorporate a sentence or two which sounds like an ending—a short summary of the main points of the speech, perhaps, or the repeat of a phrase that most embodies what the speaker has hoped to convey. It is valuable to think of the last sentence or two as something which might produce applause. Phrases which are perfectly appropriate to signal this are: "In closing..." or "I have one last thing to say..."

Once done—fully written, or the main

208

points set down on 3″ x 5″ index cards—the next problem is the actual presentation of the speech. Ideally, a speech should not be read. At least it should never appear or sound as if you are reading it. An audience is dismayed to see a speaker peering down at a thick sheaf of papers on the lectern, wetting his thumb to turn to the next page.

How to sound spontaneous

The best speakers are those who make their words sound spontaneous even if memorized. I've found it's best to learn a speech point by point, not word for word. Careful preparation and a great deal of practicing are required to make it come together smoothly and easily. Mark Twain once said, "It takes three weeks to prepare a good ad-lib speech."

Don't be fooled when you rehearse. It takes longer to deliver a speech than to read it. Most speakers peg along at about 100 words a minute.

Brevity is an asset

A sensible plan, if you have been asked to speak to an exact limit, is to talk your speech into a mirror and stop at your allotted time; then cut the speech accordingly. The more familiar you become with your speech, the faster you can deliver it.

As anyone who listens to speeches knows, brevity is an asset. Twenty minutes are ideal. An hour is the limit an audience can listen comfortably.

In mentioning brevity, it is worth mentioning that the shortest inaugural address was George Washington's—just 135 words. The longest was William Henry Harrison's in 1841. He delivered a two-hour 9,000-word speech into the teeth of a freezing northeast wind. He came down with a cold the

209

following day, and a month later he died of pneumonia.

Check your grammar

Consult a dictionary for proper meanings and pronunciations. Your audience won't know if you're a bad speller, but they will know if you use or pronounce a word improperly. In my first remarks on the dais, I used to thank people for their "fulsome introduction," until I discovered to my dismay that "fulsome" means *offensive* and *insincere*.

"Why should you make a speech? There are four big reasons (left to right): to inspire, to persuade, to entertain, to instruct. I'll tell you how to organize what you say."

On the podium

It helps one's nerves to pick out three or four people in the audience—preferably in different sectors so that the speaker is apparently giving his attention to the entire room—on whom to focus. Pick out people who seem to be having a good time.

How questions help

A question period at the end of a speech is a good notion. One would not ask questions following a tribute to the company treasurer on his re-

tirement, say, but a technical talk or an informative speech can be enlivened with a question.

The crowd

The larger the crowd, the easier it is to speak, because the response is multiplied and increased. Most people do not believe this. They peek out from behind the curtain and if the auditorium is filled to the rafters they begin to moan softly in the back of their throats.

What about stage fright?

Very few speakers escape the so-called "butterflies." There does not seem to be any cure for them, except to realize that they are beneficial rather than harmful, and never fatal. The tension usually means that the speaker, being keyed up, will do a better job. Edward R. Murrow called stage fright "the sweat of perfection." Mark Twain once comforted a fright-frozen friend about to speak: "Just remember they don't expect much." My own feeling is that with thought, preparation and faith in your ideas, *you* can go out there and expect a pleasant surprise.

And what a sensation it is—to hear applause. Invariably after it dies away, the speaker searches out the program chairman, "—just to let you know I'm available for next month's meeting."

Gey Plimpton

It's time to make a speech. Try revising a persuasive essay as a speech. Follow Plimpton's advice and get some note cards and outline the main points of your argument. Be sure to include specific examples or stories to breathe life into your ideas. Use the binoculars and don't be a wimp. State your opinions firmly. Pound your fist on the podium. Leave time at the end of your speech for a question and answer period.

How to write a business letter

Some thoughts from Malcolm Forbes
President and Editor-in-Chief of Forbes Magazine

International Paper asked Malcolm Forbes to share some things he's learned about writing a good business letter. One rule, "Be crystal clear."

A good business letter can get you a job interview.

Get you off the hook.

Or get you money.

It's totally asinine to blow your chances of getting *whatever* you want—with a business letter that turns people off instead of turning them on.

The best place to learn to write is in school. If you're still there, pick your teachers' brains.

If not, big deal. I learned to ride a motorcycle at 50 and fly balloons at 52. It's never too late to learn.

Over 10,000 business letters come across my desk every year. They seem to fall into three categories: stultifying if not stupid, mundane (most of them), and first rate (rare). Here's the approach I've found that separates the winners from the losers (most of it's just good common sense)—it starts *before* you write your letter:

Know what you want

If you don't, write it down—in one sentence. "I want to get an interview within the next two weeks." That simple. List the major points you want to get across—it'll keep you on course.

If you're *answering* a letter, check the points that need answering and keep the letter in front of you while you write. This way you won't forget anything—*that* would cause another round of letters.

And for goodness' sake, answer promptly if you're going to answer at all. Don't sit on a letter—*that* invites the person on the other end to sit on whatever you want from *him*.

Plunge right in

Call him by name—not "Dear Sir, Madam, or Ms." "Dear Mr. Chrisanthopoulos"—and be sure to spell it right. That'll get him (thus, you) off to a good start.

(Usually, you can get his name just by phoning his company—or from a business directory in your nearest library.)

Tell what your letter is about in the first paragraph. One or two sentences. Don't keep your reader guessing or he might file your letter away—even before he finishes it.

In the round file.

If you're answering a letter, refer to the date it was written. So the reader won't waste time hunting for it.

People who read business letters are as human as thee and me. Reading a letter shouldn't be a chore—*reward* the reader for the time he gives you.

Write so he'll enjoy it

Write the entire letter from his point of view—what's in it for *him*? Beat him to the draw—surprise him by answering the questions and objections he might have.

Be positive—he'll be more receptive to what you have to say.

Be nice. Contrary to the cliché, genuinely nice guys most often finish first or very near it. I admit it's not easy when you've got a gripe. To be agreeable while disagreeing—that's an art.

Be natural—write the way you talk. Imagine him sitting in front of you—what would you *say* to him?

Business jargon too often is cold, stiff, unnatural.

Suppose I came up to you and said, "I acknowledge receipt of your letter and I beg to thank you." You'd think, "Huh? You're putting me on."

The acid test—read your letter *out loud* when you're done. You

"Be natural. Imagine him sitting in front of you—what would you say to him?"

might get a shock—but you'll know for sure if it sounds natural.

Don't be cute or flippant. The reader won't take you seriously. This doesn't mean you've got to be dull. You prefer your letter to knock 'em dead rather than bore 'em to death.

Three points to remember:

Have a sense of humor. That's refreshing *anywhere*—a nice surprise

210

in a business letter.

Be specific. If I tell you there's a new fuel that could save gasoline, you might not believe me. But suppose I tell you this:

"Gasohol" – 10% alcohol, 90% gasoline – works as well as straight gasoline. Since you can make alcohol from grain or corn stalks, wood or wood waste, coal – even garbage, it's worth some real follow-through.

Now you've got something to sink your teeth into.

Lean heavier on nouns and verbs, lighter on adjectives. Use the active voice instead of the passive. Your writing will have more guts.

Which of these is stronger? Active voice: "I kicked out my money manager." Or, passive voice: "My money manager was kicked out by me." (By the way, neither is true. My son, Malcolm Jr., manages most Forbes money – he's a brilliant moneyman.)

"I learned to ride a motorcycle at 50 and fly balloons at 52. It's never too late to learn anything."

Give it the best you've got

When you don't want something enough to make *the* effort, making *an* effort is a waste.

Make your letter look appetizing – or you'll strike out before you even get to bat. Type it – on good-quality 8½" x 11" stationery. Keep it neat. And use paragraphing that makes it easier to read.

Keep your letter short – to one page, if possible. Keep your paragraphs short. After all, who's going to benefit if your letter is quick and easy to read?

You.

For emphasis, underline impor-

tant words. And sometimes indent sentences as well as paragraphs.

Like this. See how well it works? (But save it for something special.)

Make it perfect. No typos, no misspellings, no factual errors. If you're sloppy and let mistakes slip by, the person reading your letter will think you don't know better or don't care. Do you?

Be crystal clear. You won't get what you're after if your reader doesn't get the message.

Use good English. If you're still in school, take all the English and writing courses you can. The way you write and speak can really help – or *hurt*.

If you're not in school (even if you are), get the little 71-page gem by Strunk & White, *Elements of Style*. It's in paperback. It's fun to read and loaded with tips on good English and good writing.

Don't put on airs. Pretense invariably impresses only the pretender.

Don't exaggerate. Even once. Your reader will suspect everything else you write.

Distinguish opinions from facts. Your opinions may be the best in the world. But they're not gospel. You owe it to your reader to let him know which is which. He'll appreciate it and he'll admire you. The dumbest people I know are those who Know It All.

Be honest. It'll get you further in the long run. If you're not, you won't rest easy until you're

found out. (The latter, not speaking from experience.)

Edit ruthlessly. Somebody ~~has~~ said that words are ~~a lot~~ like inflated money – the more ~~of them that~~ you use, the less each one ~~of them~~ is worth. ~~Right on.~~ Go through your entire letter ~~just~~ as many times as it takes. ~~Search out and~~ **A**nnihilate all unnecessary words, ~~and~~ sentences – even ~~entire~~ *paragraphs*.

Sum it up and get out

The last paragraph should tell the reader exactly what you want *him* to do – or what *you're* going to do. Short and sweet. "May I have an appointment? Next Monday, the 16th, I'll call your secretary to see when it'll be most convenient for you."

Close with something simple like, "Sincerely." And for heaven's sake sign legibly. The biggest ego trip I know is a completely illegible signature.

Good luck.

I hope you get what you're after.

Sincerely,

Malcolm S. Forbes

Think of a job you would really like to have, but are perhaps totally unqualified to get. Now write a business letter applying to that job, using some of the good advice from our friend Malcolm Forbes. You could also try making all the mistakes Forbes talks about and write a truly awful letter, then go back and make it ring true.

211

How to read faster

By Bill Cosby

International Paper asked Bill Cosby—who earned his doctorate in education and has been involved in projects which help people learn to read faster—to share what he's learned about reading more in less time.

When I was a kid in Philadelphia, I must have read every comic book ever published. (There were fewer of them then than there are now.)

I zipped through all of them in a couple of days, then reread the good ones until the next issues arrived.

Yes indeed, when I was a kid, the reading game was a snap.

But as I got older, my eyeballs must have slowed down or something! I mean, comic books started to pile up faster than my brother Russell and I could read them!

It wasn't until much later, when I was getting my doctorate, I realized it wasn't my eyeballs that were to blame. Thank goodness. They're still moving as well as ever.

The problem is, there's too much to read these days, and too little time to read every word of it.

Now, mind you, I still read comic books. In addition to contracts, novels, and newspapers. Screenplays, tax returns and correspondence. Even textbooks about how people read. And which techniques help people read more in less time.

I'll let you in on a little secret. There are hundreds of techniques you could learn to help you read faster. But I know of 3 that are especially good.

And if I can learn them, so can you—and you can put them to use *immediately*.

They are commonsense, practical ways to get the meaning from printed words quickly and efficiently. So you'll have time to enjoy your comic books, have a good laugh with Mark Twain or a good cry with *War and Peace*. Ready?

Okay. The first two ways can help you get through tons of reading material—fast—*without reading every word*.

They'll give you the *overall* meaning of what you're reading. And let you cut out an awful lot of *unnecessary* reading.

1. Preview—if it's long and hard

Previewing is especially useful for getting a general idea of heavy reading like long magazine or newspaper articles, business reports, and nonfiction books.

It can give you as much as half the comprehension in as little as one tenth the time. For example, you should be able to preview eight or ten 100-page reports in an hour. After previewing, you'll be able to decide which reports (or which *parts* of which reports) are worth a closer look.

Here's how to preview: Read the entire first two paragraphs of whatever you've chosen. Next read only the *first sentence* of each successive paragraph.

Then read the entire last two paragraphs.

Previewing doesn't give you all the details. But it does keep you from spending time on things you don't really want—or need—to read.

Notice that previewing gives you a quick, overall view of *long, unfamiliar* material. For short, light reading, there's a better technique.

2. Skim—if it's short and simple

Skimming is a good way to get a general idea of light reading—like popular magazines or the sports and entertainment sections of the paper.

You should be able to skim a weekly popular magazine or the second section of your daily paper in less than *half* the time it takes you to read it now.

Skimming is also a great way to review material you've read before.

Here's how to skim: Think of your eyes as magnets. Force them to move fast. Sweep them across each and every line of type. Pick up *only a few key words in each line*.

Everybody skims differently.

You and I may not pick up exactly the same words when we skim the same piece, but we'll both get a pretty similar idea of what it's all about.

To show you how it works, I circled the words I picked out when I skimmed the following story. Try it. It shouldn't take you more than 10 seconds.

My brother Russell thinks monsters live in our bedroom closet at night. But I told him he is crazy.

"Go and check then," he said.

I didn't want to.

Russell said I was chicken.

"Learn to read faster and you'll have time for a good laugh with Mark Twain—and a good cry with War and Peace."

"Am not," I said.

"Are so," he said.

So I told him the monsters were going to eat him at midnight. He started to cry. My Dad came in and told the monsters to beat it. Then he told us to go to sleep.

"If I hear any more about monsters," he said, "I'll spank you."

We went to sleep fast. And you know something? They never did come back.

Skimming can give you a very good *idea* of this story in about half

"Read with a good light—and with as few friends as possible to help you out. No TV, no music. It'll help you concentrate better—and read faster."

the words—and in *less* than half the time it'd take to read every word.

So far, you've seen that previewing and skimming can give you a *general idea* about content—fast. But neither technique can promise more than 50 percent comprehension, because you aren't reading all the words. (Nobody gets something for nothing in the reading game.)

To *read faster and understand most*—if not all—of what you read, you need to know a third technique.

3. Cluster—to increase speed and comprehension

Most of us learned to read by looking at each word in a sentence—*one at a time.*

Like this:

My—brother—Russell—thinks—monsters…

You probably still read this way sometimes, especially when the words are difficult. Or when the words have an extra-special meaning—as in a poem, a Shakespearean

play, or a contract. And that's O.K.

But word-by-word reading is a rotten way to read faster. It actually *cuts down* on your speed.

Clustering trains you to look at *groups* of words instead of one at a time—to increase your speed enormously. For most of us, clustering is a *totally different way of seeing what we read.*

Here's how to cluster: Train your eyes to see *all* the words in clusters of up to 3 or 4 words at a glance.

Here's how I'd cluster the story we just skimmed:

My brother Russell thinks monsters live in our bedroom closet at night. But I told him he is crazy.

"Go and check then," he said.

I didn't want to. Russell said I was chicken.

"Am not," I said.

"Are so," he said.

So I told him the monsters were going to eat him at midnight. He started to cry. My Dad came in and told the monsters to beat it. Then he told us to go to sleep.

"If I hear any more about monsters," he said, "I'll spank you."

We went to sleep fast. And you know something? They never did come back.

Learning to read clusters is not something your eyes do naturally. It takes constant practice.

Here's how to go about it: Pick something light to read. Read it as fast as you can. Concentrate on seeing 3 to 4 words at once rather than one word at a time. Then reread

the piece at your normal speed to see what you missed the first time.

Try a second piece. First cluster, then reread to see what you missed in this one.

When you can read in clusters without missing much the first time, your speed has increased. Practice 15 minutes every day and you might pick up the technique in a week or so. (But don't be disappointed if it takes longer. Clustering *everything* takes time and practice.)

So now you have 3 ways to help you read faster. Preview to cut down on unnecessary heavy reading. Skim to get a quick, general idea of light reading. And cluster to increase your speed *and* comprehension.

With enough practice, you'll be able to handle *more* reading at school or work—and at home—*in less time.* You should even have enough time to read your favorite comic books—and *War and Peace*!

The Skimming Challenge : Find a newspaper or magazine and a timer. Set the timer for ten minutes. In ten minutes preview and skim at least 5 articles or stories. When the timer rings scribble down a few facts which you remember about each story. Report them to the class.

9

Revising Writing and Teaching

The Writer's Toolbox

Five tools for Active Revision Instruction

by Laura Harper

Laura Harper, a middle school teacher from Yakima, Washington, developed ideas in *After THE END* to meet the needs of her middle school class. Her article, published in *Language Arts*, is a great example of how concepts of craft can help students to own their own revision process. It's also a great example of how ideas in books like *After THE END* or this book can be adapted to meet the needs of your individual students. Teaching writing is an art, and arts evolve through trial and error. When we take risks in our teaching, the way Laura Harper does, we tap into the deep wells of experience in our students and anything can happen.

These revision tools provide students with a set of easily accessible options for getting their jobs done in writing.

> Revision is body work, overhaul
> Ratcheting straight the frame
> Replacing whole systems and panels
> Rummaging heaps of the maimed.
> With blowtorch and old rubber hammer
> Pound and pull, bend, use your 'bar
> Salvage takes sweat but it pays well
> (Though never rule out a new car.)
> —Dethier, 1994, p. 43

I used to think of my classroom as a workshop. I set it up so that my seventh graders had the tools they needed to get their jobs done. Instead of the hammers, nails, and drills of a traditional workshop, I provided a trunk full of writing supplies—paper, markers, reference books, and stationery. Instead of blueprints, lumber, and scrap metal, I organized a file cabinet holding brainstorming lists and drafts and writing logs. Instead of being filled with the sounds of grinding and hammering, this workshop was filled with pencils scratching, fingers typing, and students conferring. "Functional," I thought as I looked around the room. I was proud that my students had all the tools they needed for effective writing.

Yet, two years after setting up the writing workshop, I had a nagging feeling that some of the most important "tools" for writing were missing. Yes, my students had choices. They had time. Certainly, they had the physical tools they needed. Yet, their final drafts and the steps they took to write them suggested that they lacked some basic tools. My students didn't know *how* to revise.

Revision seems like a natural process in books such as Nancie Atwell's (1987) *In the Middle* and Linda Rief's (1992) *Seeking Diversity*. These books suggest that, if you ask good questions during conferences and provide plenty of time for writing, students will be able to re-see their drafts and, thus, revise. I discovered, however, that student conference partners didn't hear or couldn't articulate the weaknesses in each others' writings. If a partner did find something that needed work, the writer most often would simply add or delete a couple of words and pronounce the revision a success. After years of just being told "Revise!" without further explanation, my students had become furtive recopiers, adding a few words here and there and using neater handwriting to revise their drafts.

In addition, my students' revision difficulties were compounded by other language factors. Two-thirds of them came from limited English backgrounds—the majority speaking Spanish as a first language, with most of the other students from Native American homes. Most of my students lived in poverty, with three-fourths receiving free or reduced lunches. In addition, with parents working seasonally in agriculture, many of my students were migrant, spending time each year traveling south to Mexico and back. As a result, they wrote and read significantly below grade level. They had limited vocabularies and ways of expressing themselves in English. They had almost no natural "ear" for how English should sound.

Try only to explain your *own* revision process, and it quickly becomes clear why it is a difficult thing to teach, even to the most able students. Revision is, according to Donald Murray (1987), "one of the writing skills least researched, least examined, least understood, and—usually—least taught" (p. 85). My students, like the inexperienced writers studied by Nancy Sommers (1980), "understood the revision process as a rewording activity" (p. 381). In addition to their limited English backgrounds, they "lacked . . . a set of strategies to help them identify the 'something larger' that they sensed was wrong" in their writing (p. 383). My students needed toolboxes full of strategies, or "tools," with which to pound, saw, drill, and otherwise rebuild their writing.

What should a Writer's Toolbox do for writers? Well, consider what makes toolboxes so valuable to carpenters or mechanics. First, toolboxes keep tools immediately accessible. Carpenters or mechanics can grab their hammers or wrenches instantly and put them to quick use. A Writer's Toolbox must do the same. I wanted my students to have quick access to revision options and not waste time in needless mental blocks or

> *After years of just being told "Revise!" without further explanation, my students had become furtive recopiers, adding a few words here and there and using neater handwriting to revise their drafts.*

endless rewordings. Second, toolboxes provide carpenters and mechanics flexibility. They have a range of tools from which to choose, tools appropriate to each job. Likewise, I wanted our toolboxes to contain a range of choices, or techniques, to expand my students' flexibility in making revisions.

Fortunately, I found a source for these tools. During our reading workshop time, I read Barry Lane's (1993) *After the End,* and I was eager to try some of his revision ideas with my students. I gave each of them a 5" by 8" manila envelope that would serve as a "toolbox" and stay in each student's writing folder. During the following six weeks, we filled the toolboxes with five of Lane's revision "tools": Questions, Snapshots, Thoughtshots, Exploding a Moment, and Making a Scene.

Questions

When I became engaged to be married, my students cross-examined me for all the details. I took this to be the perfect way to introduce our first tool, or revising technique, called Questions. I stood at the front of the room and said, "Last month, my boyfriend asked me to marry him." I paused and looked around the room. "Any questions?"

"Where were you?" yelled Erin, probably surprised by the opportunity to quiz me about my life outside of school.

"How did he ask?" asked Jamie, followed by giggles from classmates.

"How did you feel?" called Melanie, with more giggles.

I quickly scrawled the questions on the board until I was out of room. When I finished, one curious student ventured, "Are you really going to answer these?"

I stalled. Before I would answer their questions, I said I wanted them to try Questions themselves. I asked them to pair up, read aloud the drafts of writing they were currently working on, and then write down any questions they had as they listened. There was only one rule: No yes/no questions allowed. One student, Monica, was asked by her partner how she felt when she realized that her house had been robbed. Andrew's partner asked him to tell more about the setting of his story, a favorite swimming hole. Elena's partner asked what made Elena's aunt, who had recently passed away, so special. Then, the students selected the most appealing questions about their drafts and freewrote on them.

In her first draft, Elena listed a few of the things her and her aunt liked doing together. She said that her aunt "had a baby boy named Anthony," and went on to write: "When my brothers would fall asleep, after playing with Anthony and his toys, Angie and I would go in the kitchen and make cookies."

After our Questions session, Elena decided to describe a specific time when she helped her aunt take care of Anthony:

> As I was pushing Anthony in his rocker, his short brown hair blew in the breeze. He was laughing and clapping his hands. "Mama!" he called. As I walked to put him down, he hugged me with his hands. They looked like his mother's. I put his socks on and his pants. His chubby legs moved around in the air.

The Questions technique not only allowed Elena to add a few paragraphs in response to her partner's questions, but more importantly, it prompted her to rethink her story. Her first draft, which had been a rather impersonal expository piece explaining her sadness at her aunt's death, evolved into a narrative that vividly portrayed their close relationship.

While revising, Elena experienced what Murray (1987) refers to as "a process of discovery." He asserts that "writers much of the time don't know what they are going to write . . .[and they] use language as a tool of exploration to see beyond what they know" (p. 90). The Questions technique reinforces this idea, especially for students writing in non-native languages. It slows the writing process so that new angles and memories can be expressed bit by bit. It also can be used to push drafts in new directions as new discoveries are made.

I wanted my students to have some way to keep this revision technique handy, just as carpenters keep their tools ready for quick access. I knew that, for middle-schoolers, simply putting the technique in their notes wouldn't be enough. The "tool" would grow rusty with disuse and would eventually be lost. They, like the twelfth graders observed by Janet Emig (1971), needed a way to "translate an abstract directive . . . into a set of behaviors" (p. 99). Since most of my students were non-native users of English, creating "scaffolding," or temporary structures for building language skills, was especially important in the development of their English (Boyle & Peregoy, 1990). I wanted them to have something tangible—like a manipulative in mathematics—so they could remember the steps of the technique and begin to use them on their own. We needed to make actual Questions "tools" to put inside our toolboxes. To that end, we brainstormed about the technique's basic steps and then wrote them on index cards. Each student put a Questions index card, or tool, in his or her Writer's Toolbox, or manila envelope, which then went into his or her writing folder.

Finally, to save time for me as well as to make the technique easier for my students to use, I wanted us to have a shorthand with which we could communicate about our revisions. I wanted us, for example, to be able to jot notes to each other recommending that certain tools be used in certain places. As Lane (1993) notes, "though each writer's process is different, a shared language helps writers . . . to gain control" of the writing process. To that end, we created a symbol for the Questions technique, a fat question mark with a circle around it. Instead of writing a lengthy comment such as, "Try having a conference on this passage to see if you can get some more information," we could simply draw the fat question mark symbol on a draft. The writer would know at a glance to try a Questions conference. Peer conferences and teacher conferences, both crucial in helping non-native English speakers gain confidence in their writing (Mendoca & Johnson, 1994; Zhang, 1995), became more focused. Having created and practiced using our first tool, we were ready to move on.

Snapshots

I wish I had a nickel for every time I scrawled "Describe" or "Explain" or "Give more detail" next to an imprecise sentence in my students' writing. To double my earnings, I wish I had a nickel for every time my students, having read my scrawled comments, simply added a word or two, believing they had done what I had asked. Sentences such as "I walked into my bedroom" actually became worse after complying with my margin comments, turning into "I walked into my big, blue, full, messy bedroom." Although it is true that my students *did* need to do better jobs describing, explain-

ing, and giving more detail, my suggestions did not help them discover the kinds of details that would bring their stories to life.

Information is critical to the revision process. During revision, writers need ways to "gather new information or to return to their inventory of information and draw on it" (Murray, 1987, p. 93). They need ways to re-enter their stories and actually "see characters walking or hear characters speaking" (Murray, 1987, p. 90). Like William Faulkner, they must be able to "trot along behind [their characters] with paper and pencil" (Murray, 1987, p. 101).

The Snapshot, our second revision tool, allows writers to do these things. It forces them to focus on close, physical detail and move from describing "preconceived thoughts and feelings to an objective reality that's both more mysterious and compelling" (Lane, 1993, p. 37). In other words, Snapshots provide a structure for the very thing we incessantly implore our students to do: Show, don't tell.

By way of introducing my students to the tool, we first looked for some good descriptions by authors we were reading, from Gary Soto to Gary Paulson. I offered an excerpt from *Little House in the Big Woods* (Wilder, 1989), which I had found in Lane's (1993) description of Snapshots:

> Ma kissed them both, and tucked the covers in around them. They lay there awhile, looking at Ma's smooth, parted hair and her hands busy with sewing in the lamplight. Her needle made little clicking sounds against her thimble and then the thread went softly, swish! through the pretty calico that Pa had traded furs for. (p. 33)

I asked my students to notice how Wilder, as she describes Ma's sewing, is freezing the action and painting "boxes within boxes" of descriptions (Lane, 1993, p. 33). I wanted to give them a visual representation of how Wilder had accomplished this. In a box the size of a Polaroid snapshot, we drew the scene described, including the lamp, Ma, and the kids in bed. Then, in a second box the same size, I drew a "zoomed in" picture of the same scene, but with only Ma, letting her figure fill the entire frame. As a result, she was larger, and it was possible to see details of her hair and her sewing. Last, in a third box the same size, I drew only Ma's hands, zooming in on the details of the needle and thimble, and even the design of the calico fabric, so that they became clearer.

Students practiced by taking Snapshots of nearby classmates. They either wrote a description of what they saw or drew a picture from which they were then able to write. After taking Snapshots, they were ready to try

217

them in their current drafts. Students paired up and began looking for places in their partners' writing where they had trouble visualizing what was going on. The partners marked three or four of these places with our symbol for Snapshots, a small outline of a camera.

During one Snapshot conference, Amber's partner told her to add a Snapshot to a scene in which Amber is getting a new punk haircut. Amber had written in her original draft: "The chair rumpled as I wiggled. The razor buzzed along my neck. I could feel the hair falling, and I didn't exactly want it to anymore." She began by unlocking more of the memories she had of this scene and finding places for them in her story. First, she drew a picture of the scene at the exact moment the haircut began, with the action frozen. In a box on her paper, she sketched herself nervously seated in a barber's chair. Then, she wrote a paragraph describing what she saw and what the picture helped her remember. Under the drawing, she described the scene:

> I sat there squirming, the blue plastic of the chair crumpled and cracked under me. The tightness of all the clips and hair ties made my head throb. I could hear the razor buzzing. I couldn't believe I was doing this.

Next, Amber picked a part of the picture she thought would be interesting to zoom in on. She chose her head as it was being shaved on one side. In another box, she drew a second picture, one that zoomed in on her head so that it nearly filled the entire box. Then, Amber wrote a second paragraph, describing what she could see in her second drawing. Under this box, she wrote what she saw:

> I felt my hair falling to my shoulders, then to the floor. The razor vibrated behind my right ear, making me giggle. I tried as hard a I could not to move. I didn't want her to cut me.

Finally, Amber zoomed in one last time. She selected the part of her second picture that was the most interesting to her, and, with the action frozen, zoomed in on it in a third picture. She took an almost microscopic perspective, sketching the bristly hairs that remained on her head. Under this third box, she described the memories that the drawing triggered:

> The tiny bristles left behind itched, but I didn't dare scratch them. The beautician still had the left side to shave. As the razor pulled away from my head, I scrunched my neck back. The bristles jabbed into my skin, and I felt a tear come to my eye. What if she messed it all up? It would be impossible to grow back.

Through the Snapshot technique, Amber discovered things about her story that she thought she had forgotten. Instead of being commanded to "Describe more" or "Be more specific," she was given a strategy by which to recreate the experience. Having been given a strategy instead of an abstract comment, she elaborated more on physical sensations, such as the "tightness of all the clips and hair ties," as well as on her own emotional state. Amber *showed* what it was like to be getting this drastic haircut, instead of only *telling* about it. Like

> *Through the Snapshot technique, Amber discovered things about her story that she thought she had forgotten.*

Robert Frost, she experienced the "surprise of remembering something I didn't know I knew" (as quoted in Murray, 1987, p. 101).

After completing our Snapshots and finding places for them in our drafts, we made our Snapshot tool. We brainstormed about the basic steps of drawing and then writing the Snapshot. Whenever we are reading a draft and have trouble picturing a character or a setting in our minds, we simply draw a small camera in that spot, confident that the writer will know how to fix the problem. This symbol is probably our most frequently used.

Thoughtshots

Helping students create vivid descriptions of the concrete stuff of their stories is challenging. However, this challenge pales in comparison to the difficulty my students had portraying the internal landscapes of their characters. They struggle with describing how their characters feel and what their characters think. At best, my students resort to simply telling. They write statements like "He felt confused" or "She was mad" or "I couldn't wait." At worst, they leave out their characters' thoughts and feelings completely, resulting in stories populated with unthinking robots. Indeed, characters in middle school students' writing often "exist merely to serve the plot" with no attention given to their "internal reflection" (Graves, 1994, pp. 288–289). No wonder realistic characters are so rare in their writing. Thoughtshots, our third tool, give writers ways to move inside their characters and show what their characters are feeling.

To get a better understanding of how professional authors move inside their characters, my students and I turned to our novels. We flipped through examples from our independent reading as well as from books like *Walk Two Moons* (Creech, 1994), *Fallen Angels* (Myers, 1988), and *Catherine, Called Birdy* (Cushman, 1994).

We listed three basic things that authors do to portray the internal reflections of their characters: (1) characters have flashbacks, triggering their memories of related events or causes; (2) characters have what we called "flashforwards," predicting the outcomes of their actions and anticipating what people will say and think; and (3) characters have what we called "brain arguments," debating with themselves about what is going on and what they should do about it.

Once again, I asked my students to read their current drafts aloud to their partners and look for three or four places where they would like to know what the characters were thinking. Then, the students set to work, choosing one such place and giving characters flashbacks, flashforwards, and brain arguments.

Maria's story was about an incident that happened while she babysat her brother. He decided to fry the legs of a frog he had caught in the backyard, a tense situation for any babysitter. Her first draft contained only one line of thoughts or feelings: "I was bored." Maria's partner suggested that she write a Thoughtshot to describe what it was like when her parents came home. Maria began with a flashforward:

> I heard the rattling of a car engine coming closer to our house. Could it be my parents? I thought. I could picture my mom's face in my mind when she sees that we have two frogs in the kitchen. I know she'll throw away the pans and dishes we used. I hope they know it was all my brother's fault.

Then, she added a flashback:

> I remember when my brother and I had made my mom a mud cake for her birthday. She had thought it was real chocolate, probably because we had put real candles on it. It wasn't long before she found out it was mud, after all. Why don't I ever say anything against my brother's ideas?

Last, Maria wrote a brain argument, showing the way she argued with herself about what to do to stay out of trouble:

> I started feeling the sweat on my hands when the door shut. "Quick, in my room," my brother whispered. "Should I stay where I am or hide with my brother?" I asked myself. Why should I leave if I didn't do anything bad? I'm getting out of here. Before I knew it, I was in my brother's room leaning against the door.

By adding Thoughtshots to her story, Maria not only lets her readers know what her characters are thinking but also does some rather sophisticated characterization. From these brief paragraphs, we get both a history of this brother-sister relationship as well as a glimpse of Maria's desire to be seen as "good." This characterization was something Maria did with little difficulty once she was given a strategy, essentially a set of behaviors, rather than an abstract command to "develop these characters."

To keep this strategy easily accessible, we discussed and wrote the steps for writing Thoughtshots on index cards and put them in our toolboxes. We then decided on the thought bubble as our symbol, our shorthand way of saying, "I'd like to know what this character is thinking right here. Let me inside!"

Exploding a Moment

"Time to the writer is like play dough in the hands of a toddler" (Lane, 1993, p. 65). Writers are in control of time in their stories, and they can shape it according to their purposes. Yet, my students were not able to stretch out the exciting moments of their stories. They rushed through climactic events—motorcycle crashes, high-dive plunges, and romantic advances—in a matter of one or two sentences. Their stories more than lacked suspense. Major life events in their stories were almost laughable because of the cursory treatment they received. Exploding a Moment makes writers the masters of time in their stories. It links together Snapshots and Thoughtshots by using action, thus allowing writers to stretch the exciting seconds of their stories into what seems like hours, creating suspense for the reader to savor.

I brought my kitchen timer to school when I introduced the Exploding a Moment tool. I read aloud an excerpt from *The Chosen* (Potok, 1967), one paragraph at a time, getting students to time the length of each one.

Exploding a Moment . . .(allows) writers to stretch the exciting seconds of their stories into what seems like hours, creating suspense for the reader to savor.

We then looked at what actually happened in each paragraph—a wind-up, a pitch, a return throw from the catcher, a second pitch, and, finally, a hit. While the entire action in *real time* probably took less than two minutes, the *story time* took twice as long.

The students identified the exciting moments, including the time preceding, during, or subsequent to the exciting moments, in their own drafts. Salvador picked the moment when he was being chased by a dog; Israel, the few seconds before he gave a girl a Valentine present; and Felicia, the instant when she knew she was locked in the trunk of a car. They estimated how long these exciting moments lasted in real time. Then, they read the exciting moments in their drafts to determine the story time. Most students found that, instead of making their exciting moments last as long as they did in real life, they actually were cutting them to less than one-tenth the actual time. The students inserted the symbol for the Exploding a Moment technique—a stick of dynamite—into these scenes.

Felicia was writing a story about a time, during an especially aggressive game of hide-and-seek, when she had gotten locked in the trunk of a car. In an early draft, she told the story in an abbreviated way: "I was playing hide and seek, and I thought I would hide in the trunk of a white car." However, by Exploding a Moment, she broke this moment down into smaller actions. She realized there were actually four events that she had been lumping together: One, she climbed into the trunk; two, she pulled the trunk almost closed; three, her brother pushed the trunk closed; and, four, Felicia kicked and screamed to be let out. Now, Felicia wanted to explode the moment by using these four actions as the main ideas for three paragraphs and by adding Snapshots and Thoughtshots to each one.

In her first paragraph, Felicia paced herself and described only her first action: her entry into the trunk. She blended with this single action some fragments of Snapshots and Thoughtshots:

> I crawled into the trunk, onto the hard but padded floor. I looked to see if he was there. I glanced back at the door. As soon as I saw him coming, my face pinched into a worried frown. I slowly lay down. I grabbed the steel white rim of the trunk and pulled on it until it reached the tip top of the lock. I could see a little, just enough to peak. It looked like a line of light between the trunk door and the car.

Already, Felicia had created more suspense, taking the reader inside the trunk with her. She then showed, in slow motion, the next action, again blended with mini-Snapshots and Thoughtshots:

> "Where is he?" I asked myself. I could no longer see through the small opening of light that had come into the trunk. It was completely silent. No one was to be seen. I looked out, raising the trunk lid a little. He sneaked around, looked right at me, eyeball to eyeball, and slammed the door shut. I pushed. I kept on pushing. It was locked!

Finally, Felicia moved to the final action, her response, which was made more vivid by including her thoughts and some physical details:

> I panicked. "Open this trunk right now!" I said. I kicked at the door. How could he open it, though? I asked myself. He didn't have the keys. I started to feel sweat roll down my body. I kicked and kicked and kicked. What could I do? All I could do was wait. I felt bruises forming, and my legs started to sting. It was dark, and I just lay there. I was burned out with no energy left. It was all silent.

This passage of Felicia's story, which originally could be skimmed over, if not skipped entirely, was expanded into three suspenseful paragraphs.

Exploding a Moment allows students to tell important parts of their stories in slow motion, and, in the process, it helps them remember. "One unexplored skill which might help our understanding of . . . revision," suggests Murray (1987), "is the writer's use of memory" (p. 95). He theorizes that writing actually "unlocks information stored in the brain" (p. 95). Exploding a Moment allows us to access information locked in the brain, resulting in both more descriptive writing on the part of the author and more suspenseful entertainment for the reader.

Making a Scene

At the root level, revision means "to re-see." According to Sommers (1980), inexperienced writers frequently have an "inability to 're-view' their work again . . . with different eyes" (p. 382). Furthermore, non-native English speakers, with which my classroom was filled, need additional help remembering that their drafts are temporary, that they can make extensive changes to their writing without focusing on conventions (Diamond & Moore, 1995). Our fifth revision tool, Making a Scene, works as a diagnostic tool that helps students see their writing through new eyes. Like a mechanic's lift, this tool allows students to take a better look at their writing and see if it is balanced.

Many students only use one element of narrative writing: action. Their stories read like laundry lists of things their characters did. Few student writers and conference partners know when a piece of writing needs more dialogue or description or internal reflection to flesh out the action in the story. The Making a Scene tool helps students evaluate their drafts for the four main ingredients of narrative writing—action, dialogue, Snapshots, and Thoughtshots—and allows them to see where and how often they used each type. We began by designating one marker color for each main ingredient in narrative writing: blue for action, yellow for dialogue, red for Snapshots (here being used to include almost any physical description), and purple for Thoughtshots (or internal description). The students then traded drafts and underlined every line in one of the four colors. Some drafts were almost completely underlined in blue; others had no yellow; others had huge blocks of red; but only a few drafts had a rainbow of colors. In case the colors didn't get the message across boldly enough, we also tallied the percentages of each type of writing in the drafts. Suddenly, my students could "re-see" their drafts.

Monica, writing about the robbery of her house, saw that she needed to add more dialogue and action to her

> *Furthermore, Making a Scene helps students . . . realize the importance of drawing from all four elements of narrative writing in order to create balanced scenes.*

story. Nearly two-thirds of her story was Snapshots; 17% was Thoughtshots; 14%, action; and a mere 2%, dialogue. Angelica's story about her family's recent move was overloaded with action at the expense of physical detail: 44% of her story was action; 22%, Thoughtshots; 18%, dialogue; and only 6%, Snapshots. Even students who had balanced the elements of their writing more proportionally could "see" areas of their drafts where they could better blend the elements, mixing thoughts with descriptions, combining dialogue with action. With the evidence in front of them, my students had reasons to revise and saw possibilities for doing so. Furthermore, Making a Scene helps students as they draft new stories. They realize the importance of drawing from all four elements of narrative writing in order to create balanced scenes.

Our symbol for Making a Scene is the black and white board that a movie director clicks shut when crying, "Action!" Placed in our toolbox, it became our fifth tool for revising.

Conclusion

Like the toolboxes of any skilled craftsmen, the Writer's Toolboxes give my students a set of easily accessible options for getting their jobs done. As a result, my room works more like my vision of a real writing workshop. However, I still have a few nagging questions. First of all, what other tools might be added to my students' toolboxes? For example, what tools work well in other genres, such as expository or persuasive writing? What tools might work better with students with other

language backgrounds? Second, I wonder what methods are most effective in teaching these revision techniques. Is it important, as one group of students advised me, to perform all of these techniques on one piece of writing? Would it be more effective to scatter these throughout the year? Third, and most importantly, what effect does the toolbox have on related areas of the reading and writing workshop? How do these tools change students' approaches to conferencing, to reading, to prewriting, and to drafting? My sense, as I listen to writing conferences and book groups, is that these tools, with frequent use, become internalized and improve my students' abilities as conference partners, readers, and drafters.

Despite the inevitable need for fine-tuning, the Writer's Toolbox—by increasing choices and by creating a common language—strengthens my students' ownership over their writing. Tait, a reluctant reviser at the beginning of the school year came to this conclusion after our Writer's Toolbox unit: "I used to think revision was just a waste of time, but now I've seen what revising can do to a story." Brian, a student instantly frustrated by comments like "Describe more," also came to understand the purpose of revising: "My ideas about revision have really changed. Now, I can do more to help my writing, to make it better. At the beginning of the year, I didn't understand it. Now I do." In fact, when questioned in an anonymous survey, all of my students said they would definitely use these revision techniques in the future. By giving them a way to talk about, to make decisions about, and eventually to perform revisions, the Writer's Toolbox transformed my students from recopiers to writers more in control of their craft. After all, that is what a writing workshop is all about.

References

Atwell, N. (1987). *In the middle: Writing, reading, and learning with adolescents*. Portsmouth, NH: Heinemann.

Boyle, O. F., & Peregoy, S. F. (1990). Literacy scaffolds: Strategies for first- and second-language readers and writers. *The Reading Teacher, 44,* 194–200.

Creech, S. (1994). *Walk two moons.* New York: HarperCollins.

Cushman, K. (1994). *Catherine, called Birdy.* New York: Clarion.

Dethier, B. (1994). Eddie's full service rewrite. *English in Texas, 25,* 43.

Diamond, B. J., & Moore, M. A. (1995). *Multicultural literacy: Mirroring the reality of the classroom.* White Plains, NY: Longman.

Emig, J. (1971). *The composing processes of twelfth graders.* Urbana, IL: National Council of Teachers of English.

Language Arts

Graves, D. H. (1994). *A fresh look at writing.* Portsmouth, NH: Heinemann.

Lane, B. (1993). *After the end: Teaching and learning creative revision.* Portsmouth, NH: Heinemann.

Mendoca, C. O., & Johnson, K. E. (1994). Peer review negotiations: Revision activities in ESL writing instruction. *TESOL Quarterly, 28,* 745–769.

Murray, D. M. (1987). Internal revision: A process of discovery. In C. R. Cooper & L. Odell (Eds.), *Research on composing: Points of departure* (pp. 85–103). Urbana, IL: National Council of Teachers of English.

Myers, W. D. (1988). *Fallen angels.* New York: Scholastic.

Potok, C. (1967). *The chosen.* New York: Simon and Schuster.

Rief, L. (1992). *Seeking diversity.* Portsmouth, NH: Heinemann.

Sommers, N. (1980). Revision strategies of student writers and experienced adult writers. *College Composition and Communication, 31,* 378–388.

Wilder, L. I. (1989). *Little house in the big woods.* Santa Barbara, CA: Cornerstone Books.

Zhang, S. (1995). Reexamining the affective advantage of peer feedback in the ESL writing class. *Journal of Second Language Writing, 4,* 209–222.

Laura Harper teaches seventh-grade English, reading, and social studies at Toppenish Middle School in Toppenish, Washington.

Laura Harper
Toppenish Middle School
104 Goldendale Ave.
Toppenish, WA 98948

Remembering Teachers

When Liz Mandrell started writing about her teachers she didn't think she could remember, yet with each fragment of a memory another one arose, and before long she had written *Trial by Error in the Halls of Ignorance*, a tribute to the powerful memory of the pen. After you read Liz's piece, see if you can write about all the teachers you have had. What will you remember once you start turning the knob on those binoculars?

TRIAL BY ERROR IN THE HALLS OF IGNORANCE
by Liz Mandrell

The day I told my English Comp teacher she was going to hell was the day I sealed my occupational fate. From that moment on, the Revenge gods, who were working for Mrs. Cochran, took over my life, vowing that I would feel the same stinging humiliation at the hand of a smart aleck, self-obsessed, sanctimonious student as Mrs. Cochran had felt when I pronounced her eternal destination there in first period English Comp. Now every time I hear a student challenging my beliefs, I hear my own self-important voice hurtling towards Mrs. Cochran's desk on that bright November morn. My brother, however, totally disagrees with this theory of occupational choice. He thinks the teaching profession was chosen for me by a collective hiss from all the bespectacled multitudes who lay claim to my educational process. "They all had it in for you, Liz," he says. "And now, like a pack of old grandparents, they sit back and watch you raise this generation of students." Maybe he's right.

My teachers did give me an early start at classroom management. I was always the kid in charge when the teacher left the room. Liz, you take the names on the blackboard of children who misbehave; Liz, you watch the lunchroom while I go smoke a cigarette; Liz, you grade these papers, dust the erasers and average my six weeks grades while I mess around with Coach Dix in the boiler room. I always felt uncomfortable with this rewarding authority, so I usually launched some big anti-establishment rally (this was in the '70's), so when the teacher came back and anarchy was reigning, I was the one and only one to blame.

But to answer the questions as to whether I chose my profession or it chose me, I have no answer. I had always thought my career choice was motivated by the slings and arrows I had suffered at the hand of the philistines who were running the classrooms where I sat. Maybe if I became a teacher, I could heal from all the emotional scars grade school and junior high left on me. Maybe if I had the red book, maybe if I called out the roll up yonder in a clear cool voice, maybe then I would have some power in my life and be able to tell the MCI guy where to get off. But if I became a slovenly secretary, answering phones and plodding at the data terminal, I would be held in bondage with the horrific memories of my educational past, memories of plastic recorders, memories of stewed tomatoes, memories of Presidential fitness, memories where only the names have been changed to protect the innocent, memories, memories, memories of…

Elementary school!! I was completely terrorized by Mrs. Elwood Norton. Why did anyone name a girl Elwood, I queried in my seat on the back row. I wanted to be up front; I wanted to shine under Elwood's bifocaled stare, but she put me on the back row with Gladys Dibble. Gladys Dibble, who stood six feet tall in the first grade, Gladys Dibble, whose dad was the only Hell's Angel in three counties, Gladys Dibble, who critically injured Joey Taggart when he spit on me at recess, Gladys Dibble, who sniffed 4,000 lbs. of snot back into her sinuses every day. Blow it out, I wanted to scream. Blow it all out! Her condition seemed to accelerate at afternoon milk break when we, as a class, became a veritable symphony of plastic straw suckers, our straws like rosened fiddle bows scraping every resonant cavern of the milk carton in search of the last drop of moo. Gladys out-sipped and out-sniffed all of us with her sinus in B minor concerto. To this day, I don't drink chocolate milk, but I did manage to struggle into second grade.

Mrs. Patterson wore no bra beneath her gauzy disheki-blouses (this was the 70's) and one day during reading…incidentally, I was in with the Wombats, which I thought was a really cool name for a reading group until I found out Wombats were burrowing marsupials in the badger family…but one day during reading her left breast fell right out, practically planting itself on the table. The earth tilted, planets spun and we all stared, eyes big as skeet plates, at the still jiggling dollop of humanity on our reading table. Mrs. Patterson reached down. "Excuzay Mwoi," she said and flopped herself discreetly back into the gauzy depths of her blouse. And there we were, six little wombats scarred forever.

Next grade, girl meets teacher. Teacher meets girl. Girl meets the paddle. Mrs. Crane The Pain made a pretense of liking me, but this was her first year teaching and frankly, she was threatened by my daunting command of the English language. I was using words like "plethora' and "castigate" just to get her goat. My sister who was in college was teaching me these words at night, plying me with Snickers bars if I could use a word correctly in three different sentences five minutes after learning the word. So Mrs. Crane The Pain got me on a legality. I was talking during quiet time, the subpoena read. Actually, it was right  after lunch and I was picking greens out of Janie Snow's braces, but The Pain wouldn't listen to my defense. Out in the hall, she bellowed. She had long, straight, unadorned hair and a long, straight, unadorned paddle. Standing there, with the sickle-like paddle poised above me, she looked like some tall, gaunt specter from Teacher Hell. But I lived through it, and I think I came to greater consciousness through The Pain, which was all the better since I needed my wits about me when I entered Sergeant Major Skinner's room.

Sergeant Major Skinner was a retired marine sergeant who called us all by our last names until one day, impudent strumpet that I was, I said, "Ahem…Sergeant Major

Mister Sir, instead of Farmer, I would pree-fer to be called Liz." "You'll be sitting on the wall during recess, Farmer, and you'll pree-fer that." I did sit there, but I didn't like it. In fact, I though hateful thoughts about Sergeant Major Skinner all during recess and when he had a mild heart attack three weeks later, I thought for sure I'd caused it. I know now it was his Type A personality and high cholesterol diet, but as a ten-year-old child, I was struck by my own powers. Maybe I could even cure Gladys Dibble's sniffleitis. I tried for several nights, chanting incantations and hexes, but to no avail; I was a mere human, savage and crude in my miracles.

Mr. Reese verbalized my hunches when he called me a savage as I pushed Augusta Walker out of the line at the water fountain. That's where savagery begins in life at the water fountain line and it extends right on to the grave in the form of corporate claims and vertical ladders of power. Mr. Reese should have told me then the way things were in life – he should have praised my barbarian ways, but not being a big fan of savagery, I suppose he let me flounder on, learning life's lessons the hard way as I stumbled on to...

Sixth grade! Ruby Butler, her make-up caked about her neck like a priest's collar, ate raw eggs and cleaned her toenails at her desk every morning. No lie. I liked her, and she liked me, but the other kids were scared to death of her. The woman would kill for Campbell Soup labels. I was the youngest of a big family, so Mom strapped big bales of labels to my back every Monday for Mrs. Butler. One day I told her those SRS reading labs really stunk, so she pounded James Michener's *Chesapeake* on my desk and said, "Read this." And I did, barely making it through the prehistoric first chapter, but speeding through the chapters on illicit love between Captain Matt Turlock and Susan Steed. I brought the book back to Mrs. Butler, lying it reverently on her table, placing my hand on the top and swearing, "I read it all." She quizzed me with several questions in front of the class, and when I answered them to her satisfaction, she kissed me square on the mouth. I can still feel her catfish whiskered lips covering mine to this day.

Seventh and Eighth grade were pretty much a blur. I hated the move from my tiny rural elementary to the middle school building in town. The halls smelled funny and all the rich snobs from St. Mary's Catholic School for Queers and Turds were there. My science teacher picked his nose and hit kids with a yard stick, my social studies teacher was a pimp of some kind and my P.E. teacher was so beautiful, I felt like puking at the gangling reflection of my own naked budding body in the locker room mirrors. But the shining light of my middle school day was Mrs. Whitney's class. She taught English and was about 150 years old. Her skin looked like a saddlebag and she used to drape her arm over her suspiciously pregnant looking stomach and walk around lecturing thusly. She had put two husbands in the grave already, but got married again that year to some old gentleman whose name she refused to take. "My name's so long now, they'll have to double truck my obituary," she crocked. We joked about their honeymoon night, retching at the thought of Mrs. Whitney in a black silk teddy, slinking toward the bed, having deposited her teeth in a glass by the sink. But Mrs. Whitney was loads of fun. We had to memorize a poem every month. I still remember some of them. She made us square off for the Reagan-Carter debate. She said things like, "Great balls of fire," and

"Don't just sit there like a bump on a pickle," and "You're squirming' like a hen on a hot rock," and "Fiddle dee dee." Years later, I realized Scarlett O'Hara must have been her idol. Even now, I can see Mrs. Whitney sweeping into the classroom, one hand draped across her stomach, pencil waving in the other hand like a summer fan, and saying, "Grades, grades, grades. I think I shall positively scream if I hear another word about grades." She was wonderful, I thought, finally a teacher who doesn't torment me. I could go on with Mary Whitney stories, but oh, the memories, they overwhelm me…yes, all the warm, funny memories, memories, memories…

…Gilligan, Wake up! Wake up, little buddy! You were dreaming. What…huh? Oh, I'm sorry. I was talking about Mrs. Cochran, right? Damning her to hell and sealing my fate, that sort of thing?…I remember. I remember that still sliver of moment, when urged by my religious zealotry in the face of Mrs. Cochran's school renowned atheism, I called out from the back of the room, my voice ringing like a bell in the hallowed halls of Christendom, "Mrs. Cochran, I think you are sadly disillusioned, and I'm afraid you are going straight to hell." And therein lies my life, my career, my voice which was really not a choice at all, but a decision formed in the heavens that I should walk a mile in Mrs. Cochran's moccasins. Vengeance is yours, Mrs. Cochran. I'm getting my payback now.

Liz Mandrell lives in Kentucky

Quality in Writing

Interview with Barry Lane

ALL ONE

WT: How do you define and judge quality in writing?

Lane: Begin just by asking one simple question, "What is good writing?" Ask it to your class. Ask it to yourself. Think of your favorite authors. Think of the student writing that rises to the top of the pile when you take home a stack of papers. Brainstorm a list of criteria. Don't worry if the criteria are too personal.

When you are done, go over the list and combine criteria that seem to go together. Ask the questions to move from personal criteria like "the characters are interesting" to more objective criteria like "the author gives many vivid details about the character to make him interesting." Whittle down your list to a few criteria and make initials for them. Use your criteria to assess writing in a simple way that allows you to see a profile in the writing.

For example, let's say my criteria are details, purpose, flow, and humor. Simply list them down a page.

D ————————————
P ———————————
F —————————
H ———

Let's call this a race of criteria.. The lines you drew across the page show me which horse is in the lead. This gives a profile to the writing and could easily be the basis for a reflective letter about the piece. For example, I can see this piece is strongest in details and weaker in flow.

The key to assessment is the word itself. It comes from the Latin verb *assidire*: to sit beside. We are not ranking here. We are sitting beside a piece of writing and observing its qualities. We are finding a common language to talk about those qualities.

WT: How does "good" writing look and sound?

Lane: If you've read *After THE END*, you know I am a little obsessed with the notion of voice in writing. Strong writing always has some kind of voice to it. It may not be a personal, informal voice, but there is something in the prose which tells you that a person wrote it. It wasn't a list coughed up by a CD-ROM or an encyclopedia.

There are other qualities of powerful writing. Strong writing is distinct, individual, and inquiring. It asks questions it can't answer. It answers questions in peculiar and sometimes spectacular ways. It surprises itself and the reader with vivid details, dynamic organization, an intriguing purpose. It's clear but not facile, it's complex but not ambiguous. Am I starting to sound like a wine critic?

When asked to define jazz, Louis Armstrong said, "I don't know what it is, but I know when I hear it." This is the easy answer to the question, and though it might also be the best, writers and teachers shouldn't settle for it because it's too boring.

For example, if I tell you that good writing is a strong voice and you show me a piece with little voice that you know is wonderful, then we have a dialogue going. You can say it's the detail that really makes a piece of writing shine. Someone else can say it's the way the piece is organized.

And still another can say you're all wrong. "It's the way the guy puts his socks on." We are talking now, and writers like to talk about writing because it helps them to know what to strive for.

My favorite way to create criteria is to take to class a piece of really bland writing. Here's one of my favorites:

The Sad Man
The sad man ran.
The sad man ran to Dan.
Dan had a fan.
Dan can fan the sad man.

Tell the class this is wonderful and ask them what they think. When they say, "No, it is not wonderful," ask them why. Make a list. If you want, have kids rewrite this piece of writing in groups of three. Begin by asking questions. Have kids answer those questions in a revised story. When they share their new creations, notice the qualities that make it better. (I've been doing this exercise for five years, and I've never met a group which revised this piece and it came out worse.)

In *After THE END* I interviewed kids about the difference between basals and real literature. They said things like, "In a basal you got a boy and and a girl and a dog. Tell me why I should be interested?"

We can train kids to have an ear for good writing, and they will be able to recognize and define the qualities of good writing with a common specific language.

WT: Do criteria for "good" writing change with different purposes and genres? If so, how?

Lane: The most fundamental criteria don't change very much. For example, vivid and explicit detail is as important in a short story as it might be in a business letter or research paper. Vermont teachers, after several years of passionate debate, came up with

"...like toddlers exploring limits of their universe, strong writers will stretch the rules and expectations of any genre."

five generic criteria: purpose, organization, details, voice and tone, and grammar, usage and mechanics. (To find out more about this, I recommend Geof Hewitt's excellent book on this subject, *The Portfolio Primer*, published by Heinemann.) After assessing work from different genres, most teachers in Vermont will tell you that these criteria do work very well in every genre but poetry. Portfolio teachers in Kentucky have had a similar experience.

This makes poets I know very happy. Because poems work on so many different levels and poetic form and language can vary so much from poem to poem, it is very difficult to assess it with consistent criteria. Though we could spend time inventing a poetry rubric (and some people are), in the end all rubrics, all attempts to assess anything are about consistency and uniformity and, let's face it, the best poetry is not. Though I agree it's very important that writing teachers set common standards and share a common language to drive teaching in a sensible direction, let's

not fool ourselves into thinking we can figure it all out. Let's leave a little mystery, myth, and magic. You can't make rubrics out of fire and blood, but you can make poems of it.

What's more interesting to me is how we can mix and expand genres. I just picked up a fascinating book by Tom Romano called *Writing with Passion* (Boynton/Cook, 1995. See review on p. 40). Romano teaches at the college level and believes that students learn when they take risks with genres. The research paper can become poems in his class. Poems can metamorphize into lab reports. The word genre itself implies convention. Romano believes that it's the writer's job to play with conventions and genre to achieve a higher purpose. I heartily agree. When I was in school I wrote reams of comedy and satire, but I soon stopped showing it to my teachers because it was not considered an appropriate genre for school. I wish I had had Romano as a teacher.

We need to continually expand and explode the notion of genre inside and outside school. George Orwell did not know that he was writing a narrative essay when he wrote *Shooting an Elephant*. He was telling a story. He was trying to say something about British imperialism. Editors never ask writer's for five-paragraph themes or expository writing. Forms or genres, like assessment, are also about conformity and, like toddlers exploring limits of their universe, strong writers will stretch the rules and expectations of any genre.

WT: How do the criteria for quality differ by the age (grade level) of the writer?

Lane: Very little. I have taught college students and first graders in the same day. I can see the same qualities emerging in their work. I see detail. I see voice. I see various forms of organization. I worry sometimes when I hear teachers talk about what's developmentally appropriate for certain age levels. My experience shows me that students often rise to the expectations of their teacher. Read Ralph Fletcher's Book *What a Writer Needs* (Heinemann) to see powerful writing from all ages side by side.

I once was teaching in a K-8 school in Vermont. I had a class with the eighth graders in the morning and the third graders in the afternoon. I was doing what I thought was an advanced lesson with the eighth graders and a simpler one with the third graders. On the second day one of the third graders asked me why I hadn't done the fun lesson I'd done with the eighth graders with them. Apparently, Trevor, one of the eighth graders involved in a big buddy program, had taught the "advanced" lesson to the entire third-grade class. After that day I vowed not to limit what I do with third graders until I'd seen with my own eyes.

Qualitative shifts in writing through the grades can also tell us a lot about how we teach. For example, first graders often write with more voice than twelfth graders. Is this developmental? I don't think so, but it might tell us a bit about what primary school teachers value and high school teachers don't.

WT: How can teachers give students effective feedback about their progress and the quality of their writing?

Lane: To begin with, let's talk about what doesn't work. This is what Jerry Seinfeld says about his writing teacher's feedback:

"I always did well on essay tests. Just put in everything you know on there, maybe you'll hit it. And then you get the paper back from the teacher and she's written just one word across the entire page, 'vague.' I thought vague was kind of 'vague.' I'd write underneath it, 'unclear,' and send it back. She'd return it to me, 'ambiguous.' I'd send it back to her, 'cloudy.' We're still corresponding to this day.

> *"Wean students from holistic numbers and letter grades by putting the focus on specific criteria, assessment, and the writing itself."*

Hazy, muddy..."(*SeinLanguage*, Bantam). Seinfeld's frustrating experience with teacher feedback was the same as mine in school. My teachers scribbled cryptic notes on my paper, and in my mind I scribbled nasty notes back to them. In *After THE END* I have a chapter called "Don't fix my story, just listen to me: a guide to conferencing and co-dependency." The goal of all writing teachers is to shrink the line to their desk. If you have 160 students, you need 160 teachers-in-training, not because you're lazy, but because, when it comes right down to it, your job is *their* job.

Of course, everyone could do more with more time and fewer students, but what's also needed are tools to help students take control over their own learning. These self-assessing students don't come magically. We need to train them with critical guidelines. Make self-reflection and assessment a habit in your classroom. Develop a consistent language to discuss and assess writing. Wean students from holistic numbers and letter grades by putting the focus on specific criteria, assess-

ment, and the writing itself. (Read Linda Rief's wonderful book *Seeking Diversity* to get a glimpse of what this looks like in the classroom).

Some of you are probably thinking *what about grades.* I have to grade. Parents want grades. In the past, grades have been seen as a sign of quality. I was teaching at a university where the Dean decided to raise academic standards. He called all the faculty together and told them to give more Cs. This had nothing to do with raising standards because every teacher had a different notion of what a "C" was, and those notions of quality were never discussed, assessed, or even talked about in a specific way.

Likewise, I once held up a piece of very mediocre writing at a conference and asked the teachers what they thought of it. A high school teacher in the front row said, "That's a B." Then she went on to say, "You know I can teach the B, but I can't teach the A." I thought to myself, if grades mean anything (and I'm not convinced they do), isn't the "A" the only grade we should be teaching?

Some teachers in Kentucky have given up grading individual papers and created grading rubrics. For example, an A student shows evidence of reading 30 minutes each night; is able to write thoughtful responses to the reading, which relate it to his/her life; shows evidence of revision in writing; and can write insightful reflections on what they are learning, etc. These teachers have decided that if they have to grade, they want to grade more than a few quizzes, tests, or papers. They want to grade what they are trying to teach, i.e., a lifelong love of reading and writing. Moreover, they want their students to use the rubric to assess and grade themselves on their progress. If you have ever done this, you will know that students are very good at it. Most teachers find that students are tougher on themselves than their teacher is.

The only way to raise the quality of writing in a school is to create, share, and celebrate the specific criteria for that quality with everybody on a regular basis. When parents start asking "what can she do" instead of "what did she get," we'll know we're making progress. When high-school students ask "what did I learn" instead of "what did I get," we'll know the new day is upon us. Until that day we must continue educating everybody, especially the most difficult people.

One thing I've learned about education is that if you keep telling and showing it over and over, most people will get it. Here's a line many portfolio teachers say to me at my workshops: "My worst enemies have become my greatest allies once they understood what I was doing."

WT: If teachers understand quality, can they teach toward it? Can they assess it?

Lane: Yes and yes. Understanding notions of quality and learning to assess writing can drive curriculum in a very specific and positive way. However, in my travels around the country, I have seen obstacles to teachers understanding quality. In many states, for example, they have mastery or performance tests. They sound like a good idea, but many times teachers stop their best teaching practices and start teaching to a recipe which will help students perform better on the test. Ironically, these kids would do better on most mastery tests if teachers just forgot about the test and taught students to develop a lifelong passion for writing. Even more ironic is that these tests were put in place to drive curriculum in the aforementioned positive direction. I remind teachers of this wherever I go. I ask them, "What's the worst that can happen to you if you forget the test and employ your best teaching practices in the classroom?"

The tragedy of American education is that the head does not know what the hand is doing, but gives

> *"What's the worst that can happen to you if you forget the test and employ your best teaching practices in the classroom?"*

orders anyway. If superintendents are really interested in total quality management, they should be spending at least half their time in classrooms, working with the teachers and students who create that quality. This kind of accountability will go much further than the little numbers and graphs that seem to occupy so much of their precious time.

These administrators would also know that when W. Edwards Demmings (the father of TQM) visits a company like General Motors, the very first thing he does is to impose a moratorium on all types of testing because it creates winners and losers. The goal of TQM is to create a team of "winners." Only then, when people are working together with high self-esteem, when it's safe to take risks, can we start defining the skills and levels of performance and learn how to specifically teach to them.

My experience shows me that many administrators and school boards talk about raising quality in education and empowering teachers, but few are willing to take the important political

risks to accomplish their goals. Close your eyes now and imagine a superintendent who says to his school board, "For the next two years let's take the $300,000 we are giving for CTBS and Iowa tests and use it to pay teachers for time to meet for staff development so that they can develop their own method of assessment and standards of quality in instruction. We can bring in consultants to help them, but our goal is to involve all teachers, community members, and the students themselves in the process of raising real standards in our schools."

Show me a nation of school superintendents with this type of chutzpah, and I'll show you a nation where quality is more than just a buzz word.

WT: What practical strategies can teachers use to emphasize and encourage quality in writing in their classrooms?

Lane: I believe that teachers can teach concepts, to get students excited about the possibilities of craft in writing. I've written three books about these concepts, so I guess you could say it's driven my curriculum in a major way. Most of these concepts I learned as a writer first and a teacher second. I recommend that you do the same. These concepts include: leads; details as binoculars instead of wallpaper; snapshots and thoughtshots (two types of detail that replace the mindless maxim "Show don't tell" with "There's a time to show and a time to tell, turn turn turn..."; exploding moments (writing in slow motion); and building scenes (crafting dialogue).

My experience tells me that students get bored with their writing when they don't know their options. I see the teacher as someone who shows them a new concept and says, "What could **you** do with this?"

Teachers and schools can also publicly share and celebrate the qualities of powerful writing. Assessment should never be seen as slicing apart a piece of writing. It should be about celebrating the reasons we see something or even why we love something. Read-alouds, literary teas, benchmarking sessions, bulletin boards of criteria and writing, poetry readings, and peer conferences can all be tools for exploring in a very specific way what we value and what we don't.

WT: What closing comments do you have for our readers?

Lane: Luciano Pavoratti told the *New Yorker* that "there are two types of singers. One who is doing everything very easily. The top note for him is like a—peanut! He just picks it off! And there are singers who have a little trouble with the top note, but they give you their heart. For me, personally, I like the singer who makes you feel something very important. The first kind comes out of the schools, and they have all the pyrotechnics. So? So? I think you need a little effort. A cry. Pain. Something there to make you think it's true—to the singer and to the audience."

I think it's important for writing teachers to always remember that in the end, beyond everything, writing is a powerful form of human expression. Roland Barthes defined literature as "the question minus the answer." I've worked in prisons and seen men with sixth-grade educations write 200-page novels in my class. I've seen newly-literate adults write about painful memories that moved a huge audience to tears. Yes, skills are important, and lord knows we need to find a way to make our best quality teaching and writing accountable to both students and parents, but at the end of the day, I feel best about the student who writes from the heart, who asks the questions that don't have the answer.

In my book *Writing as a Road to Self-Discovery* (Writer's Digest Books, 1993), I've written about many such students of all ages. Writing that book taught me to value *potatoes*, the stuff that grows under the surface which the writer and reader need to find out more about. There needs to be something at stake beyond making perfect sentences or finishing assignments or scoring high on tests, beyond portfolios and rubrics, as Pavoratti says, "A cry. Pain. Something to let you know it's real." If we keep this always in mind, we won't lose our way. 🍎

Barry Lane's books include Discovering the Writer Within *(with Bruce Ballenger),* After THE END, Writing as a Road to Self-Discovery, *and* The Portfolio Sourcebook. *For information about his seminars and in-service work call: 1-800-613-8055.*

For many of us, grammar and spelling were the two qualities most assessed when we were in school. In today's student-centered classrooms, children from the earliest ages are learning to be self-editors. The red pen is not a weapon if it's in the writer's hands.

I wrote the following piece to help diffuse the tension and fear teachers still have about grammar and spelling. Try reading this piece to your class and enlist them to join the Grammar Police. (This piece was excerpted from *Discovering the Writer Within* copyright ©1989 by Bruce Ballenger and Barry Lane. Used with permission of Writer's Digest Books, a division of F&W Publications, Inc.)

Grammarnoia

The story you are about to read is true. Only the grammar and punctuation have been changed to protect the innocent.

He was in his office late at night. He was writing. There were three loud raps on the door. He scratched out sentences. He hid paper under the file cabinet. He pulled the paper from his typewriter and stuffed it in his mouth.

The door exploded open and two men barged in. Both wore tweed sportcoats with wrinkled copies of Strunk and White in the breast pockets. They stood in a cloud of chalk dust, flailing their red Flairs.

"Grammar Police. Drop the pen!"

They flashed their IDs. Both full professors. Harvard '56, Columbia '64. They yanked the piece of yellow second copy from his mouth and ransacked the drawers.

"Run-ons," the older one said, scoring his pen over the wrinkled piece of paper.

"Comma splices," the other man said. "Gerunds everywhere."

They rolled the teacher away from the desk and faced him against the wall.

"But I take a process-oriented approach," the teacher said.

"Sure buddy, we've heard that before. Spell necessary."

"I'm not spelling anything till I see my lawyer."

"Punctuate this sentence." They shoved a piece of paper into his lap. "THE MAN WHO WAS HAPPY EATING WHEATIES LIKED OTHER CEREALS TOO."

"I'm not punctuating anything."

"How long have you been teaching at this university?"

"A year."

(continued on next page)

(continued from p.7)

"Put it in a complete sentence."

"I have been teaching at this university a year."

"Put it in the pluperfect."

"I taught—"

"Book him."

"But this is only a first draft."

"Sure, buddy, and we're going on our first little ride downtown. Maybe you can have a little talk with the spelling squad, too. Spell necessary."

"It begins with N-E,"

"You hear that Joe? We've got a real Phi Beta Kappa on our hands here."

They laughed as they slid bits of crinkled paper into their manila envelopes.

"You can't do this. There's nothing wrong with being ungrammatical as long as you do it in the privacy of your own room with a consenting piece of paper."

They thumbed through their Strunk and Whites in unison.

"Listen to this, Meathead: 'There's no excuse for grammatical ambiguity.'"

"But what about content? What about subject? What about voice? What about me?"

They clamped two steel parentheses over his wrists.

"We'll deal with you, don't worry."

In the squad car on the way to the station they asked him how he could expect to teach college freshman to write when he could barely punctuate a sentence himself. He was silent, his mind recalling all the spelling bees from which he was eliminated in the first round; his eyes peering through the gallons of red ink on every essay he had ever handed a teacher.

"I was a victim of an ungrammatical childhood," he told the judge. "My mother spoke in fragments. My father always hesitated in mid-clause. In their eyes, I was parenthetical. I lived between the commas."

The judge wore a commencement robe and mortar board. Hanging from the tassels were dashes, semicolons, periods.

"Spell necessary," he said.

"Hopeless."

"No, necessary."

"Impossible."

"No, necessary."

He had looked up the word at least 3,000 times in his lifetime, and he still could not be sure if there were one *c* and two *s*'s or one *s* and two *c*'s.

He closed his eyes and imagined the firing squad—10 high school English teachers with horn-rimmed glasses and eraser-pink ears. His hooded body slumped meekly in the chair. *Long live meaning*, he would cry at the last moment, or *Substance over form forever.*

"N-E-C-"

In his mind there were two *c*'s, but suddenly, at the very last moment, one of them floated away like a balloon into the stratosphere.

"E-S-S-A-R-Y. Necessary."

"Indeed, necessary," the judge said.

He was paroled the next morning and was last seen chasing run-ons through a parking lot in New Jersey."

Failure: Nature's Path to Revision

Good teaching is about flying by the seat of your pants, knowing that your best lesson plan isn't the one in your book, but the one you think up in the shower each morning. Sadly, the world doesn't always promote this type of risk-taking. On the other hand, that's probably why it's called risk-taking. The following piece about failure was first published in *OOps: What We Learn When Teaching Fails*, edited by Brenda Miller Power and Ruth Shagoury Hubbard, published by Stenhouse of York, Maine. When we dare to failure we sometimes see the big picture which informs our teaching beyond all the curriculum goals.

One, Two, Buy Velcro Shoes: What Greg Taught Me

BARRY LANE

To all those aides who know why Ed

is so Special

His arms would stiffen like two-by-fours at his side. His face would distort into a grotesque mask as if he were being poked with hot irons. His eyes would close tight in horror, "She's comin' back!" he'd shout, patting his chest like a penitent as his whole body recoiled in terror. "It's all right, Greg," another voice inside him would reply. "She's gone, Greg." Greg was about to tie his shoe, and each time I tried to teach him he turned into a B-movie monster.

I was Greg's personal care attendant, which was another way of saying I was the guy who was supposed to follow Greg around and try to teach him something, which was another way of saying I was the interpreter of Greg's cryptic messages, which was another way of saying I was the guy who cleaned up Greg's messes.

Greg was a sixteen-year-old boy with autism being schooled at a private school for the retarded in the early 1980s, when such institutions were still politically correct in New Hampshire. They even still used the word *retarded* then, though two years later the move to *developmentally disabled* gained prominence. Labels are an institution's way of saying, Don't I know you from somewhere? and Greg was one to defy all labels; though *autism,* a term created by psychologist Leo Kanner in the 1950s to describe fourteen characteristics exhibited by schizophrenics, seemed to fit him fairly well.

He was about five feet tall with straight black hair that stuck up in several directions. He walked on his toes (one of Kanner's signs) and clucked often. Children with autism also often exhibit self-abusive behaviors, which in Greg's case involved walking along brick walls with the right side of his face pressed against the brick. He had stopped most of this activity by the time I met him, though the scabs and scars were still there. Some people with autism are savants like Dustin Hoffman's character in the movie *Rain Man,* but Greg's afflictions involved various types of other brain damage, which

233

meant he had little of what we might call normal speech. He did a lot of parroting. ("Go in the house, Greg?" I'd say. Greg's reply, "Go in the house.") In his file the label *severe and profound* was used to describe Greg's problem. This seemed to me the most apt and fitting description of·Greg I had seen. One look in his eyes and you saw the severity of his pain, and· the more I got to know Greg the more I became aware of just how profound a human being he was.

Greg will learn to tie his shoe with minimal assistance. This was the sentence that tormented my life. It was written in Greg's IEP, which stands for Independent Educational Plan, but because of that line I started referring to it as Greg's ITP or Independent Torture Plan. Goals like *Greg will undo the twist tie on a loaf of bread* or *Greg will make himself chocolate milk and drink it* were easy. Even goals like *Greg will learn to shave his face without losing the eyebrows* were not too difficult to master. But this tying-the-shoes thing got the worst of him every time we tried it.

First let me explain that the way they tied shoes at this school was different from the way you or I learned to tie shoes. I remember learning from Gary Fagan, an older boy in the neighborhood, when I was four. I remember how proud I was when I showed my mother. It was the "through the loop" stage that made the breakthrough for me. I can still remember how it felt when I pushed the loop through and almost magically the laces formed a bow. I remember quickly undoing it to see if it was luck or if I could repeat my success, and when I did it again and again I could feel a swelling sense of pride. Contrary to my own popular belief, I was educable, knowledge would stick to me, and I could demonstrate this for years by tying my shoe.

To teach Greg this daring feat, I was asked to break it down into several stages. These stages are, of course, etched in my memory like the Doublemint Gum jingles of my childhood:

Left hand: cross drop.
Right hand: cross drop.
Left hand
under the triangle.
Take both ends and
pull tight.
(repeat)
Take both ends and
pull
but leave a little hole.
Left through the hole
going away from you.
Right through the hole
going toward you.
Pinch both loops and
Pull tight.

Most days we couldn't get past the first two stages without Greg having a major tantrum. One day he ripped a shower curtain right off the rod in a Brando-like moment of utter contempt and outrage. It was after that hair-raising experience that I decided tying the shoe might not be quite as important as understanding what was happening inside Greg when he tried.

I began studying more about autism and I learned some startling facts. Because children with autism are left-brain deficient, they have great difficulty conceptualizing time with words. Most of us know today is today and tomorrow is tomorrow. We think, It's 8:00 A.M. now, I will finish breakfast and go to the store to buy milk at 8:30. Many people with autism can't have that thought because it requires an abstract concept of time. In other words, the only way a kid like Greg can structure time is in the present with in-grained routines and rituals that give him the same sense of order that we construct in thought. I remember reading a story in which a mother of a seven-year-old boy with autism described a major tantrum her son had on the way to school. She thought the routine was no different from any other day until she remembered she had passed a car that day. When you depend on external routines for mental clarity, just about any inevitable variation becomes an Orwellian assault on your thoughts.

That's when I started thinking seriously about the deeper implications of being Greg. If you had no way of creating time in your head, there was nothing to say that the past was past. The expression "Time is the great healer of all wounds" would not be true, because everything that had ever happened to you would continually happen to you in each moment of your waking life. There would be no past to escape, no future to hide in. If all humanity were like Greg, we would live the eternal return. We wouldn't have the luxury of saying, World War II happened before we were born; it would be happening right now, and we would be powerless to stop the painful thoughts unless we could be distracted by the present long enough to engage in some activity like stirring Hershey's syrup into a glass of milk. The pain trapped in Greg's gentle face suddenly began to make sense.

I began to pay closer attention to Greg's words when he had his tantrums. "She's comin' back," he'd say, his face contorted in excruciating pain. I asked Greg, "Who is she?" and Greg would reply, "Who's she?" his face still twisted with pain. The other most consistent voice was one that said, "It's all right, Greg, calm down." This was not a consoling voice but more a self-annihilating one. "Who's saying that?" I asked. "Who's saying that?" Greg parroted again. I realized this was getting us nowhere when Greg started saying my questions as part of his repertoire. I was just adding another disembodied voice to the confusion.

Then I began to investigate Greg's past. The social worker had told me a little about Greg's family. They were Portuguese, a big Catholic family. They loved each other but expressed it by shouting insults and hitting and calling up guilt. They had refused most respite care and Greg's younger brothers took care of him to fill in for his older brother who had recently left home to join the service. They had little money but were not poor in spirit, Just in passing she told me that Greg's maternal grandmother had taken him alone for summers when he was a young child. She had taught him to speak but died suddenly when he was five.

A month later I interviewed Greg's mother about his grandmother. I had gotten to know her well through the summer program I designed for Greg at his house. In her words, "Greg wouldn't speak for anyone but his Nana." His Nana took him for the summer when he was three and taught him to play peekaboo. She nurtured him and loved him so hard, he would pine away when she brought him back home in August to his big confusing family. Nana's sudden death of a stroke at fifty years old was a shock to everybody. On the way to the funeral Greg's mother and dad had stopped at Nana's house to get something. Greg was with them and bolted out of the car and into the house in front of them. He started looking for Nana in closets, in drawers, under beds. He kept shouting, "Peekaboo Nana, Nana Peekaboo." Greg's mother was greatly distressed and kept telling her husband, "That kid. That kid. Do something about that kid." Her husband finally grabbed young Greg by the shoulders, sat him down on Nana's bed, and in a stern voice said, "SHE'S GONE, GREG! ALL GONE! NO MORE! SHE'S NEVER COMING BACK!" Greg's mother described her son's reaction, "His head tipped over, his eyes closed, and he didn't speak again for eight years."

After hearing that story it was clear where Greg's tantrums came from. With no concept of time how could five-year-old Greg process grief? You or I would be able to reflect on a painful memory as something buried years in the past. For Greg, ten years ago was today waiting to happen over and over. A trigger as simple as tying a shoe would propel that moment into the present. Since Greg was four or five when he lived with his Nana, I could only speculate that, like me, that was the year he was learning to tie his shoes.

The next time Greg went to tie his shoe I put my theory to work. "Cross drop," I said, initiating the painful process. Greg's arms turned to timber and his head recoiled in that twisted mask of sadness. "She's comin back," he muttered as his eyes squeezed shut. "Greg," I said, "she loves you." I will always remember the moment that followed. Greg's entire body seemed to deflate as though an icy wind had stopped blowing and a warm sun was now shining over him. "She loves you," I said again. And this time his eyes opened wider than I'd ever seen and he turned to me, and with the wonder of a small child said, "She loves you, Greg."

No, Greg never learned to tie his shoe, and it was about a month later that I gave up and bought a pair of gray running shoes with Velcro fasteners with my own money. I confess I did not follow Greg's IEP with the same zeal after that day. Greg taught me that the forest was not the sum of the trees but something larger and far more magnificent than I ever imagined possible. My IEP has not been the same since.

Table of Appendices

The following appendices help supplement the material found in the main body of the Toolbox.

I   —   Lesson Review

II   —   Leads

III   —   Snapshots

IV   —   State Departments of Education

V   —   Some Great Resources

VI   —   Great Rubric

VII   —   Spanish Translation of Key Pages

VIII   —   Best Books

I

Lesson Review

The following reviews some central revision mini-lessons which I teach at my seminars. If you want more background, I suggest you read the first five chapters of *After THE END*, or come to a seminar.

1) Share what you write with your students' next class (especially if this is not your habit). Remember you can't teach pottery without getting hands messy. Make it a habit to write and share with them. Model insecurity.

2) Teach the binoculars first.

   a) Think of three details about your room
   b) Write them down with space between
   c) In groups of three turn the knob on each others binoculars
   Note: another way to model the binoculars with young students who don't know what questions are but know how to ask them is. "I have a dragon. What do you want to know about my dragon."

3) Build on the above with one of my favorite comedy writing exercises.
   a) Write a sentence like; He/she had strange taste in clothes.
   b) In groups of three or four kids brainstorm details
   c) Taking each detail one at a time kids turn the knob on it by asking more and more questions. Note: Remember to model that "Is or Are or Did" questions don't work as well as What or Where or When or Who or How questions.

4) Teach Snapshots and Thoughtshots

   a) Begin by reading some or create a blurry one like I did with you, then ask them to turn the knob on your binoculars.
   b) Tell students that next time they are stuck and write a sentence like, "My dad is driving the car," they can do for themselves what they did for you. ASK QUESTIONS to turn the knob.
   c) Now take your magic camera and take a snapshot of someone in our family. The first question to answer is where are they?
   d) When you get stuck, as all writers do all the time. Take out your binoculars and do for yourself what your partners did for you.
   e) Your can also draw a picture of your snapshot.
   f) Now write a thoughshot either in the mind of the person or a thought you have about them or that moment. Notice the difference.

5) Teach Exploding Moments Next

   a) Model by reading and talking about slow motion in films. When does a filmmaker decide to use slow motion? Act it out. Why not make the whole film in slow motion.

   b) Now that we know about snapshots, thoughtshots and the binoculars we have some great tools for exploding moments.

   c) Here is the prompt. If you were making a film of your like. Where would you use slow motion? Fill a whole page with one moment that only lasted a few seconds of minutes. Don't introduce it. Just jump right in. When you get stuck, as all writers do, try this. If you have written snapshots for your last two sentences try writing a thoughtshot. If you have written thoughtshots try writing a snapshot. Use your binoculars. How do you turn the knob? ASK QUESTIONS!

6) Teach Growing Leads from Potatoes

   Tell a story and ask for questions. Write them down but don't answer them until you have a board full. Show them how each question digs a new potato. Make a story circle as a whole class or in small groups. Turn questions into leads.
   Remember some other ways of celebrating and teaching leads. Lead boards. Lead writing contests. Revising leads from published books. Encourage students to do what many writers do. Write many leads and choose the one that makes you want to write the most.

7) Encourage students to use concepts of craft on their own to make revision and writing more fun. Example: Is there a place to add a snapshot or thoughtshot in your story? Is there a place to explode a moment? If there is, put an arrow there and get a blank piece of paper. Insert it into your draft. If you don't have a computer, revise like you have one.

II

Some Leads

Leads from Middle School

When you have a lead writing contest at Halloween you are in for trouble. Though the following leads may not be considered great literature, the students had a great time writing them. And when your students enjoy writing leads, I can assure you they will write more of them.

All of a sudden there was a unidentified flying object hovering over the hay field..

As I saw the blood drip under the door, I knew something was wrong.

My elbow hurt, but the pain of losing was even worse.

As a classroom full of hungry kindergartners sat in a circle munching on their snacks, suddenly, they heard a loud noise that shook the building beneath them.

She hopped across the mossy rocks, carefully avoiding the rushing current of the waterfall. In mid step, she felt her foot begin to slip. Screaming, she helplessly plunged into the roaring water. 20 years later, a young girl sat on a mossy rock gazing at the waterfall.

The foamy white jaws and white teeth as sharp as knives of a dangerous dog nipping at my heels with a ravenous force sent adrenaline to my brain to run faster as the rabid crazed dog continued to chase me down the street.

I saw the two eyes staring back at me, and took another step.

As we wandered along the deserted beach, the moonlit disc was full in the sky and shone a path across the slowly rolling waves. We both smiled at the perfect moment. The tiny grains of sand were tickling our feet as he ran his callused fingers through my silky, straight, long hair that sheered under the glistening stars.

I stared into the unforgiving darkness and once again saw the hooded men on horses. They were riding after me. I began to run, but toppled over the chair that was in my way, and I knew it was over.

Out of the dark blue sky came a silver shining metal block, a plane. It spun in 360's and made the trees ruffle as its nose came diving down towards the earth. The pilot knew his only way out was ejection, but all he could see was grass.

I was driving down the road one afternoon when I saw the bird flying at me, and the first thing that went through my mind was, how good was his aim.

I saw a dark green light flash. Then suddenly it was black and ebony again. He felt a three fingered hand touch his shoulder. He wondered "where am I".

As I stumbled through the thick jungle brush, I aimed my AK-47 at the commander's head. A million thoughts ran through my mind, as I waited for the "go" signal.

As I ran through the dimly lit hallway, I could hear the roar behind me. They got louder and louder and ever louder! Then all of a sudden, it went black.

On that freezing cold night, I felt my hands and chin go into uncontrollable vibrations as my eyelids settled over my eyes for what I had expected to be the last dream I would ever dream.

As I walk down the dark hall, I see two glowing eyes. My thought was that I should scream but my parents will get mad and start to yell at me. They probably would have said that I was crazy.

Suddenly, as he leaned against the wall, it gave way and the man stumbled into a room of terror.

"As the old man approached they began to smell the terrible stench that haunted them for weeks.

He walked into the dark room and saw two bright eyes just staring at him.

The big scary dog was coming toward me and he wasn't stopping.

The lights went dark and I felt a clammy hand on my shoulder. I closed my eyes hoping I was dreaming when the hands wrapped around my throat. I stood stiff and I couldn't breath.

The stranger walked by with a smirk on his face and hiding something in his pocket.

She fell to the ground. Her heart was racing. She look around. No one in sight except for the shadows surrounding her.

In a flash, Mark got a glimpse of the killer. Himself! But not, Mark had a schizophrenic twin brother.

Leads from Literature

When Mrs. Fredrick C. Little's second son arrived, everybody noticed that he was not much bigger than a mouse.

Stuart Little E.B.White

Robin drew the coverlet close around his head and turned his face to the wall.

The Door in the Wall Marguerite De Angeli

Now, I don't like school, which you might say is one of the factors that got us involved with this old guy we nicknamed the Pigman.

The Pigman Paul Zindel

I am keeping this journal because I believe myself to be in some danger and because I have no other way of recording my fears.

The Ocean, John Cheever

The first week of August hangs at the very top of the summer, the top of the live-long year, like the highest seat of a Ferris wheel when it pauses at its turning.

Tuck Everlasting Natalie Babbitt

I am a white man and never forgot it, but I was brought up by the Cheyenne Indians from the age of ten.

Little Big Man, Thomas Berger

Nobody was really surprised when it happened, not really, not at the subconscious level where savage things grow.

Carrie, Stephen King

I am living at the Villa Borghese. There is not a crumb of dirt anywhere, nor a chair misplaced. We are alone here and we are dead.

Tropic of Cancer, Henry Miller

We've got a ranch house.

The Beans of Egypt Maine, Carolyn Chute

You don't know about me without you have read a book by the name of *The Adventures of Tom Sawyer*; but that ain't no matter.

The Adventures of Hucklebury Finn, Mark Twain

Samuel Spade's jaw was long and bony, his chin a jutting V under the more flexible v of his mouth.

The Maltese Falcon, Dashiell Hammett

The jury said "Guilty" and the judge said "Life" but he didn't hear them.

The Mansion, William Faulkner

When we moved into our locker the third day of seventh grade, about the first thing Louise did was to stick this gross mirror onto the back wall.

The Fastest Friend in the West, Vicki Grove

What my father said was, "You pays your dime, you takes your choice," which, if you don't understand it, boils down to him saying one thing to me: Get out.

LIES, Ethan Canin

Ma lasted a year after Pa was gone. That's how I came to live with Granpa and Granma when I was five years old.

The Education of Little Tree, Forrest Carter

As the homing pigeon flew over the houses, thirty-four-year-old Daniel Bernoulli stopped to watch. How wonderful it must be to fly, he thought, and how swiftly a bird was able to go from here to there; his own trip from Russia had taken an entire two months. traveling by horse drawn coach.

Five Equations That Changed the World, Michael Guillen

Now that you have cleared your mind, you are ready to embark upon the path and taste of the tree of knowledge—but first you must learn to discriminate so you are not embarking up the wrong tree.

Driving Your Own Karma, Swami Beyondananda a.k.a. Steve Bhaerman

What is a Woman?

Woman as Other, Simone de Beauvoir

In spite of over two thousand years of contact, Westerners and Arabs still do not understand each other.

Proxemics in the Arab World, Edward T. Hall

Kennedy Space Center: June 18, 1983. The astronaut van stopped in front of the launchpad and Dr. Sally Ride, mission specialist, and the four other members of the crew peeked out the window.

Sally Ride Shooting for the Stars, Jane Hurwitz and Sue Hurwitz

Dark and Stormy Night Contest Winners

The countdown had stalled at T minus 69 seconds when Desiree, the first female ape to go up in space, winked at me slyly and pouted her thick, rubbery lips unmistakably--the first of many such advances during what would prove to be the longest, and most memorable, space voyage of my career.

--Martha Simpson, Glastonbury, Connecticut (1985 Winner)

The bone-chilling scream split the warm summer night in two, the first half being before the scream when it was fairly balmy and calm and pleasant for those who hadn't heard the scream at all, but not calm or balmy or even very nice for those who did hear the scream, discounting the little period of time during the actual scream itself when your ears might have been hearing it but your brain wasn't reacting yet to let you know.

--Patricia E. Presutti, Lewiston, New York (1986 Winner)

The notes blatted skyward as the sun rose over the Canada geese, feathered rumps mooning the day, webbed appendages frantically peddling unseen bicycles in their search for sustenance, driven by Nature's maxim, "Ya wanna eat, ya gotta work," and at last I knew Pittsburgh.

--Sheila B. Richter, Minneapolis, Minnesota (1987 Winner)

Like an expensive sports car, fine-tuned and well-built, Portia was sleek, shapely, and gorgeous, her red jumpsuit molding her body, which was as warm as the seatcovers in July, her hair as dark as new tires,her eyes flashing like bright hubcaps, and her lips as dewy as the beads of fresh rain on the hood; she was a woman driven--fueled by a single accelerant--and she needed a man, a man who wouldn't shift from his views,
a man to steer her along the right road, a man like Alf Romeo.

--Rachel E. Sheeley, Williamsburg, Indiana (1988 Winner)

To Enter the Bulwer-Lytton Fiction Contest

The rules to the Bulwer-Lytton Fiction Contest are childishly simple:

Sentences may be of any length (though you venture beyond 50 or 60 words at your peril), and entrants may submit more than one, but all entries must be "original" and previously unpublished.

Gastropoda mail entries should be submitted on index cards, the sentence on one side and the entrant's name, address, and phone number on the other. (For electronic submissions, see below.)

Entries will be judged by categories, from "general" to detective, western, science fiction, romance, and so on. There will be overall winners as well as category winners.

The official BLFC deadline is April 15 (a date Americans associate with painful submissions and making up bad stories). In truth, though, we will judge anything submitted by the middle of June (or perhaps even by the 1st of July).

Send your entries to:
Bulwer-Lytton Fiction Contest
Department of English
San Jose State University
San Jose, CA 95192-0090

The camel died quite suddenly on the second day, and Selena fretted sulkily and, buffing her already impeccable nails--not for the first time since the journey began--pondered snidely if this would dissolve into a vignette of minor inconveniences like all the other holidays spent with Basil.
   --Gail Cain, San Francisco, California (1983 Winner)

The lovely woman-child Kaa was mercilessly chained to the cruel post of the warrior-chief Beast, with his barbarous tribe now stacking wood at her nubile feet, when the strong, clear voice of the poetic and heroic Handsomas roared, "Flick your Bic, crisp that chick, and you'll feel my steel through your last meal."
   --Steven Garman, Pensacola, Florida (1984 Winner)

III

Snapshots

Julie Sherman's fifth graders zoom in on their subjects in these short snapshots. Once you know what a snapshot is, you can add it to your writing.

Her soft hands touched the silver spoon as it pushed its way through the cookie dough. She wiped her hands delicately on the beige apron, then she looked outside the quiet falling white snow as she took a sip of hot chocolate out of her purple cow mug. The smell of chocolate chip cookies filled the room. Her face had a tired relaxed expression. The only sound was the wood crackling on the fire and the golden dog snoring on the maroon rug.

Sarah

As the two men come into the pit, the referee yells "PIT". The two chickens fly together. Feathers fly as the hatch leaves the gray staggering sideways and down from the shock of being rattled to death. Blood flies everywhere. The matching hatch crows and stands there proud of his accomplishment. He walks over to the gray to finish him off. The gray lays there feeble and weak as blood flows from his beak.

Edward

My eyes big and bulging, my hands tightly gripping the hard cold damp bar as the roller coaster goes so fast on that 50 foot drop. And my mouth opens wide, so wide that I have to scream. I could probably even swallow a whole elephant. My stomach feels as though it has exploded inside of me. I am being jerked, swayed and pulled side to side, up and down. The damp iron smell makes me feel sick and with all the screaming my head is so dizzy I feel like fainting.

Tammy

Me and my four friends are standing behind 4 desks attached together enjoying our cheese pizza covered with tomato sauce. I am drinking my Dr. Pepper from a white styrofoam cup. My silver plated necklace is glimmering from the light above. Other kids are sitting at their wood and metal desks enjoying their different varieties of pizza. The smell of pizza makes me even more hungry.

Gary

The girl sits on the rough leather seat of the boat. As she leans her head over the side of the boat, cool crisp water sprays her face. As the boat slows down she can see all around her. The sky is beautiful, dark magenta. Bright orange and dark pink colors the sky. From across the water, comes a family of ducks swimming toward the boat. The father duck has a beautiful green neck and blue wings. The mother duck is brown and the baby ducklings are bright yellow. From one area of the small mossy island a crane is washing his white feathers. Not far away another brown duck is building a nest in the moss. Little minnows are swimming about very quickly through the water. The smells of the animals and grassland is fresh in my nose and you can hear the ducks quacking softly.

Carla

As the man sweeps the floor vigorously he looks in great amazement at the three thousand stag heads and skulls of old times ago. The man feels as if he is surrounded by wicked prison wire just taunting him to try and break out. The man looks ahead to see a massive mounted stag head. It has ten wickedly sharp antlers on its head and regretful eyes of cold marble, but still he keeps on sweeping.

Tristan

Bedtime

Read the following persuasive essay by a 4th grader. Can you find a place where you think an extra snapshot will make the piece stronger.

I know kids should pick their own bedtimes. WHY? Because I am a kid. We know how much sleep we need. We know how much time it will take to get our homework done. Besides that it is not fair because your parents get to watch T.V. T.V is sometimes learning. And if you are not tired you just lay in bed and do nothing when you could be reading. And if you have a younger sister or brother they should go to bed earlier than you should. I know kids should pick there own bedtimes. By the age of 8 we are old enough to make all our own decisions.

Listen for Snapshots

David, a college freshmen, wrote this 1st draft about an ill-fated trip to the supermarket. After you read this essay to your class ask them to pretend they are having a conference with the author. What parts did you like best? What did you want moré of? What did you want less of? Practice using some of the conference forms in Part 3.

The Gypsies

I was not well-behaved as a child; most people who knew me thought me to be a holy terror. I was the kid on the block who discovered that if you organized your friends into groups (i.e. assign some kids to throw rocks and cause havoc, while others watched for adults), you could accomplish much greater destruction than if you simply ran around like a bunch of fools. All this was due to my reading Sergeant rock comic books at an early age. In second grade, my father went in for an "emergency conference" with my teacher, meaning I was being a royal pain and not behaving myself on the playground like all the other little boys and girls did. He was gone for about four hours, and when he returned, I was yelled at for about the same length of time. On such instances my parents would threaten: "If you don't straighten up your act, we are going to sell you to the gypsies!" This threat usually worked, at least for two or three days, and after it wore off, I was back to being a brat once again.

One Friday, my mother caught me trying to lasso the chickens. We had about twenty or so in our barn, and that night when my father got home, I was yelled at for an hour and once again they used the gypsy threat. I was beginning to feel that there was no truth to this threat since I still got away with most of the normal tricks, yet there seemed to be something different about this lecture that separated it from all the others; there was no grounding or removal of television privileges, they just walked away after they finished their speech. I sat there wordless, not knowing what to think.

The next day was Saturday and I awoke promptly at 7:30, got dressed and ran downstairs so I could watch Scooby Doo, but just as my hand reached out to the television, my mother yelled, "No T.V., you're going grocery shopping with me."

God has created no greater torture for an eight year old that can possibly compare with grocery shopping on a Saturday morning. We had to get in the car and drive fifteen miles to a supermarket because "It gave the best coupons," and fifteen miles is a long distance when you're missing your favorite cartoon. All the way to the market, I hoped the car would get a flat tire or develop engine trouble, so we would have to go home, groceryless.

We arrived at the supermarket and parked the car far from the entrance; usually no spaces are within a sensible distance to the doors, so you have to carry the groceries half a mile to the car.

When we got inside the supermarket, I would stand and read magazines because my mother wouldn't let me push the cart since I would race it up and down the aisles. I was in luck, the store had the new issue of *Mad* magazine; I would be occupied the entire time my mother was in the store. I read through the entire magazine and I saw no sign of my mother. Curious, I decided to walk through the store to look for her. I walked past every aisle twice—still no sign of her. Panic hit me; then I realized, what if she did really sell me to the gypsies.

I saw the picture clear in my mind. My dad was paid off last night by the leader of the caravan, and my mother would leave me alone in the store for the gypsies to pick up. At least she could have said good-bye.

Panicking, I looked for possible abductors. Then I saw her, the queen of the gypsy pack. She stood looking through the spaghetti. Gypsies always eat Italian food, I remembered. She had long, black hair that was twisted into a pigtail, which ran straight down her back. On her ears were two long silver earrings with pearls on the ends. Her coat was old and tattered; stains were covering random portions of it. The large maroon pants she wore were partially tucked into her boots, which were both covered in a heavy layer of mud. Her husband was walking down the aisle towards her.

He had a small pencil mustache that stood out on his chubby face. He was a stout little man, dressed in work clothes that were decorated with splotches of paint. In a thickly accented voice, he told his wife to hurry up. So the gypsies must be working nearby, I thought. My mouth fell open at the sight of the two of them. Where did they park their wagon, I wondered; I didn't see it in the parking lot.

I turned and ran through the entire store. My mother wasn't leaving me with any gypsies! Then I saw her trying to escape down aisle twelve. The distance to her seemed like an eternity; I ran and ran and finally caught her before she made it to the processed foods.

"Why did you leave me for the gypsies? I'll be good, you'll see. Please buy me back," I protested.

"What are you talking about? Quite being silly," she said. "I've been looking all over the store for you. I told you never to wander off while I'm shopping. Come on, I'm ready to leave."

After passing through the checkout, we loaded the groceries into the car. This is too easy, I thought. I made sure to fasten my seatbelt so no gypsy could rip me out of the car when we stopped at the stoplights on the way home.

For the rest of the weekend I felt ill at ease at home. I feared that in the middle of the night, my parents would bundle me up in my sheets and put me on the curb for a roving band to pick up. Then I probably wouldn't even realize what happened until I woke up in a gypsy caravan with some hairy gypsy lady trying to shove mush down my throat.

I decided to be on my best behavior for the rest of the month. My parents couldn't sell me if I was well-behaved, I thought. This thought backfired, because my mother thought I was sick and made me stay in the house as soon as I got home from school. There is just no way **to come out on top, some weeks.**

IV

Your State Department of Education Needs you!!!

It's time to write your state department and report to them on the status of their latest state test. Include specific examples of student work to make your case. If you get an intriguing or inspiring response, please send them with your address to Discover Writing Company PO Box 264 Shoreham, VT 05770 Your work may be published in a later edition of The Reviser's Toolbox and provide inspiration on how individual teachers can create meaningful change.

ALABAMA
Dr. Edward R. Richardson
Superintendent of Education
Alabama Dept of Education
Gordon Persons Office Building
50 North Ripley Street
P.O. Box 302102
Montgomery, AL 36130-2101

ALASKA
Dr. Shirley J. Holloway
Commissioner of Education
Alaska Dept of Education
801 West 10th Street, Suite 200
Juneau, AK 99801-1894

ARKANSAS
Mr. Raymond J. Simon
Director
General Eduation Division
Arkansas Dept of Education
Four State Capitol Mall, Room 304A
Little Rock, AR 72201-1071

CALIFORNIA
Ms. Delaine A. Eastin
Superintendent of Public Instruction
California Dept of Education
721 Capitol Mall
Sacramento, CA 95814

COLORADO
Dr. William J. Moloney
Commissioner of Education
Colorado Dept of Education
201 East Colfax Avenue
Denver, CO 80203-1799

CONNECTICUT
Dr. Theodore S. Sergi
Commissioner of Education
Connecticut Dept of Education
165 Capitol Avenue
Room 305 State Office Building
Hartford, CT 06106-1630

DELAWARE
Dr. Iris T. Metts
Secretary of Education
Delaware Dept of Education
Townsend Building
401 Federal Street, Suite 2
Dover, DE 19903-1402

FLORIDA
Mr. Frank T. Brogan
Commissioner of Education
Florida Dept of Education
Capitol Building, Room PLOB
Tallahassee, FL 32301

IDAHO
Dr. Anne C. Fox
Superintendent of Public Instruction
Idaho Dept of Education
Len B. Jordan Office Building
650 West State Street
P.O. Box 83720
Boise, ID 83720

ILLINOIS
Dr. Joseph A. Spagnolo, Jr.
Superintendent of Education
Illinois Board of Education
100 North First Street
Springfield, IL 62777

INDIANA
Dr. Suellen K. Reed
Superintendent of Public Instruction
Indiana Dept of Education
State House, Room 229
200 W. Washington Street
Indianapolis, IN 46204-2798

IOWA
Mr. Ted Stilwill
Director of Education
Iowa Dept of Education
Grimes State Office Building
East 14th & Grand Streets
Des Moines, IA 50319-0146

KANSAS
Dr. John A. Tompkins
Commissioner of Education
Kansas Dept of Education
120 South East Tenth Avenue
Topeka, KS 66612-1182

KENTUCKY
Dr. Wilmer S. Cody
Commissioner of Education
Kentucky Dept of Education
Capitol Plaza Tower
500 Mero Street
Frankfort, KY 40601

LOUISIANA
Mr. Cecil J. Picard
Superintendent of Education
Louisiana Dept of Education
626 North 4th Street 12th floor
Baton Rouge, LA 70804-9064

MAINE
Mr. J. Duke Albanese
Commissioner of Education
Maine Dept of Education
23 State House Station
Augusta, ME 04333-0023

MARYLAND
Dr. Nancy S. Grasmick
Superintendent of Schools
Maryland Dept of Education
200 West Baltimore Street
Baltimore, MD 21201

MASSACHUSETTS
Mr. Frank Haydu
Interim Commissioner of Education
Massachusetts Dept of Education
350 Main Street

Malden, MA 02148-5023

MICHIGAN
Mr. Arthur E. Ellis
Superintendent of Public Instruction
Michigan Dept of Education
608 West Allegan Street 4th Floor
Lansing, MI 48933

MINNESOTA
Mr. Robert J. Wedl
Commissioner
Minnesota Dept of Children Families and
Learning
726 Capitol Square Building
550 Cedar Street
St. Paul, MN 55101

MISSISSIPPI
Dr. Richard A. Boyd
Interim Superintendent of Education
State Dept of Education
Central High School Building
P.O. Box 771
359 North West Street
Jackson, MS 39201

MISSOURI
Dr. Robert E. Bartman
Commissioner of Education
Missouri Dept of Elementary
& Secondary Education
205 Jefferson Street, 6th Floor
Jefferson City, MO 65102

MONTANA
Ms. Nancy Keenan
Superintendent of Public Instruction
Montana Office of Public Instruction
1227 11th Avenue
Helena, MT 59620-2501

NEBRASKA
Dr. Douglas D. Christensen
Commissioner of Education
Nebraska Dept of Education
301 Centennial Mall, South, 6th Floor
P.O. Box 94987
Lincoln, NE 68509-4987

NEVADA
Mrs. Mary L. Peterson
Superintendent of Public Instruction
Nevada Dept of Education
700 East 5th Street
Carson City, NV 89701-5096

NEW HAMPSHIRE
Dr. Elizabeth M. Twamey
Commissioner of Education
New Hampshire Dept of Education
101 Pleasant Street
State Office Park South
Concord, NH 03301

NEW JERSEY
Dr. Leo F. Klagholz
Commissioner of Education
New Jersey Dept of Education
P.O. Box 500
Trenton, NH 08625-0500

NEW MEXICO
Mr. Michael J. Davis
Superintendent of Public Instruction
New Mexico Dept of Education
Education Building
300 Don Gaspar
Santa Fe, NM 87501-2786

NEW YORK
Mr. Richard P. Mills
Commissioner of Education
New York Education Dept
111 Education Building
89 Washington Avenue
Albany, NY 12234

NORTH CAROLINA
Dr. Michael E. Ward
Superintendent of Public Instruction
North Carolina Dept of Public Instruction
Education Building
301 North Wilmington Street
Raleigh, NC 27601-2825

NORTH DAKOTA
Dr. Wayne G. Sanstead
Superintendent of Public Instruction
North Dakota Dept of Public Instruction
State Capitol Building, 11th floor
600 Boulevard Avenue, East
Bismarck, ND 58505-0440

OHIO
Dr. John M. Goff
Superintendent of Public Instruction
Ohio Dept of Education
65 South Front Street, Room 810
Columbus, OH 43215-4183

OKLAHOMA
Ms. Sandy Garrett
Superintendent of Public Instruction
Oklahoma State Dept of Education
Hodge Education Building
2500 North Lincoln Boulevard
Oklahoma City, OK 73105-4599

OREGON
Mrs. Norma Paulus
Superintendent of Public Instruction
Oregon Dept of Education
255 Capitol Street, NE
Salem, OR 97310-0203

PENNSYLVANIA
Dr. Eugene W. Hichok, Jr.
Secretary of Education
Pennsylvania Dept of Education
333 Market Street, 10th Floor
Harrisburg, PA 17126-0333

RHODE ISLAND
Mr. Peter McWalters
Commissioner of Education
Rhode Island Dept of Elementary
 & Secondary Education
Shepard Building
255 Westminister Street
Providence, RI 02903

SOUTH CAROLINA
Dr. Barbara S. Nielsen
State Superintendent of Education
South Carolina Dept of Education
1006 Rutledge Building
1429 Senate Street
Columbia, SC 29201

SOUTH DAKOTA
Ms. Karon L. Schaack
Secretary of Education
South Dakota Dept of Education
 & Cultural Affairs
700 Governors Drive
Pierre, SD 57501-2291

TENNESSEE
Dr. Jane Walters
Commissioner of Education
Tennessee Dept of Education
Sixth Floor, Gateway Plaza
710 James Robertson Parkway
Nashville, TN 37243-0375

TEXAS

Dr. Michael A. Moses
Commissioner of Education
Texas Education Agency
William B. Travis Building
1701 North Congress Avenue
Austin, TX 78701-1494

UTAH

Dr. Scott W. Bean
Superintendent of Public Instruction
Utah State Office of Education
250 East 500 South
Salt Lake City, UT 84111

VERMONT

Dr. Marc E. Hull
Commissioner of Education
Vermont Dept of Education
120 State Street
Montpelier, VT 05620-2501

VIRGINIA

Mr. Paul D. Stapleton
Superintendent of Public Instruction
Virginia Dept of Education
P.O. Box 2120
Richmond, VA 23218-2120

WASHINGTON

Dr. Teresa Bergeson
Superintendent of Public Instruction
Washington Dept of Public Instruction
Old Capitol Building, Washington & Legion
P.O. Box 47200
Olympia, WA 98504-7200

WEST VIRGINIA

Dr. Henry R. Marockie
State Superintendent of Schools
West Virginia Dept of Education
1900 Kanawha Boulevard, East
Building 6, Room B-358
Charleston, WV 25305

WISCONSIN

Mr. John T. Benson
Superintendent of Public Instruction
Wisconsin Dept of Public Instruction
125 South Webster Street
P.O. Box 7841
Madison, WI 53702

WYOMING

Ms. Judy Catchpole
State Superintendent of Public Instruction
Wyoming Dept of Education

V

Great Resources

Here is a short list of resources for your school and classroom.

Potato Hill Poetry 888-5-POETRY

A first rate, award winning newsletter and fabulous workshops by Andrew Green which leave you wanting to write poetry till the cows come home.
361 Watertown st. Newton, MA 02158

The Write Traits 1-800-825-1739

Vicki Spandel is a woman with a mean rubric (see the next appendix). She will make you love to assess writing (no small feat). Using a wealth of student examples and a ton of published literature, Vicki will show you how assessment can drive instruction in a positive direction.

Teachers and Writers Collaborative

(5 union square west/ New York NY 10003)
These people publish the most intelligent, yet practical books on the teaching of writing, especially poetry. Their books are all written by writers who work in the schools. Get their catalogue. You won't be sorry.

Adbusters Magazine 1-800-663 1243

If you liked subvertising in chapter 5 you will like this magazine. Your students can submit satirical ads to their regular contests.

Discover Writing Company 1-800-613-8055

Inservice workshops and residencies on writing and laughing across the curriculum, Revision and Portfolio Assessment. Come visit our all new website for a lesson plan and to get more information:

www.discoverwriting.com

VI

Good Rubric

Heard any good rubrics lately? Here's the best one I know. Designed by teacher/author, Vicki Spandel it actually wants to be read. Your students will pick up on the clear, homespun language. The assessment guide itself models good writing--a rarity in my travels.

You can find the two sided version on pages 177 and 178. The following sheets are written in the first person and are designed to give students a personal connection with the criteria. Use them with your class and watch their ability to assess their writing grow.

For more information call *The Write Traits* at 1-800-825-1739. Ask for Annie or Tiffany.

Idea Development

- *Knowing what I want to say*
- *Focusing on the main point*
- *Adding important details*
- *Getting rid of "filler"*
- *Identifying the purpose*

5 **My paper is clear, focused, and full of important details. I know my purpose (why I'm writing).**
- You can tell I know a lot about this topic. I thought about it before writing.
- I can sum this paper up in one clear sentence: _____ .
- I chose details that were interesting or would give a reader new information; I left out information or facts everyone already knows ("filler").
- Once you start reading, you will not want to stop.
- You can picture what I'm talking about. I *show* things happening in my writing; I don't just *tell* you about them.
- The purpose of this paper is _____ (to tell a story, give an opinion, explain something, etc.).

3 **It's a good beginning. You can get the general idea of what I'm trying to say. I need more details, though.**
- If I knew more about this topic, I could make it more interesting.
- Some of my "details" are really filler—things most readers probably know.
- More examples would help make my writing believable and informative.
- My topic feels *too* big. No wonder I don't have room for details.
- I give readers the big picture. But if they want to know more, they'll have to "fill in the blanks."
- What's the *one main thing* I'm trying to say? I don't think it really stands out yet.
- I'm *pretty* sure my purpose is to _____ (tell a story, give an opinion, explain something, etc.).

1 **I'm just figuring out what I want to say.**
- Help! I need a LOT more information before I'm ready to write!
- I'm still thinking on paper. It just rambles on without saying much.
- I need details, details, *details!* Plus I need to get rid of the junk—the stuff I wrote just to fill space.
- A person reading this couldn't really picture anything yet. It's still out of focus.
- Could I sum this up in one sentence? Are you kidding? *I'm* not even sure yet what my main point is.
- Is this a story? A how-to paper? My opinion? Who knows? I'm not sure *what* my purpose is.

Adapted from *Creating Writers*, Spandel and Stiggins, New York: Longman, 1997, pp. 112-116. Used with permission.

Organization

- **Putting things in order**
- **Writing a lead**
- **Writing a conclusion**
- **Linking ideas together**

5 **My paper is as clear and easy to follow as a good road map.**
- My beginning (lead) pulls readers right in.
- Every detail falls in just the right place.
- You never feel lost.
- Everything in this paper relates to my main point or main story.
- You never wonder how one idea connects to another. I made those links clear.
- My paper ends in a good spot. My ending makes you think.

3 **If you pay attention, you can follow my paper pretty well.**
- Most things are in order. I might move *some* things around, though.
- I have a lead. It might not grab you, but hey—it's *there!*
- Most details relate to my main point or story, but now and then, I wander a little.
- Now and then, you might say, "What does *this* have to do with anything?"
- I tried to link ideas together. Sometimes, I tried *so* hard that my transitions (*My first point, My second point, My final point, etc.*) got in the way. I overdid it.
- I have a conclusion. It needs work, but I have one.

1 **Hey—do you see any pattern here? I don't!**
- I'm not sure where I'm going—so it's pretty hard for me to guide a reader!
- A beginning? Actually, I just started in . . .
- I pretty much wrote things down as I thought of them. I'm not sure they're in any kind of order.
- Things are kind of jumbled together, like junk in the attic.
- Linking ideas? I haven't gotten that far yet. I'm not sure what goes with what.
- The main point? I guess that's for the reader to figure out!
- An ending? Not really. I just stopped writing when I ran out of ideas.

Adapted from *Creating Writers*, Spandel and Stiggins, New York: Longman, 1997, pp. 112-116. Used with permission.

Voice

- *Putting yourself into your writing*
- *Thinking of your audience*
- *Liking your topic—and letting it show!*
- *Matching voice to purpose*

5   **My personal fingerprints are on this piece of writing.**
- You can hear my voice in every line.
- You can tell I care about this topic.
- I know who my audience is, and I used a voice that is right for that audience.
- I also know my purpose (to tell a story, to write a business letter, to make an argument), and I used a voice right for that purpose.
- I write with confidence—because I know my topic well.
- When I read this piece aloud, I like the sound of it.
- My voice will get—and hold—your attention.

3   **You will probably hear *moments* of voice in this writing.**
- Sometimes this sounds just like me. Other times it sounds as if anyone could have written it.
- I don't mind this topic, but it doesn't exactly fascinate me. I guess you can tell that sometimes.
- I know who my audience is, but I didn't really think about making my voice just right for them.
- I also know my purpose (to tell a story, to write a business letter, to make an argument), but I didn't really try to match my voice to that purpose.
- I'd be more confident if I knew a little more about this topic.
- When I read this piece aloud, I like parts of it.
- You might notice my voice—but I'm not sure it would make anyone sit up and listen.

1   **I don't feel as if I put that much energy into this writing. I'm not sure it sounds like me. Maybe it doesn't have much voice. Or maybe it's the *wrong* voice.**
- I don't hear my voice in this writing.
- I do not find this topic interesting, so why try to make it interesting for others?
- I'm not sure who my audience is. Would this voice suit them? Beats me.
- Matching voice to purpose? What *is* the right voice for a story? A business letter? A personal essay? A letter to the editor? I have to think about this.
- I don't know enough about this topic yet to sound confident.
- I don't like my writing that much when I read it aloud. It's just not me. And it sure won't get anybody's attention.

Adapted from *Creating Writers*, Spandel and Stiggins, New York: Longman, 1997, pp. 112-116. Used with permission.

Word Choice

- *Painting word pictures*
- *Finding the right words*
- *Avoiding fluff (nice, special)*
- *Favoring strong verbs*

5   **The words and phrases I've chosen seem <u>exactly right</u> to capture my thoughts and feelings.**

- Every word or phrase helps make my meaning clear.
- Words are used correctly. I *know*—I checked.
- You can tell I am writing to inform (or persuade or amuse) my reader—not to impress someone with overdone language.
- I used some everyday language, but in a slightly new and appealing way.
- Do you have some favorite words or phrases in this piece? I do.
- I counted on good strong verbs (*squash, wheedle, cajole, renounce*) and precise nouns. You won't find mountains of modifiers weighing down my writing.
- I avoided the big word choice pitfalls: redundancy; vague, fluffy language (*nice, special, great, exciting*); jargon; and overblown, flowery language that annoys some readers.

3   **My language communicates; it gets the job done.**

- You can understand my basic meaning. Some language is too general, however (*We had a fun time*).
- Most words are used correctly. I didn't often stretch hard, though.
- Here and there I might have tried to impress my reader—even if it took a thesaurus to do it.
- I may have forgotten to define some technical terms (if used).
- Favorite words or phrases? Let's see . . . maybe *one or so . . . where was it?*
- Strong verbs? What's wrong with *is, are, was, were?* And you can't have too many marvelous modifiers—*can* you?
- Did I get <u>overly</u> flowery in spots? (*Her wild mane of hair cascaded tumultuously over her pearly shoulders.*) Well, chalk it off to romantic novel syndrome.

1   **What does this mean? I'm not sure myself.**

- Some of this wording is so vague I don't know if it means anything: *It was really fun and stuff, but then, you know, a lot of stuff changed in some ways.*
- I think I misused too many words: *She had a <u>magnanimous</u> hole <u>emanating</u> from the toe of her stocking.*
- A lot of my redundant phrases get a little redundant. That happens a lot.
- Inflated or jargonistic language makes my paper ponderous and hard to read: *I endeavor to imitate the goals that society has ratified.*
- I can picture my reader saying, *"Oh, come off it!"* OR maybe, *"What on earth does he/she mean??"*

Adapted from *Creating Writers*, Spandel and Stiggins, New York: Longman, 1997, pp. 112-116. Used with permission.

Sentence Fluency

- Giving it readability
- Varying length
- Varying beginnings
- Reading aloud to see how it sounds

5   **It's a little like music—or poetry. It flows, it has rhythm, and it's easy to read aloud.**
- A long sentence here, a short sentence there: you won't get bored.
- Read through my sentence beginnings; notice the variety.
- I have used connecting phrases to show how ideas relate: *however, then, next, after a while, besides, moreover, on the other hand, because, when*, etc.
- "Filler" has been cut, so my sentences are lean, direct, and to the point.
- You can read this writing with expression. It makes sense—*and,* it has style.

3   **This text hums along. Sentences are clear and readable.**
- It could be smoother, but it has some good moments.
- I've noticed something about my sentences. Most are about the same length. Maybe I should shorten some. Maybe I should lengthen others.
- I guess I did get into a rut with sentence beginnings. I guess I could use more variety. I guess I'll fix that.
- I have used *some* connecting phrases: *however, then, next, after a while,* etc. A few more would not hurt.
- A few sentences, like this one, are just a little on the wordy side and could stand to be cut so they wouldn't be quite so wordy.
- OK, so it's not musical yet, but you can read it aloud if you take your time.

1   **This is a challenge to read aloud. Even for me.**
- The way I've written some sentences just go right into the next sentence it's confusing to figure out where does the second sentence begin?
- I put in so many connecting words—*and, so then, because*—that it's like I was trying to write one big sentence!
- Some parts are choppy. Some sentences are too short. They need to be longer. They need to be graceful. They need to be combined.
- Some of my sentences are way, way too long and also way, way too wordy like I was just writing to keep the pencil moving or something. Some have missing.
- This is VERY HARD to read aloud *even if you practice*. It's not smooth, and some of it doesn't even make sense.
- I need to make this sound more like the way people talk.

Adapted from *Creating Writers*, Spandel and Stiggins, New York: Longman, 1997, pp. 112-116. Used with permission.

Conventions

- Proofreading
- Editing
- Checking sources to make sure it's right
- Using editing tools (dictionary, handbook, spell checker, etc.)

5   **I know my conventions and it shows. This is ready to publish. I know because I proofread it—*carefully*.**
- An editor wouldn't have much to do on this paper; you'd have to hunt for errors.
- The text is clean, edited, and corrected.
- Spelling, punctuation, capitals and grammar are all correct.
- Paragraphs show where I switch topics or where a new person begins to speak.
- Only light touch-ups would be required to polish the text for publication.
- A reader will breeze right through this text; it's easy to mentally process.
- Well-used conventions help make meaning clear.

3   **My conventions are getting there. You'll probably notice a few errers, but they won't keep you from understanding the meaning.**
- I read through it. I made some corrections. I'd need to do more if I wanted to publish it.
- Spelling is correct on simple words. On more dificult words, you might find some miner errors.
- I think i did a pretty good job on capitals.
- My punctuation, is pretty good except I'm not sure about all my commas and I might have used too many exclamation points!!
- It reads like a second draft—not too rough, but definitely needs work.
- Conventions aren't strong enough to enhance meaning, but they don't really get in the way, either.

1   **This paper needs editing! You might need to read it once to decode it, and then again to think about the meaning.**
- Evin looking thru hear I see lots of erors.
- My speling needs work, so does my punctuation so do My Capital letters?
- I might have some errors in grammar. My subjects and verbs doesn't always agree.
- I scribbled this down In a Big Hurry. i haven't had time to edit it yet it needs work
- Problems with conventions get in the way of meaning.

Adapted from *Creating Writers*, Spandel and Stiggins, New York: Longman, 1997, pp. 112-116. Used with permission.

VII

Spanish Translatons of Key Pages

Translated by Stephen Pollard   pcpollard@worldnet.att.net

Excavar una Papa Hoy

Una papa crece debajo de la superficie en una obra de escritura. Es la cosa que el/la lector(a) y el /la escritor(a) quieren excavar. Escucha las siguientes oraciones de entrada. ¿Qué preguntas se te ocurren mientras escuchas?

Yo tenía seis años cuando mi madre me enseñó el arte del poder invisible.
Amy Tan

Tú no eres el tipo que estaría en un lugar como éste a esta hora de la mañana.
Luces brillantes ciudad grande   Jay McInerney

No debes decírselo a nadie, mi madre dijo, "Lo que te voy a decir."
La mujer guerrera   Maxine Hong Kingston

El nombre que mi familia me llama es Muchacha Madrugadora porque me levanto temprano y siempre estoy pensando en algo.
La muchacha madrugadora   Michael Dorris

1) Cuéntales a unos amigos una historia o lee algo en que estás trabajando.

2) Tus amigos pueden escuchar y pueden escribir preguntas curiosas en tiras de papel.

3) Toma tu pregunta favorita y conviértela en una nueva oración de entrada contestándola en una o dos oraciones.

   Por ejemplo:
   ¿Qué tan grande era el perro?

   Era el perro más grande que jamás he visto.

   ¿Es una historia verdadera?

   Tal vez no me lo creas pero lo que sigue es una historia verdadera.

4) Trata de encontrar una nueva oración de entrada para una de tus historias en tu diario de escritura.

La Ropa Loca Se Vuelve Más Loca

Con un(a) compañero(a) de clase, pon en una lista algunos detalles en la columna a la izquierda para hacer que la oración borrosa se ponga clara. Acuérdate de que los detalles son cajas adentro de otras. Si tu primer detalle es que los pantalones tienen unos diseños de puntos, enfoca los binoculares haciendo girar el botón hasta que los diseños de puntos estén en forma de peras moradas y rosadas. Escribe otros detalles tuyos más específicos y locos en la columna a la derecha.

A él/ella le gustaba la ropa loca.

1er detalle

Más específico

Pantalones rojos

Pantalones acampanados de color rojo brillante

El Hombre Triste Revelado

¿Jamás has pensado en la historia verdadera detrás de una oración cuando lees? Ahora tienes tu oportunidad. Ves que se dejaron algunos espacios grandes entre cada renglón en este cuentito para que escribieras tus preguntas acerca de cada oración. ¿Por qué corría el hombre triste? ¿Cómo se llamaba? Usa tus preguntas para revisar la historia. Sigue girando el botón de tus binoculares para que la historia se haga más interesante.

El hombre triste

El hombre triste corrió.

El hombre triste corrió hasta Francis.

Francis tenía un abanico.

Francis puede abanicar al hombre triste.

Haciéndole Preguntas A Un Personaje

En ficción, los personajes se desarrollan mientras más nos hacemos preguntas acerca de ellos. Los binoculares pueden ayudarte a desarrollar un personaje antes de que empieces tu historia. Aquí tienes algunas preguntas básicas que debes hacer acerca de un personaje. Emparéjate con alguien y háganse preguntas acerca del personaje. Hagan listas o telarañas acerca de su personaje. Dibujen dibujos también. Acuérdense de que las historias son de personajes con problemas y metas verdaderos. Sigan haciendo preguntas para ayudar a que los problemas y los metas de su personaje se desarrollen y cambien.

Nombre: Edad: Altura: Peso:

Familia y amigos:

Una cualidad positiva destacada:

Una cualidad negativa destacada:

Problema: Meta:

Caja Postal 414

Las Tías

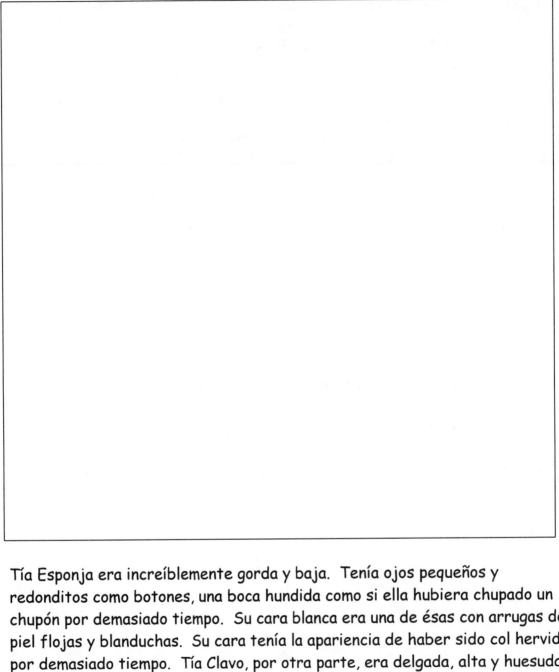

Tía Esponja era increíblemente gorda y baja. Tenía ojos pequeños y redonditos como botones, una boca hundida como si ella hubiera chupado un chupón por demasiado tiempo. Su cara blanca era una de ésas con arrugas de piel flojas y blanduchas. Su cara tenía la apariencia de haber sido col hervido por demasiado tiempo. Tía Clavo, por otra parte, era delgada, alta y huesuda, y se ponía unos anteojos de aros de acero. Ella sujetaba los anteojos en su nariz con un ganchito. Su voz era chillona y sus labios eran largos, estrechos y mojados. Cuando ella se enojaba unas burbujas de baba se le salían de la boca mientras hablaba.

Reventar un Momento

Si tú fueras un(a) director(a) haciendo una película acerca de tu vida, ¿dónde usarías partes a cámara lenta? Piensa en momentos alegres, momentos tristes, momentos cariñosos. Habla con amigos y despiértense las memorias adentro de sus cabezas.

Cuando estés listo(a), escribe en una hoja aquél único momento. No vayas al día siguiente ni luego en ese día. Quédate allí. No escribas con letras grandes ni agregues palabras de sobra solamente para llenar la hoja. Por otra parte, permítete permanecer en tu momento disfrutándolo anotando tus imágenes de él usando estas ideas.

★ Usa tus binoculares: enfoca los lentes prestándoles atención a los sonidos, a los olores, a los sabores y a lo que ves.

★ Lee tu última oración. Si es una foto trata de cambiar a una foto mental o si es de puras fotos mentales cambia y agrega fotos sólo.

★ Si sólo logras llenar media hoja, vuelve al escrito para agregarle unas fotos o fotos mentales.

★ Ciérrate los ojos y imagina que estás otra vez allí en tu momento. Espera a que vengan las palabras.

Aquí hay algunas sugerencias de algunos momentos para reventar. Haz una lista de tus momentos mientras que hables con tus compañeros de clase.

- Un momento en que te perdiste
- Un momento en que se te perdió algo o alguien
- Un momento doloroso se te ocurrió
- Un momento alegre se te ocurrió
- El momento cuando tú llegaste a los Estados Unidos
- Un momento que es gracioso ahora, pero no en ese entonces
- Un momento de que casi no te acuerdas
- Un momento decisivo en un juego

Los Binoculares de Matemáticas

En el libro **Math Curse** por Jon Szeiska, el personaje principal ve problemas de matemáticas por todos lados. ¿Y tú? ¿En cuántos problemas pudieras haber pensado desde cuando te levantaste esta mañana hasta ahora mientras lees esto? Saca tu binoculares de matemáticas y empieza a girar el botón. En la columna a la izquierda, escribe unos datos verdaderos que encuentras en periódicos, libros o en tu vida cotidiana. En la de la derecha, escribe algunas preguntas de matemáticas acerca de los datos que has encontrado.

Ejemplo: Sylvester Stallone ganará 60 millones de dólares por sus tres próximas películas. (fuente USA Today)

Mi pregunta: Asumiendo que él trabaja 40 horas a la semana, ¿cuánto ganará a la hora?

Yo calculé $9,615.38 por hora.
No es mal trabajo, ¿verdad?

Datos

Un caballito del diablo come, como promedio, unos 300 zancudos al día.

Preguntas

¿Cuántos zancudos comerá en una semana?
Si traes a tu casa diez caballitos del diablo, ¿cuántos zancudos comerán en un mes?

Los Clasificados

Trata de escribir un anuncio de <se busca>. Tienes que hacerlo pidiendo alguien o algo de las ciencias, las matemáticas, las ciencias o cualquier materia académica. Empieza poniendo en una lista los datos acerca de tu individuo o cosa. Entonces desarrolla tu anuncio usando los datos que tienes.

Se busca:

Benito Juárez: Tiene que ser bajo; alrededor de 5'2" a 5'5". Tiene que ser indio zapoteca. A él, tienen que gustar los derechos de todos aun los pobres. Esta persona, además, debe de ser justo. Tiene que ser abogado, político y guerrero. Los cobardes no vengan, sólo los valientes. Llame al 555-6754. Pregunte por Poder del Pueblo

Se busca:

La selva tropical: Debe ser capaz de producir cantidades grandes de oxígeno del monóxido del carbono. Debe ser capaz de criar 1/3 de las especies de plantas en la Tierra y de proveerle al mundo entero medicinas.
No pierdas esta oportunidad de crecer en este campo nuevo.
Llama al 1-800-233-9008 y pregunta por La Tierra Quemada

Se busca:

Se busca:

Se busca:

El Problema y la Papa

Una vez que tiene un problema tu personaje, la próxima pregunta que se hace es cuál es la papa que está debajo del problema, la cosa que te pregunta el por qué. La papa es la causa del problema. Por ejemplo, si tu protagonista se llama Mateo y su problema es que golpea a la gente, la próxima pregunta que tienes que hacerte es, **¿por qué**? A lo mejor es que su hermano le dé palizas. Tal vez su papá se le muriera y Mateo esté enojado. Quizá él no pueda leer muy bien y eso le frustra. Puede ser que sean todas estas cosas.

Escribe el problema de tu personaje al lado izquierdo y después anota unas papas que crecen debajo de su problema a la derecha. Acuérdate de que las papas no son los problemas sino que son las causas que muchas veces se esconden enterradas fuera de la vista.

Problema

Papa

¿Qué se me queda en la mente?

Título_____ Borrador#_____ Escritor(a)_____

Fecha _____ Lector(a) _____

¿Qué se me queda en la mente?

Opino que...

Una cosa que el/la escritor(a) hará es:

La Conferencia con el/la Maestro(a)
¡Hazla tú mismo(a)!

Título_____Borrador#_____Escritor(a)_____

Fecha _____ Maestro(a) ficticio(a) _____

Tu maestro(a) está demasiado ocupado(a) para reunirse contigo hoy, pero necesitas mucho una conferencia. ¿Qué harás? Es fácil. Pretende que vas a reunirte con él/ella. Escribe un diálogo de lo que se van a decir acerca de tu escrito.

Escritor(a):

Sr./Sra. _____:

Escritor(a):

Sr./Sra. _____:

Una cosa en la cual trabajaré:

Yo Quiero Más.

Título_____	Borrador#____	Escritor(a)_____
Fecha _____	Lector(a) _____	

Yo quiero más acerca de...

Yo quiero menos acerca de...

El plan del escritor o de la escritora...

Mi Crítico Interior

Título_____ Borrador#____ Escritor(a)_____

Fecha _____ Lector(a) _____

Tu crítico interior aprueba cuando oye algo que hace sentido. Antes de una conferencia, anota lo que tu crítico interior te dice acerca de tu escrito. Entonces, anota lo que te dice tu crítico interior después de la conferencia. ¿Cómo cambiaron tus ideas?

Opiniones de mi crítico interior antes:

Opiniones de mi crítico interior después:

¿Cómo cambiaron mis ideas de los cambios en mi escrito?

El Boleto de Conferencia para el/la Maestro(a)

Título _____ Borrador# _____

Escritor(a) _____ Fecha _____

1_____fecha_____

2_____fecha_____

3_____fecha_____

4_____fecha_____

¿Cómo ha cambiado la forma de escribir?

La Conferencia de la Pregunta Curiosa

En una conferencia de la pregunta curiosa el/la escritor(a) lee su escrito mientras el/la lector(a) escucha y anota preguntas curiosas en una hoja de papel. Las preguntas curiosas no se pueden contestar que sí o que no sino que surgen según el ínteres que el/la lector(a) tiene en la historia. Cuando escribes preguntas curiosas, debes considerar lo siguiente.

- ¿De qué quiero saber más?
- ¿Qué parte me deja pensativo(a)?
- ¿Qué parte queda sin explicación?
- ¿Qué más quieres saber del personaje principal?
- ¿Qué te confunde?
- ¿Qué partes te tenían muy entretenido(a) y qué partes te tenían aburrido(a)?
- ¿A cuál de los personajes querías conocer más?
- ¿A qué opinones les hacían falta hechos para respaldarlas?
- ¿Qué ideas te dejan perplejo(a)?

La Conferencia de la Pregunta Curiosa

1) El/La escritor(a) lee su escrito en voz alta mientras su compañero(a) escucha y anota preguntas durante y después.

2) El/La escritor(a) recoge las preguntas y entonces vuelve a su escrito a los lugares adonde las preguntas lo/la refieren.

3) Trata de contestar las preguntas más interesantes. Agrega las respuestas a las preguntas en forma de fotos, fotos mentales o en forma de diálogo, etc...

4) Lee el escrito con y sin las revisiones. ¿Se mejora tu escrito?

Conferencias de Tiempo

En una conferencia de tiempo, el/la lector(a) y el/la escritor(a) buscan lugares en los cuales pueden manipular el tiempo adentro de un escrito. Podemos hacer marchar más lento el tiempo reventando momentos o agregando sucesos. Podemos hacer marchar más rápido el tiempo acortando el diálogo o escribiendo con menos descripción un evento en vez de darle muchos detalles (véase capítulo 4). Aquí tienes algunas cosas en las cuales puedes fijarte cuando tratas de sentir el paso del tiempo.

- ¿Ocurre la acción en tiempo real? Si es así, ¿empieza lo suficientemente tarde en el día o podemos hacer más corta la mañana y ir a la parte buena más temprano?

- ¿Hay demasiado diálogo? ¿Es el diálogo necesario? Es decir, ¿revela información importante o es que se pudiera reemplazar con una frase como ésta y no omitir datos importantes? *Hablaron un ratito.*

- ¿Hay un suceso o momento que ocurrió muy rápidamente sin mucha explicación? Por ejemplo, "Él robó el banco y se fue a la casa."

- ¿Hay más momentos importantes en la historia. Si es así, ¿se les dedica más tiempo a estos momentos más importantes?

Una Conferencia de Tiempo
1) Lee en voz alta la historia. Préstales atención a las partes emocionantes y también las partes aburridas.
2) Marca las partes buenas y busca maneras en las cuales puedes expandirlas con más detalles, fotos o fotos mentales o diálogos.
3) El/La lector(a) debe escoger al menos una parte lenta que el/la escritor(a) pudiera quitar o acortar.
4) El/La escritor(a) toma las mejores sugerencias y vuelve a escribir. ¿Se mejora el escrito?

Una Conferencia de La foto

En una conferencia de la foto, el/la lector(a) busca algunos lugares en un borrador donde él/ella quiere más detalles físicos. Tales lugares son marcados con un ☐. El/La escritor(a) puede decidir a qué lugares les conviene más la foto y él/ella puede escribir una foto que describe más esos lugares. Una foto puede ser una oración o una frase solamente o hasta uno o dos párrafos enteros. El largo no es importante. Lo que sí es importante es lo que el/la escritor(a) dice y cómo lo dice mejor. Aquí tienes unas ideas que te pueden ayudar. Para más ayuda, véanse los capítulos 2 y 3.

- Describe los gestos y los movimientos del personaje.
- Pinta el escenario con una descripción de un lugar.
- Escucha los sonidos y lo que se dice.
- Enfócate mucho para poder usar detalles físicos de una persona o lugar.
- Trata de usar más que uno de los cinco sentidos.
- Pinta un sentimiento en el escenario sin decir qué sentimiento es.

Algunas Reglas

1. Empieza buscando lugares en los cuales puedes agregar fotos.

2. En una hoja aparte, el/la escritor(a) escribe una foto para agregar.

3. Lee la sección con la foto, entonces, leéla sin ella. Pregúntale al (la) lector(a) si es mejor.

4. Repite estos pasos. Acuérdate de que la escritura es una obra de arte como la fotografía, y todas las obras de arte se desarrollan al tanteo.

Una Conferencia de la Foto Mental

En una foto mental, el/la lector(a) posiblemente puede buscar lugares en los cuales opiniones, pensamientos retrospectivos o conflictos internos se pueden colocar en un escrito. Busca momentos en los cuales lo físico esté demasiado descrito. Busca momentos en los cuales tu personaje aproveche de estar pensativo. Por ejemplo:

- Una decisión importante se le acerca al personaje y éste tiene que analizar sus opciones
- Un personaje miente y piensa en las consecuencias
- Una canción causa que el personaje se acuerde de una memoria.
- Un personaje dice algo que no quería decir y piensa en lo que ha pasado
- Un asunto de consciencia le pesa mucho
- Algo tiene que arrelgarse

Una Conferencia de la Foto Mental

1. Lee el borrador en voz alta.

2. Busca lugares en los que vas a agregar las fotos mentales.

3. El/La escritor(a) escribe unas fotos mentales en una hoja blanca y luego las mete en su escrito.

4. Lee el escrito con y sin lo que agregaste. ¿Es mejor?

¡Pruébalo!

En la escritura expositiva el usar los binoculares muchas veces significa que tienes que enfocar los lentes en los hechos para poder respaldar las opiniones borrosas, pero a veces tenemos que echarle más que un vistazo a lo que escribimos para que estemos seguros de que escribimos hechos u opiniones.

Ahora tenemos la oportunidad de practicar. En tu diario de escritura dibuja una línea vertical en el medio de la hoja. Al lado izquierdo, escribe algunas opiniones. Al lado derecho, escribe algunos hechos que respalden las opiniones que escribes. Es posible que tengas que ir a la biblioteca para encontrar un hecho específico. Por ejemplo:

Opinión (¿No me lo crees?)

Hecho (Te lo probaré)

La Tierra es contaminada por productos químicos venenosos.

Un promedio de 21 derrames tóxicos ocurren en los Estados Unidos cada año.

Hay más osos negros en Nueva Hampshire hoy que había en 1900.

Había un número estimado de 50 osos negros en Nueva Hampshire en 1900. El Departamento de la Pesca y Cacería de Nueva Hampshire estima que hay 2,500 osos hoy.

La fuerza nuclear en el país anteriormente llamado la Unión Soviética es peligrosa.

Entre 1993 y 1998 hubo 418 accidentes nucleares en el país de Ukraine.

La Historia de 3 Actos

Muchas historias y casi todas las películas de Hollywood se pueden dividir en tres actos; la Introducción en la cual el problema básico o el conflicto se presenta; la Complicación en la cual las cosas se ponen más complicadas y también donde otros problemas surgen y finalment. La Resolución se presenta donde los problemas se arreglan de alguna manera u otra. Abajo encontrarás un análisis de los 3 actos de la Cenicienta. Después de estudiar este análisis, trata de establecer los tres actos de una de tus historias.

La Cenicienta

Introducción: Ella quiere ir al baile y entonces la Hada Madrina se le aparece y con magia hace su deseo la realidad, pero le advierte a la Cenicienta lo que va a suceder si ella no sale para las 12:00. El problema o el conflicto se presenta en la Introducción.

Complicación: Aunque lo pasa muy bien en el baile, ella sale demasiado tarde y mientras se marcha corriendo, deja su zapatilla de vidrio. Las hermanas suyas hablan de la princesa pero no creen que fuera su hermanastra.

Resolución: El Príncipe decide buscar a su Princesa y eventualmente él encuentra el pie correcto al que le queda la zapatilla. La historia empieza tristemente pero termina alegremente.

Comentario: Creo que la resolución de la Cenicienta es demasiado corta. Si yo fuera a reescribir la historia, agregaría más acerca de la búsqueda de la Cenicienta o haría el final más largo. Los escritores de Walt Disney, en realidad, hicieron esto. Inventaron algunos ratoncitos que ayudaron a que la Cenicienta se escapara de un cuarto que tenía la puerta cerrada con llave.

Los 3 Actos de mi Historia

Abajo hay 3 cajas en las cuales tú puedes definir los 3 actos de una historia que ya has escrito o de una que estás por escribir. Después de que escribas o de que dibujes los tres actos, pregúntate qué acto es el más fuerte y cuál puede estar más desarrollado poniéndole un obstáculo más grande en el problema o un cambio en la trama.

Título _____

Introducción

Complicación

Resolución

La Conferencia de Revisión

Ven a una conferencia de revisión leyendo para buscar uno o dos tipos particulares de revisión. Estos tipos pueden ser determinados por el/la maestro(a) o el/la escritor(a). Por ejemplo, si he trabajado en empezar mis oraciones con letra mayúscula o en escribir párrafos fuertes, yo le pediría al (la) lector(a) que buscara errores de ese tipo o que encierre con círculo lugares donde hice eso muy bien. Aquí tienes unas áreas gramaticales en que puedes enfocarte.

Letras Mayúsculas: ¿Todas las oraciones empiezan con letra mayúscula? ¿Llevan todos los nombres propios letra mayúscula?

Oraciones: ¿Están todas las oraciones completas? ¿Usas una variedad de diferentes tipos de oraciones?

Párrafos: ¿Es la obra escrita en párrafos? ¿Empieza un nuevo párrafo con un nuevo hablador?

Voz: ¿Es la voz constante? Es decir, ¿suena como la voz del autor?

Coma: Usa la coma después de la salutación de una carta, una lista de cosas y para separar una frase subordinada de una frase independiente.

Mi Boletín de Gramática

Aquí tienes una manera de seguir lo que ya sabes de la gramática y en lo que necesitas trabajar. Llena el boletín de gramática abajo. Agrégale un escrito tuyo. Encierra con círculo y ponles números a los lugares que demuestren lo que ya sabes de la gramática y en lo que trabajas.

1) Lo que sé:

2) En lo que trabajo:

La Lista de Verificación del Revisor

- ¿A mí, me gusta la entrada o puedo encontrar o escribir otra mejor?
- ¿Dónde puedo usar los binoculares?
- ¿Dónde puedo meter una  o una ?
- ¿Hay un momento en que puedo ?
- ¿Dónde puedo desarrollar más el escenario?
- ¿Dónde puedo cambiar el ?

VIII

A Few Good Books

This is a very short list of books to help you teach writing. I've tried to be very selective and specific. There are many more books you might find useful from professional book publishers such as Heinemann and Stenhouse. I have also included some children's literature.

Teaching the Craft of Revision

What a Writer Needs by Ralph Fletcher

This book is packed with wise advice and great student examples on the craft of writing. Fletcher writes with the kind of warmth, sincerity and insight that only comes from a practicing writer who loves to share what he has learned in the trenches.

After THE END: Teaching and Learning Creative Revision by Barry Lane

I wrote this book to show teachers and students the joy of revision. It's organized around well-tested mini-lessons to create a passion for revision in your students

Crafting a Life by Donald Murray

If writing teachers could have a Delphi Oracle, it would be Donald Murray. His original book, *A Writer Teaches Writing,* will tell you all you need to know to get started. This small book condenses Murray's crystal clear insights about the craft of writing. When you put it down, you will pick up a pen.

Craft Lessons by Ralph Fletcher and Joann Portalupi

This book is packed with lessons on the craft of writing for students 1-8. This is a "must have" for any teacher looking to strengthen the reading/writing connection in their class.

Revising the Research Assignment

The Curious Researcher by Bruce Ballenger

This is the only book you will need to teach research writing at any grade level. Though it was originally written as a freshman English text for college, Ballenger writes with such voice and his examples are so illuminating, you'll want to adapt his ideas for your 2nd graders. If you are under the academic delusion that expository writing should be boring, you need this book.

Writing with Passion **by Tom Romano**
This personal book explores the notion of the multi-genre research paper. If you enjoyed the wacky research reports in chapter 6, this book will show you how to develop these ideas into longer assignments.

Assessment Driving Instruction

Creating Writers **by Vicki Spandel and Richard Stiggins**
This classic book will clue you in to how assessment will drive your teaching in a positive direction. Written with warmth and good humor, the authors lead you by the hand through the Promised Land of authentic assessment. Dozens of student examples light the way. This book can take your writing classroom, your school or district to the next level.

Portfolio Primer **by Geoff Hewitt.**
Hewitt was one of the architects of Vermont's Statewide Portfolio program so he knows about portfolios from the inside out. But this book is not just another talking-head telling you that assessment is good for you. A poet himself and a teacher in the schools, Hewitt relates his razor sharp insights to real children and their writing.

The Portfolio Sourcebook **by Barry Lane and Andrew Green**
Andy Green and I wrote and compiled this book to go along with our portfolio workshops. It contains much useful information and forms to help create a classroom where portfolios make sense.

Starting a Writer's Workshop

Seeking Diversity **by Linda Rief**
This book shows what a great teacher can do even though they teach in a flawed system. Rief's writing/reading classroom runs on its own steam and Rief shows you how yours can do the same.

A Fresh Look at Writing **by Donald Graves**
Donald Graves' years of wisdom as a writing guru are condensed into this practical book. You'll find a useful chapter on conferences and many good suggestions to try out with your students. It's the book to grab for when things get tough.

The Writer's Notebook **by Ralph Fletcher**
This book is a wonderful guide for young people on keeping a writer's notebook. Fletcher uses many examples of student writing to back up his sound ideas on living the writer's life.

Discovering the Writer Within **by Barry Lane and Bruce Ballenger**
First published in 1989, Bruce Ballenger and I wrote this book because we couldn't find a textbook that mirrored the way we taught. It leads the reader through 40 days of activities that mirror a process approach to teaching.

Writing as a Road to Self-Discovery **by Barry Lane**
I wrote this book to find the big potatoes, those stories at the core of our being. It has been popular as a text in high schools and as a resource for elementary and middle school teachers.

History Books

The History of US **by Joy Hakim**
This 10 volume series is written with a marvelous voice. Hakim lures the reader into a love of history with stories, questions, her own opinions and stunning illustrations. Use this book in social studies and to model what real writers do when faced with expository assignments.

Lies My Teacher Told Me **by James Lowen.**
This best selling history book analyzes twelve of the most widely used American History textbooks and shows us what they leave out in order to sell books.   You may not agree with Lowen's ideas about history, but this book will get you thinking about the way history is passed down.

Not So **by Paul Boller**
This purposefully provocative book explodes all the myths about American history from Columbus to Clinton. Great modeling for students doing insightful research.

A Tabloid History of the World **by Kevin McDonough**
This clever book makes all of history into tabloid front pages. Headlines such as, "Greek Tricksters Trash Troy," help teach alliteration with good fun. Now make your own alliterative headline.

10 Favorite Picture Books

The Mysteries of Harris Burdick **by Chris Van Allsburg**
This book teaches the mystery of leads.

Zoom **by Istvan Banyai**
This wordless picture book models what surprising details emerge when the camera pulls back.

Earthlets **by Jean Willis**
This book describes babies from the alien point of view; it features great modeling for playful voices in writing.

Dancing Moons **by Nancy Wood**
This gorgeous book of Native American poetry will show you how to teach the power of chant poetry and its capacity for eliciting detail.

Counting on Frank **by Rod Clement**
Did you know the average ball point pen draws a line 7000 feet long? The protagonist of this book models what happens when we use the math binoculars all the time.

The Math Curse **by Jon Scziescka**
This famous book teaches the math binocular concept well.

The Night I Followed the Dog **by Nina Laden**
If Humphrey Bogart came back as a cocker spaniel, he would be in this book. Great voice.

I Love You Forever **by Robert Munsch**
Time passes quickly in this book of snapshots through time. Good modeling for shrinking time.

If You Give a Mouse a Cookie Laura J. Numeroff
This is your classic loop ending. Good modeling for stories which end where they begin

Mr. Blueberry **by Simon James**
This book of letters and replies is a wonderful model for a research paper. Emily writes like a poet, Mr. Blueberry like an expert. The two voices rub against each other in this warm and wonderful book.

Baby Writer **by Nigel Hall**
This is the book that made my daughter a writer at 18 months. Great modeling of the literacy process. (For purchasing info, call 1-800-613-8055.)

Teaching Bibliography

Here is some more books to enjoy and help model some of the concepts in this book.

If This is Expository Writing Why Isn't if boring .

(Great models for expository "writing with voice.)

Abraham Lincoln a photobiography   Russell Friedman
Badland, Jonathan Raban
Be Seated James Cross Giblin
Boat Book, Gail Gibbons
Boats, Anne Rockwell
Bugs, Nancy Winslow Parker
Come Back, Salmon: How a Group of Dedicated Kids Adopted Pigeon Creek and
Brought it Back to Life, Molly Cone
The Compleat Cockroach, David George Gordon
The Dead Tree, Alvin Tresselt
Dinosaurs, Gail Gibbons, (and other non fiction titles by Gibbons)
Eleanor Roosevelt, by Russell Friedman
Grossology Begins at Home: Science of Really Gross Things in Everyday Life, Sylvia
Granzei
Happy Day! Things to Make and Do, Judith Conaway
Here is the Artic Winter, Madeleine Dunphy
How We Learned the Earth is Round, Patricia Lauber (and others in the How We
    Learned Series)
I Did It, Harlow Rockwell
In Search of Nature, Edward Wilson
Insectopedia, Douglas Florian
Learning To Swim in Swaziland: a Child's Eye View of a Souther African Country,
    Nila K. Leigh
Nature's Numbers, Ian Stewart
Pickle in the Middle and Other Easy Snacks, Frances Zwelfel
Picture Book of Anne Frank, David Adler
Picture Book of Harriet Tubman, David Adler (and other Picture Book biography series)
The Popcorn Book, Tomie dePaola
Recycle!, Gail Gibbons
Soccer Is Our Game, Leila Boyle Gemme
Spooky Tricks, Rose Wyler and Gerald Ames
Springtime Surprises! Things to Make and Do, Judith Conaway
Trucks, Ray Broekel

Expository Writing Books with Pizzazz for Older Readers
Cosmos Carl Sagan
Longitude, Dava Sobel

How the Irish Saved Civilization, Thomas Cahill
Lincoln, David Herbert Donald
Ethics, Harry Stein
Beyond the Revolution, Gloria Steinham
The People's History of the United States, Howard Zinn
A Cartoon History of the Universe, Larry Gonick
Undaunted Courage, Stephen A. Ambrose
Witness to a Century, George Seldes
The Tom Peter's Seminar, Tom Peters
The Way Things Work, David McCauley
Inside the Brain, Ronald Kotulak

Books that Play with Time
(Stories told in a non-linear way)
The 18th Emergency, Betsy Byars
The Angel With the Mouth-Organ, Christobel Mattingly
A Chair for My Mother, Vera Williams
The Changing Maze, Zilpha Keatley Snyder
Dakota Dugout, Ann Turner
Fat Chance, Claude, Joan Lowery Nixon
The Frog Prince, Continued, Jon Scieszka
A Girl Called Boy, Belinda Hurmence
Grandma Didn't Wave Back, Rose Blue
The House on Maple Street, Bonnie Pryor
How My Parents Learned to Eat, Ina R. Friedman
Island Rescue, Charles E. Martin
Journey, Patricia MacLachlan
Julie of the Wolve, Jean Craighead George
Just a Dream, Chris Van Allsburg
Lost and Found, Jill Paton Walsh
The Miracle Tree, Christobel Mattingly
Miss Rumphius, Barbara Cooney
Night in the Country, Cynthia Rylant
A Proud Taste for Scarlet and Miniver, Elaine L. Konigsburg
The Quilt Story, Tony Johnston
Rapscallion Jones, James Marshall
Runa, Allison James
The Stopwatch, by David Lloyd
Sing for a Gentle Rain, Allison James
Time Train, Paul Fleishman
Watch the Stars Come Out, Riki Levinson
When I was Young in the Mountains Rylant, Cynthia
When I was Nine James Stevenson
Why the Chicken Crossed the Road, David Macaulay
The Wreck of the Zephyr, Chris Van Allsburg

Books That Play with Time for Older Readers
One hundred Years of Solitude, Gabriel Garcia Marquez
Slaughterhouse Five, Kurt Vonnegut
Fugitive Pieces, Anne Michaels
Einstein's Dreams, Alan Lightman
The White Hotel, D.M. Thomas
The Magus, John Fowles
The French Lieutenant's Woman John Fowles
To the Lighthouse, Virginia Wolf
As I Lay Dying, William Faulkner
The House on Mango Street, Sandra Cisneros
Betrayal Harold Pinter (a play that moves backwards in time. Available in video too)

Best Books for Exploding Moments
These books contain first rate slow motion moments and scenes

Hatchet, Gary Paulsen
The Sign of the Beaver, Elizabeth Speare
Charlotte's Web, E.B. White
Tuck Everlasting, Natalie Babbit
Fig pudding, Ralph Fletcher
Into the Dust,
Number the Stars, Lois Lowry
The Giver Lois Lowry
Bridge of Teribithia, Katherine Paterson
Sing for a Gentle Rain Alison James

Books with Unforgettable Exploded Moments for Older Readers
Angela's Ashes, Frank Mc Cord
The Beans of Egypt Maine, Carolyn Chute
Cold Mountain, Charles Frazier
The Death of the Detective, Mark Smith
Einstein's Dreams, Alan Lightman
Kaffir Boy, Mark Mathaban
Night, Elie Weisel
I Know Why the Caged Bird Sings, Maya Angelou
Shooting an Elephant, George Orwell
1984, George Orwell
The Things They Carried, Tim Obrien
Salvador, Joan Didion
The Dubliners, James Joyce (each short story has a moment in it)
Surfacing, Margaret Atwood
Fugitive Pieces, Anne Michaels
This Way to the Gas, Ladies and Gentlemen, Tadeuz Borowski
Hardcastle, John Yount

Unforgettable Characters – The people depicted in these stories stick with you long after the book is back on the shelf

Ace the Very Important Pig, Dick King-Smith
Agnes the Sheep, William Taylor
Amanda's Perfect Hair, Linda Milstein
Amelia Bedelia Helps Out, Peggy Parish
Amos and Boris, William Steig
Anastasia Krupnik, Lois Lowry
Annabelle Swift, Kindergartener, Amy Schwartz
Arnie Goes to Camp, Nancy Carlson
Babushka's Doll, Patricia Pollaco
The Bedspread, Sylvia Fair
Bedtime for Frances, Russell Hoban
The Best Christmas Pageant Ever, Barbara Robinson
Bridge to Terabithia, Katherine Paterson
The Bully of Barkham Street, Mary Stolz
The Burning Questions of Bingo Brown, Betsy Byars
Charlie and the Chocolate Factory, Roald Dahl
Christina Katerina and the Time She Quit the Family, Patricia Lee Gauch
Class Clown, Johanna Hurwitz
A Day No Pigs Would Die, Robert Newton Peck
Dr. Desoto, William Steig
Fritz and the Mess Fairy, Rosemary Wells
Freak the Mighty, Rodman Filbrick
Grandpa's Song, Tony Johnston
Henry and Mudge, Cynthia Rylant
I Wish I Were a Butterfly, James Howe
It's Not the End of the World, Judy Blume
The Lemonade Babysitter, Karen Waggoner
Lyddie, Katherine Paterson
Matilda, Roald Dahl
Miss Maggie, Cynthia Rylant
Miss Rumphius, Barbara Cooney
The Mouse and the Motorcycle, Beverly Cleary
Pigman, Paul Zindel
The Pinballs, Betsy Byars
Queenie Peavy, Robert Burch
Ramona the Pest, Beverly Cleary
Song and Dance Man, Karen Ackerman
Somebody Loves You, Mr. Hatch, Eileen Spinelli
Stone Fox, John Reynolds Gardner
William's Doll, Charlotte Zolotow
Wombat and Bandicoot, Best of Friends, Kerry Argent

Strong Characters for Older Readers
Catcher in the Rye, J.D. Salinger
Emma, Jane Austen
A Prayer for Owen Meany, John Irving
The Adventures of Huckleberry Finn, Mark Twain
The Bean Trees, Barbara Kingsglover
Edisto, Padget Powell
In Country, Bobby Ann Mason
Jane Eyre, Charlotte Bronte
The Tin Drum, Gunther Grass
Stones From the River, Urslula Heigi
She's Come Undone, Wally Lamb
Ironweed, William Kennedy
The Fan Man, William Kotzwinkle
Bright Lights, Big City, Jay Mcinerney
Continental Drift, Russell Banks
The Long Goodbye, and other books by Raymond Chandler

Dialogue –These books have well written dialogue.
Alexander and the Terrible, Horrible, No Good. Very, Bad Day. Judith Viorst
Amella Bedella. Peggy Parish
Anastasia Krupnik. Lois Lowry
Dr Desoto, William Steig
Ernest and Celestine Gabrielle Vincent
The Ghost – Eye Tree. Bill Martin, Jr
The Ginger Man, J.P. Dunleavy
Fig Pudding, Ralph Fletcher
Grandaddy's Place. Helen V. Griffith
The Great Gilly Hopkins, Katherine Paterson
Happy Birthday Moon. Frank Asch
Ira Sleeps Over. Bernard Waber
Jumanji. Chris Van Allsburg
Leo the Late Bloomer. Robert Kraus
Rosie and Michael. Judith Viorst
The Velveteen Rabbit, or How Toys Become Real. Margery Williams
White Dynamite and Curly Kid. Bill Martin, Jr.
Wilfred Gordon McDonald Partridge, Mem Fox
Winnie the Pooh, A.A. Milne

Great Dialogue for Older Readers
The Collected Short Stories of Ernest Hemingway, Ernest Hemingway
Pale Horse, Pale Rider, Katherine Anne Porter
Cathedral , Raymond Carver
Will You Please Be Quiet Please, Raymond Carver

© Discover Writing Press-1-800-613-8055-www.discoverwriting.com

The Color Purple, Alice Walker
The Joy Luck Club, Amy Tan
The Collected Short Stories of Isaac Babel
The Collected Stories of Stanley Elkin
The American Buffalo, David Mamet (play. Available in video)

Snapshots—Books with Vivid Word Pictures

Arctic Memories, Normee Ekoomiak
Apple Tree, Peter Parnall
Babushka's Doll, Patricia Pollaco
Buried Alive, Ralph Fletcher (poetry for teenagers)
The Changing Maze, Zilpha Keatley Snyder
Charlotte's Web, E.B. White
Chipmunk song, Joanne Ryder (and other books by Ryder)
Dakota Dugout, Ann Turner
Dancing Moons, Nancy Wood (Native American Poetry
Dark and Full of Secrets, Carol Carrick
Fox's Dream, Keizaburo Tejima
In Coal Country, Judith Hendershot
I Am the Ocean, Suzanna Marshak
I Am Wings, Ralph Fletcher (poetry for teenagers)
I Wish I Were a Butterfly, James Howe
Jemima Remembers, Crescent Dragonwagon
The Little House on the Prairie, Laura Ingles Wilder
Many Moons, James Thurber
Morning Girl, Michael Dorris
The Mousehole Cat, Antonia Barber
Owl Moon, Jane Yolen
A Prairie Boy's Winter, William Kurelek
Re-Zoom, Istvan Banyai
The Salamander Room, Ann Mazer
Sarah , Plain and Tall, Patricia MacLachlan
The Snow Speaks, Nancy White Caristom
Storm In The Night, Mary Stolz
There's More..Much More, Sue Alexander
Through Grandpa's Eyes, Patricia MacLachlan
Tuck Everlasting, Natalie Babbitt
Twilight Comes Twice Ralph Fletcher
Whale Song, Tony Johnston
When I Was Young In the Mountains, Cynthia Rylant
Winter Barn, Peter Parnall
The Winter Room, Gary Paulson
Woodpile, Peter Parnall
Zoom, Istvan Banyai

Books with Great Snapshots For Older Readers
<u>War and Peace</u>, Leo Tolstoy
<u>The Beans of Egypt Maine</u>, Carolyn Chute
<u>Love Medicine</u>, Louise Erdrich
<u>The Things They Carried</u>, Tim Obrien
<u>The Song of Napalm,</u> Bruce Weigl (poetry about Vietnam)
<u>Just Worlds</u>, Geof Hewitt, (poetry)
<u>Moby Dick</u>, Herman Melville
<u>The Long Goodbye</u> and other books by Raymond Chandler
<u>The Lady Oracle</u> and other books by Margaret Atwood

Word Play
<u>101 More Words and How they Began</u>, Arthur Steckler
<u>Dandelions Don't bite</u>, Leone Adelson
<u>English Words Grow From Latin and Greek Roots</u>, Kristin Tracy
<u>From the Horses Mouth</u>, Ann Nevins
<u>Guppies in Tuxedos: Funny Eponyms</u>, Marvin Terban
<u>Heavens to Betsy! and Other Curious Sayings</u>, Charles Funk
<u>A Hog on Ice and Other Curious Sayings</u>, Charles Funk
<u>Horsefeathers and Other Curious Words</u>, Charles Funk
<u>The King Who Rained,</u> Fred Gwynne
<u>A Little Pigeon Toad.</u> Fred Gwynne
<u>It's Raining Cats and Dogs</u>, Christine Ammer
<u>Last Names First</u>, Mary Price and Richard S. Lee
<u>More Words of Science</u>, Isaac Asimov
<u>Murfles and Wink-a-Peeps: Funny Old Words for Kids</u>, Susan Kelz
<u>Put Your Foot in Your Mouth and Other Silly Sayings</u>, James Cox
<u>Superdupers! : Really Funny Real Words</u>, Marvin Terban
<u>Talk About English: How Words Travel and Change,</u> Janet Klausner
<u>Thereby Hangs the Tale: Stories of Curious Word Origins</u>, Charles Funk
<u>What a Funny Thing to Say</u>, Bernice Kohn Hunt
<u>What's That You Said? How Words Change</u>, Snn R. Weiss
<u>Where Words Were Born</u>, Arkady Leekum
<u>Words: A Book About the Origins of Everyday Words and Phrases</u>, Jane Sarnoff
<u>Words Can Tell: A Book About Out Language</u>, Christina Ashton
<u>Words From the Myths</u>, Isaac Asimov

Word Play for Older Readers
<u>Word Play,</u> Peter Farb
<u>Anguished English,</u> by Richard Lederer
<u>The Miracle of Language, Richard Lederer</u>
<u>Wordstruck,</u> Robert McNeil
<u>The Oxford English Dictionary,</u> Now available on CD!

Parodies, Spin-offs and other Wild Revisions

Andy and the Lion, James Daugherty

Beauty, Robin Mckinley

Cinder Edna, Ellen Jackson

Cinderella Penguin, or the Little Glass Flipper, Janet Perlman

The Cinderella Show, Janet and Allan Ahlberg

Cinder-Elly, Frances Minters

Cowboy and the Black-eyed Pea, Tony Johnston

Deep in the Forest, Brinton Turkle

The Fourth Little Pig, Teresa Celsi

The Frog Prince, Continued, Jon Scieszka

Frog Princess, Alix Berenzy

The Giant's Toe, Brock Cole

I Want a Dog, Dayal Kaur Khalsa

Jim and the Beanstalk, Raymond Briggs

Little Wolf and the Giant, Sue Porter

The Once Upon a Golden Apple, Jean Little

The Paper Bag Princess, Robert Munsch

Peeping Beauty, Mary Jane Auch

Pondlarker, Fred Gwynne

Prince Cinders, Babette Cole

Prince of the Pond: Otherwise Known as De Fawg Pin, Donna Jo Napoll

The Principal's New Clothes, Stephanie Calmenson

The Stinky Cheese Man, Jon Scieszka

Ruby, Michael Emberley

The True Story of the Three Little Pigs, John Scieszka

Barry Lane's Recycled Fairy Tales (8 fractured fairy tale songs) (cd/tape)

Parodies for Older Readers

Dave Barry Slept Here: a sort of history of the United States, Dave Barry

Politically Correct Bedtime Stories, James Garner

Cartoon History of the United States, Larry Gonick

Seinlanguage, Jerry Seinfeld

A Tabloid History of the World, Kevin Mcdonagh

Julia A. Moore Bad Poetry Collections   Enter a Bad poem yourself
Julia A. Moore Poetry Contest/ Flint Public Library/
1026 Kearsley/Flint Michigan 48502

Best Poetry Guides

The Handbook of Poetic Forms, edited by Ron Padget

Poetry Everywhere, by Jack Collum and Sheryl Noethe

Today You are My Favorite Poet, Geof Hewitt

For the Good of the Earth and Sun, Georgia Heard

© Discover Writing Press-1-800-613-8055-www.discoverwriting.com

Bring Barry Lane to Your School

Barry visits many schools for inservice trainings and residencies. He's also a sought after keynote speaker for conventions. Below is a short list of some of his topics. For a complete packet of detailed information call 1-800-613-8055 or visit our website www. discoverwriting.com.

Revision: How to Teach it, Learn it, Love it!

Revision is an ongoing creative process, not simply the act of making a sloppy copy picture perfect. Based on *After THE END* and *Reviser's Toolbox,* this practical seminar or keynote is loaded with well-tested ideas for teaching the joy of revision to your students.

Writing and Laughing Across the Curriculum

Boring encyclopedia writing just doesn't cut in the age of information. This workshop is packed with quick ideas for helping students assimilate information and write expository prose with meaning, purpose and a point of view.

Laugh to Learn

"A joke is total knowledge in a Nano-second"   Steve Martin

What would Hamlet sound like as a basal reader? What would grades sound like if they could talk? Why did the administrator cross the road? Find out the answer to these important questions and understand some basics of humor and why we need it in this 60 minute keynote. Barry's stand-up comedy routine is by far his most popular keynote address.

Questioning Answers: 21st century thinking through Writing

The children of the future will write the questions at the end of the chapter, not answer them. This speech illustrates the need to get students asking questions to become successful lifelong learners and thinkers.

The Portfolio Pep Rally

Drawing on years of experience as a network leader in Vermont's writing portfolio program and practical information in *The Portfolio Sourcebook,* this keynote leads the audience to an understanding of what portfolios really are and how their assessment can drive curriculum into the next century.

Barry can come work and sing with your kids

Barry visits many classrooms and presents assemblies K-12 each year. Workshop titles include:

Digging for Details...Snapshots and Thoughtshots.. Exploding Moments
Growing Leads...Laugh to Learn....Wacky We-search We-ports...Elvis Lives

Call 1-800-613-8055 Fax 1-802-897-2084-- www.discoverwriting.com